Praise for *The Decision Intelligence Handbook*

This book builds on Dr. Pratt's first book, *Link*, stepping organizations through the collaborative—and very human—process of "designing decisions." I recommend it to anyone involved in business decision making at any level, as a means of elevating the process and delivering real, measurable, and strategic value.

—Howard Dresner, founder and Chief Research Officer at Dresner Advisory Services; author of The Performance Management Revolution *and* Profiles in Performance; *and "father" of business intelligence*

Decision intelligence is an incredibly important concept. It is critical for decision makers to understand the implications of the decisions they make. Causal diagramming and the other methods outlined in this book are powerful techniques that should be introduced into every company interested in improving its ability to react effectively to change.

—Allan Frank, president at Think New Visions, LLC; former CTO for the city of Philadelphia and CapGemini

I am thrilled to pioneer a new approach to decision making in the complex world of healthcare workforce management. Our innovative use of decision intelligence foundation models is helping hospitals address the ongoing staffing crisis and provide better patient care by capturing the best practices to make and monitor talent acquisition, enablement, and retention decisions. This book is an invaluable resource for anyone looking to make better decisions to improve healthcare operations.

—Lorenzo Martinelli, cofounder and chairperson of C-Plan.IT

Artificial intelligence today is exploding, driven by large language models (LLMs) like ChatGPT. I think of decision intelligence (DI) as the "killer app" for LLMs because DI connects this advanced technology to business outcomes with an unprecedented amount of knowledge and power. This book tells you how to harness that power.

—Teasha Cable, decision intelligence entrepreneur; cofounder and CEO of CModel.io

The Decision Intelligence Handbook

Practical Steps for Evidence-Based Decisions in a Complex World

L. Y. Pratt and N. E. Malcolm

Foreword by John Elkington

Beijing · Boston · Farnham · Sebastopol · Tokyo

The Decision Intelligence Handbook

by L. Y. Pratt and N. E. Malcolm

Published by O'Reilly Media, Inc., 1005 Gravenstein Highway North, Sebastopol, CA 95472.

O'Reilly books may be purchased for educational, business, or sales promotional use. Online editions are also available for most titles (*http://oreilly.com*). For more information, contact our corporate/institutional sales department: 800-998-9938 or *corporate@oreilly.com*.

Acquisition Editor: Michelle Smith	**Indexer:** Sue Klefstad
Development Editor: Sarah Grey	**Interior Designer:** David Futato
Production Editor: Clare Laylock	**Cover Designer:** Karen Montgomery
Copyeditor: nSight, Inc.	**Illustrator:** Kate Dullea
Proofreader: Piper Editorial Consulting, LLC	

June 2023: First Edition

Revision History for the First Edition
2023-06-21:   First Release

See *http://oreilly.com/catalog/errata.csp?isbn=9781098139650* for release details.

978-1-098-13965-0

[LSI]

Table of Contents

Foreword

When this book's authors first asked me to write this foreword, I answered with a soft "no."

Although I have often spoken of the need for system change in service of sustainability objectives, and am often told I am a system thinker, it doesn't feel that way. If you recall Robert Pirsig's long-ago book, *Zen and the Art of Motorcycle Maintenance*, he distinguished between "romantics"—people who love riding a Harley until it breaks, then kick it as they stalk off down the road—and "mechanics," who hunker down and try to fix the machine. I warned Pratt and Malcolm that I am more of a romantic than a mechanic, at a time when we need more mechanics.

Romantics, I believe, will always exist and will often be needed, but true systemic change—whether toward sustainability or simply to adapt to the complexities facing modern enterprises—increasingly needs mechanical talent. And that, bluntly, has never been me.

Undeterred, the authors doubled down, explaining that I'd hit on exactly the point of decision intelligence and of this book. Indeed, if we are to effectively galvanize ourselves to meet the level of change and disruption now required, we will need the perspectives of both the mechanic and the creative, working together.

We live in an age where two forces are colliding. First, as often happens during scientific and technological revolutions, increased specialization is creating barriers between disciplines: the exponential innovator struggles to communicate with the economist, the politician, the investor, or the executive. Each inhabits their own island of expertise, protected by bastions of jargon. But nature—and emerging economic realities—rarely respect such artificial separations.

The second force comes from a new class of cross-disciplinary problems: climate disruption drives migration and conflict; conflict affects the production and distribution of food; food scarcities drive poverty; poverty impacts the wider economy and dents tax yields, and so on, as these dynamics hamper our ability to tackle the climate crisis. Around we go, in complex causal chains, whorls, loops.

None of these problems can be solved in isolation. And such dynamics cascade from the realm of sustainability down to everyday business and policy decisions, whether you're a sweet potato grower or a government official creating a net-zero carbon emissions policy (both examples well covered in this book). Every decision maker now faces an ever more complex and turbulent world.

Throughout my career, I've observed that creative minds like mine help bridge the gaps between our perceptions and emergent realities. We need people who can use lateral thinking to spot these connections, to understand increasingly nested systems, and to locate today's crucial tipping points and tomorrow's leverage points.

I need no persuading that technologies—including earth observation, big data, and AI—are crucial in helping us to spot and solve new classes of risk and opportunity. I have visited organizations like NASA, the Woods Hole Oceanographic Institution, and DeepMind to get a sense of where we may be headed. But, full disclosure, much of the time I struggle to understand what these people are talking about. Their brains seem to work many times faster than mine–it's like drinking from a fire hose.

Nor am I alone here. Leaders worldwide are trying to become more "evidence-based" and "data-driven," but many seem to operate more from the analytical right side of their brains than the creative left side. So, the focus needs to expand from high-profile leaders to their teams and organizational cultures. We need to be less obsessed with what individuals and corporations and brands are doing and more focused on how we can create market dynamics that ensure all market actors move in the right direction—with the necessary urgency.

There is no way we can pull our economies back within our planet's limits without the help of big data, expert systems, and AI, but their contribution will only bend the relevant curves if we can blend the minds and skills of romantics and mechanics, today and tomorrow.

I found, in the following pages, that if you have the patience and are a nontechnical creative like me, you can learn how to work with technical people more effectively. This holds true whether you're a business leader or you're creating policy and shaping market incentives. I hope you'll find that here, too.

If, on the other hand, you're a technical person who feels the frustration of communicating effectively with nontechnical (or less technical) people, you can bridge the gap from the other side. This book contains a step-by-step recipe for doing so. I conclude that it should be on the reading lists of all business schools and on the desks (not just shelves) of legislators and leaders worldwide.

I suspect that few people will read this book cover-to-cover in a single sitting. But you will be well-served even if the book hovers on your desk or shelf and you read just a chapter a month. It is dense with ideas, but leavened with exercises that help us see our decisions through new lenses, in ways that can help us all to communicate better with colleagues.

Finally, and perhaps most importantly, the authors show us all how to invite a new kind of "colleague" into our thinking, conversations, and work. Decades ago I got a well-known financial-world cartoonist to draw me a picture of a boardroom table, also now featuring a fish in a business suit (symbolizing the natural world), a woman from the Global South (symbolizing the ever-expanding social agenda) and a robot (symbolizing accelerating technological progress). Today, the robots are already here. It's time to welcome them in and work out what we can do with them that we can't do without.

> — *John Elkington,*
> *cofounder of Environmental Data Services,*
> *SustainAbility, and Volans Ventures;*
> *aka the "Godfather of Sustainability"; and*
> *author of* Green Swans: The Coming Boom
> in Regenerative Capitalism

Preface

The past few decades have brought astonishing improvements in data science, business intelligence, and artificial intelligence (AI). In response, organizations are increasingly determined to weave these technologies into the fabric of their everyday decisions. Indeed, a 2019 survey (*https://oreil.ly/jPTo9*) conducted by global consulting firm McKinsey found that better decision making can benefit a typical Fortune 500 company by as much as $250 million per year.

This reflects a big opportunity to improve organizational outcomes, even as it reflects the dismal state of organizational decision making today.

But we're far from achieving this nirvana. In *Fortune* magazine (*https://oreil.ly/8jSuC*), Alan Murray and Jackson Fordyce write, "Business leaders are so overwhelmed with data they're struggling to function." And today, many "data-driven" and "evidence-based" initiatives are falling short. The reason is, simply, that decision making is not really about data: it's about achieving an organization's outcomes, with data as a key ingredient, but still secondary to business outcomes. This incorrect focus on the data itself leads to data and AI work that isn't well aligned with many organizations' outcomes and desired goals.

Smart organizations are moving, instead, to "outcome-driven" decision making, with data and technology working "under the hood" to supercharge their choices.

Along the way, a new discipline has emerged to help them, called decision intelligence (DI). DI brings AI (including generative AI technologies like ChatGPT), data, human expertise, research, and more into an integrated framework that answers two questions: "If I take this action today, in this context, what will be the outcome?" and "What is the best action to take today to maximize the likelihood that I'll reach my goals?"

DI is about ensuring that decision makers can use the most powerful technologies, and that decision-making systems present information in a way that feels natural and intuitive. DI moves organizations beyond simply using historical data, which provides information and insights about the present and past, to answering questions about the future.

Hi, we're the authors of this book, N. E. Malcolm and L. Y. Pratt. Pratt co-invented DI (with Mark Zangari) in 2010. Since then, working with our team, we've helped DI to grow into a field so promising that *Forbes* (*https://oreil.ly/35dE2*) asks whether it's "the new AI." The Gartner Group (*https://oreil.ly/K5ORm*) predicts that more than a third of large organizations will be using DI by the time this book is published; market-research firm MarketsandMarkets (*https://oreil.ly/3enfp*) projects that DI will grow to a $22 billion market by 2027; and Chinese behemoth Alibaba (*https://oreil.ly/1yF06*) names DI second on its list of top technology trends for 2023 (just after generative AI).

One of us—coauthor Pratt—wrote the first book on DI: *Link: How Decision Intelligence Connects Data, Actions, and Outcomes for a Better World*.[1] We've now built and delivered dozens of DI solutions for large and small commercial organizations, start-ups, and the public sector. DI projects—ours and those of other DI practitioners—have saved and generated many hundreds of millions of dollars for organizations worldwide, in addition to social and other nonfinancial benefits.

About This Book

This book is a practical, "roll up your sleeves" guide to how you can do DI, within your own organization or as a consultant or Decision Intelligence Service Provider (DISP) or Decision Intelligence Infrastructure Provider (DIIP) for others. It's organized around a collection of nine DI "best practice" processes. We'll walk you through each one, starting with how to decide if DI is right for your situation. We'll show you how to go about designing a decision. By the time you work through the book, you'll have a continuously improvable decision asset that is connected to data, AI, and more in a way that will drive competitive differentiation and success through better decision making.

But before we dive into the gnarly details, we feel it's important for you to understand that you can start doing DI today. Seriously, we're talking about 20 minutes from now: the time that it takes to get to the section called "Build Your First CDD, Right Now!" in the next chapter.

Decision Intelligence in a Nutshell

Simply put, DI helps organizations make better decisions. It helps decision makers understand how the potential actions they can take today (the things they can do)

---

1 L. Y. Pratt, *Link: How Decision Intelligence Connects Data, Actions, and Outcomes for a Better World* (Bingley, UK: Emerald Publishing, 2019).

could affect their desired outcomes (the things they want to accomplish). To get from actions to outcomes, DI centers around a drawing called a causal decision diagram (CDD), which acts as a "decision blueprint." The CDD lets you *design* a decision. Its purpose is to get everyone on the same page—technologists, decision makers, and even the stakeholders affected by the decision. To give you an idea of what a CDD looks like, Figure P-1 shows a very simple one.

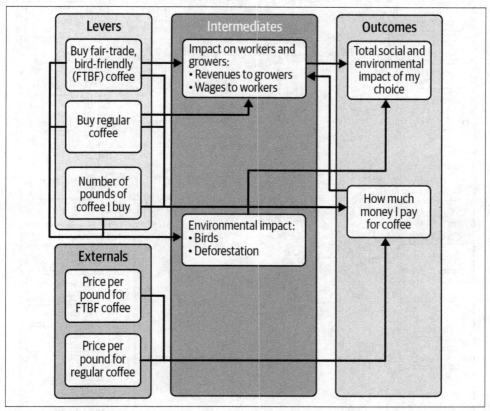

Figure P-1. A simple causal decision diagram (CDD).

We'll have more to say about CDDs in later chapters, but you can see a few things right off the bat. We draw actions on the left-hand side of the diagram and outcomes on the right. Between the two is a chain of consequences. (Note that these are *consequences*, not tasks, and are—as a rule—outside of your control after you take an action.)

Figure P-2 shows a more complex CDD, including some annotation showing where technology fits into a decision. (To look at the details, you can download a PDF from the book's supplemental materials repository (*https://oreil.ly/DIH-supplemental*).)

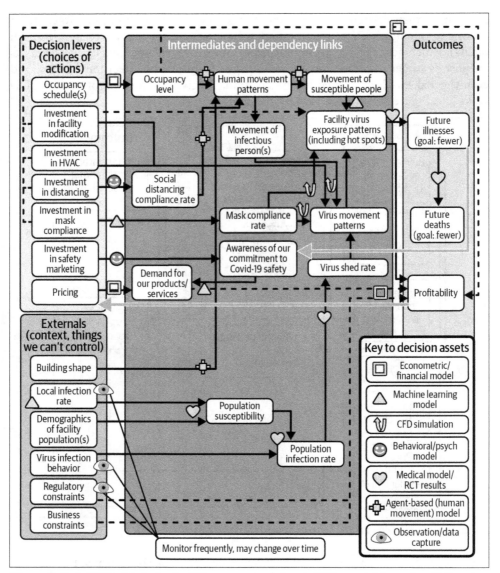

Figure P-2. A CDD that helps building managers decide "When and how should I go about opening my building and keeping people safe from the pandemic?"

To draw a CDD, you document your desired outcomes and the actions you can take to achieve them. You capture these in a diagram that also shows your understanding of the cause-and-effect chains that connect actions to outcomes. Later, if you want, you can add data, evidence, models, analytics, and human expertise that inform your decision, so that your diagram isn't just on paper but also can be simulated by a computer. In this form, the simulation based on the CDD is effectively a "decision digital twin," providing an evidence-based way to determine which actions will be most effective in achieving your outcomes. We'll walk you through the process for creating CDDs in this book.

At its most fundamental, DI is an *integration* and *design* discipline, connecting technologies together with each other and with human decision makers. And the CDD shows how these pieces fit together. Simply put, DI helps organizations leverage the best of human expertise, hand in hand with all sorts of technology. DI begins and ends with the group or person making the decision. Technology is secondary, used in support of better decisions. Not fully automated, yet not just based on human judgment, DI is a "hybrid" AI method—one of the fastest-growing technology markets (*https://oreil.ly/_ZFTk*).

The DI methodology holds that structured decision making can be represented as a set of well-defined *processes*. These follow a lifecycle, beginning with formulating the decision at hand and ending with retrospectively analyzing the effectiveness of the chosen course of action, and possibly reusing the decision or elements of it for future decisions.

That might sound like a lot, but an important aspect of DI is that it's easy to do, especially at the start. Rather than asking you to think about decisions in a new way, DI simply asks that you *document the way that you think about decisions today*. You'll find that just drawing a picture of a decision—as we'll teach you to do in the next chapter—goes a long way.

Along the way, you'll find that DI includes these important elements:

- Clearly defining decision requirements
- Representing decision making as a set of well-defined processes that follow a lifecycle, from formulating the decision to retrospectively analyzing its effectiveness and potential for reuse
- Following an iterative design process that incorporates data, analytics, and expert judgment; allows for multiple scenarios; and models different potential worlds
- Creating a CDD as a unifying graphical representation for a designed decision
- Integrating decision assets like data, human knowledge, and machine learning (ML) and AI models with elements of the CDD; this lets decisions be driven by data and more
- Emphasizing quality assurance and security
- Transforming into a decision-centric organization using organizational and cultural best practices

LLMs, OMG

As this book goes to press, ChatGPT and other large language models (LLMs) are turning the technology world upside down, supercharging writers, coders, scammers, and more. And DI is no exception. We are already seeing LLM technology provide incredibly valuable advice (*https://oreil.ly/Bd6lJ*) to our DISP clients, acting as a superpowered new collaborator in multiple phases of the DI processes you'll read about here. In particular, we've seen LLMs surface actions, externals, outcomes, and unintended consequences that no one had previously considered, helping to reduce "tunnel vision."

We see LLMs' role in DI as a sort of "super Google," giving decision modelers and decision makers much easier access to a wide range of assets that they can use to inform their decision making. But LLMs don't do action-to-outcome simulations, so they're complementary to the decision-reasoning methods we describe here.

Who Is This Book For?

This book is for you if you'd like to learn how to introduce DI to your organization or to your clients. You might be an executive who takes decisions seriously, combining the best of diverse human and computer knowledge to drive competitive advantage. You might be passionate about addressing climate change, but you know that there's a lot of earth observation (EO) data that's going unused because data scientists don't know how to connect it to decision making. You might be a data or AI consultant or an employee in one of the emerging DISP companies, looking to differentiate your practice by providing something new and valuable. You might be an ML expert who wants to maximize the value of this important technology, or a head of analytics or business intelligence who needs a way to communicate with your internal clients so that your technology helps them with better evidence-based decisions.

We've written this book for the "insurgent" bottom-up perspective, as well as for the lucky few who have obtained centralized executive sponsorship to take DI organization-wide. Indeed, we wrote this book in collaboration with a G20 central bank in the process of doing just that, and the bank has adapted this book for its internal use.

What You Will Learn

After completing this book, you will:

- Understand the kinds of decisions organizations make and which ones DI can help with
- Understand how to create, read, use, maintain, and reuse CDDs

- Have a "starter kit" of DI documents and templates that you can tailor for your organization

And you'll understand how to use DI to:

- Structure decision conversations around desired outcomes (financial or not) and actions to achieve them
- Use state-of-the-art collaborative tools to map AI, knowledge, data, and more into decisions
- Find simplicity and order amid the confusion of complex data, tools, and decisions
- Provide value to your data management projects by guiding them toward the 10% of data that has 90% of the value
- Identify ways to integrate silos within your organization
- Specify your requirements for automated decision-reasoning simulations to a software team
- Earn greater trust and credibility for your data/analytics/AI team, because you speak your customer's language

Please note that there are several topics that are *not* covered here. For instance, we don't delve into the broader societal impacts of DI or its potential for solving complex problems like the climate and pandemics. These impacts are covered in *Link*. Finally, we don't get into the technical specifics of how to build DI tools such APIs, interfaces, or AI and statistical models that interoperate with computerized DI models. Those technologies change quickly, but the principles we offer here stand on their own, independent of specific technological choices.

Assumptions This Book Makes

We do not assume that you have any specific technical knowledge. We have written this book to help all the participants in a decision-making process—not only the executives, managers, and stakeholders, but the analysts and data scientists who provide data and other evidence to decision makers.

We also do not assume that you have read *Link*. We'll introduce everything about DI that you need to know. Where *Link* was a visionary survey of the field, this book gives you actionable steps you can take to do DI, today and right now, with or without technology. This book also focuses on DI *processes*: our emphasis here is on the sequence of steps to take within your organization to make better decisions with better outcomes.

Contents of This Book

In Chapter 1, we introduce you to DI. We present a brief history of DI and explain its benefits from several points of view. You can skip Chapter 1 if you want to get started with the DI processes quickly.

The remaining chapters are organized around nine DI processes, summarized in Figure P-3.

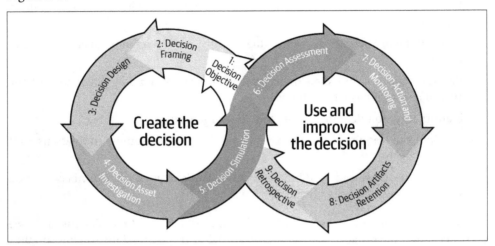

Figure P-3. The nine DI processes.

Chapter 2 gets you going with decision making. It covers the processes of creating an initial Decision Objective Statement and framing the decision design, including identifying the actions available and the desired outcomes.

Chapter 3 covers Decision Design, where you create your initial CDD.

In Chapter 4, you'll investigate the technical and data assets that can support your decision. This is called Decision Asset Investigation.

Now it's time to pull everything together to make the best decision you can. This is Decision Simulation, covered in Chapter 5.

Before you take action based on your decision, you'll want to evaluate risks, sensitivities, and uncertainties. This is Decision Assessment, the topic of Chapter 6.

Now it's time to take the action(s) you chose. In this book, we're not going to tell you how to do things once you've made a choice—we figure you're already pretty good at that. But in Chapter 7, we'll describe Decision Monitoring: how you can use your DI assets to monitor the results of your action(s) (KPIs, intermediates, outcomes, and more) as they play out in reality so that you can make quick adjustments if things drift off course.

Finally, Chapter 8 covers what you do after the decision model has been used. In Decision Artifacts Retention, you ensure that as much of the decision-making effort as possible can be reused. In the Decision Retrospective process, you'll assess and improve your decision-making processes for next time.

Conventions Used in This Book

The following typographical conventions are used in this book:

Italic

Indicates new terms, URLs, email addresses, filenames, and file extensions.

`Constant width`

Used for program listings, as well as within paragraphs to refer to program elements such as variable or function names, databases, data types, environment variables, statements, and keywords.

This element signifies a tip or suggestion.

This element signifies a general note.

Using Supplemental Materials

Supplemental material (worksheets, etc.) is available for download at *https://oreil.ly/ DIH-supplemental*.

If you have a technical question or a problem using the code examples, please send an email to *support@oreilly.com*.

This book is here to help you get your job done. In general, if example code is offered with this book, you may use it in your programs and documentation. You do not need to contact us for permission unless you're reproducing a significant portion of the code. For example, writing a program that uses several chunks of code from this book does not require permission. Selling or distributing examples from O'Reilly books does require permission. Answering a question by citing this book and quoting example code does not require permission. Incorporating a significant amount of example code from this book into your product's documentation does require permission.

We appreciate, but generally do not require, attribution. An attribution usually includes the title, author, publisher, and ISBN. For example: "*The Decision Intelligence Handbook* by L. Y. Pratt and N. E. Malcolm (O'Reilly). Copyright 2023 Quantellia, L.L.C., 978-1-098-13965-0."

If you feel your use of code examples falls outside fair use or the permission given above, feel free to contact us at *permissions@oreilly.com*.

O'Reilly Online Learning

 For more than 40 years, *O'Reilly Media* has provided technology and business training, knowledge, and insight to help companies succeed.

Our unique network of experts and innovators share their knowledge and expertise through books, articles, and our online learning platform. O'Reilly's online learning platform gives you on-demand access to live training courses, in-depth learning paths, interactive coding environments, and a vast collection of text and video from O'Reilly and 200+ other publishers. For more information, visit *https://oreilly.com*.

How to Contact Us

Please address comments and questions concerning this book to the publisher:

O'Reilly Media, Inc.
1005 Gravenstein Highway North
Sebastopol, CA 95472
800-889-8969 (in the United States or Canada)
707-829-7019 (international or local)
707-829-0104 (fax)
support@oreilly.com
https://www.oreilly.com/about/contact.html

We have a web page for this book, where we list errata, examples, and any additional information. You can access this page at *https://oreil.ly/DI-Handbook*.

For news and information about our books and courses, visit *https://oreilly.com*.

Find us on LinkedIn: *https://linkedin.com/company/oreilly-media*

Follow us on Twitter: *https://twitter.com/oreillymedia*

Watch us on YouTube: *https://youtube.com/oreillymedia*

Acknowledgments

This book would not have been possible without, first of all, the amazing team of employees and investors at Quantellia, who have stuck with us through the challenging task of creating a new discipline at the same time as we offer solutions into it. It's been a long haul, but an epic experience. There are really no words to express our gratitude for our long-suffering supporters. Of particular mention is Mark Zangari, who, as the co-inventor of DI, is the "hidden gem" behind much of what we do: his insights are woven deeply into what you will read here.

We've also been blown away by the knowledge and experience of the team at O'Reilly, especially Michelle Smith, and Sarah Grey, who took the time to learn DI so deeply while editing our draft that we consider her a contributor to the discipline!

We've also been blessed with great colleagues with whom we have built and delivered DI solutions, including Jessica Jaret, Elizabeth Nitz, Dr. John Wooten, Skye Wiersma, and Katie Harder, and in earlier days Rick Ladd, Sammy Thomas, Jennifer Fruehauf, Margaret Johnson, Allie Golon, and Janet Nemmers. We are also particularly grateful to Erik Balodis, who contributed great ideas to an early draft of this book, resulting in this article (*https://oreil.ly/EHLDY*).

Bolstering and supporting our work from outside of our organization have been friends and fans too numerous to mention. Worthy of special note are Jim Casart, Dr. David Roberts (a worldwide leader in bringing DI into academia, who also reviewed a draft of this book), Allan Frank, Robert Walker, Joseph Wiggins, VR Ferose, Håkan Edvinsson, James Parr and his team at Trillium (who are bringing DI into one of the most important domains of our time: climate resilience), Dr. Grady Booch, Dr. Cassie Kozyrkov, Jeffrey Williams, Tim McElgunn, and Linda Kemp. We got terrific feedback from a number of technical reviewers, and are grateful to Joshua Dejong, Dr. Roger Moser, Donald Farmer, Tobias Zwingmann, Anand Thakar, Jen Stirrup, and Jazmine Cable. The DI vendor community has also been of great support. Data Innovation.AI, Pyramid Analytics, Astral Insights, Agilisys, CModel, and C-Plan.IT are worthy of special note. We are also very grateful to our family members: Michael Malcolm, Dr. Annis Pratt, Dr. Faith Hopp, John Smith, Casper Smith, and Aspen Smith (and coauthor Pratt thanks her dog, Bowie, too), for their sacrifices that came from supporting this important endeavor. Co-author Pratt also thanks Landlocked Ales (whose Decision Fatigue beer flights fueled her writing).

CHAPTER 1

Introduction

"Decision-makers only use 22% of the jumble of data-driven insights they receive," Erik Larson writes in *Forbes* (*https://oreil.ly/sd1ZG*). What's going on? This is an especially important question when we think about senior leaders, whose choices are critical to the success of their organizations, and sometimes, the world.

It's sad to think that this powerful technology is having such limited impact. Technologies define an age: the printing press brought about the Renaissance, the steam engine was core to the Industrial Revolution, and computers created the "Information Age." We thought that analytics and data would have a similar impact for the better. But, as this book goes to press, the jury is still out.

There was a widespread belief for a while that "more data = better decisions," but, sadly, we're not seeing organizations—public or private—that we think are doing better than ever. Some would say things are worse.

What's going on? Part of the answer is that many organizations are facing unprecedented complexity and volatility from external factors. Globalization means that the corner store has given way to the big-box store, the pandemic has changed how we work and collaborate, and changes in media and climate mean that we're all getting used to a "new normal."

In response, many leaders and data scientists have embarked on a digital transformation journey, going from paper-based records to digitized information, then using that information to drive business intelligence (BI) and to train artificial intelligence (AI).

But data, AI, and BI aren't enough. Leading organizations are recognizing the importance of both collaborative intelligence (CI) and decision intelligence (DI): to integrate the expertise of multiple perspectives to make better decisions, leading to better outcomes. AI/BI/CI/DI: all are needed to reap the benefits of the new age. DI, from this point of view, then, is the "last mile" to realize the transformation vision.

Indeed, you can think of modern organizations as decision factories (*https://oreil.ly/6Ke_T*), using meetings, emails, and more to churn out one decision after another. As Dominik Dellermann, CEO of Vencortex, writes (*https://oreil.ly/fSyrb*): "Ultimately, the value of your company is just the sum of decisions made and executed.... [The] ability to make faster, more consistent, more adaptable and higher-quality decisions at scale defines the performance of your entire business."

But the journey to better decision making, as you might expect, includes bumps and obstacles along the road. One common roadblock is that, despite these widespread digital transformations, many organizations are still making decisions without the benefit of evidence and data that are clearly connected to business outcomes—even as the decisions they make are more important than ever.

Core to overcoming this roadblock is a more professional approach to managing the ingredients in a typical decision. How do you integrate them into a well-justified set of actions that (you have good reason to believe) will lead to the outcomes you desire? Within the volatile, complex, and uncertain environment of organizations (commercial and public), this challenge—however promising—can seem overwhelming. As decision-making expert Dr. Roger Moser told us, what's important is that "people start to focus on designing more effective and efficient decision-making processes, and new technological advancements along the data value chain (including AI/ML, data storage, data lakes, etc.) allow for a new level of professionalism in decision process design."

The good news is that a little bit goes a long way. In most organizations, people still make important decisions using 20th-century processes and "technology." Most people don't see effective and efficient decision-making processes as critical to managing decisions. They don't think of "a decision" as something that they can create collaboratively, extend, check for "bugs," reuse, and improve over time.

Indeed, a decision is a bit like a spaceship: it's something that you create with other experts from different parts of your organization, using advanced technology to reach lofty goals. Just this simple mental shift toward realizing that decisions are like other things we can build and extend can be a powerful step toward solving complex problems.

Do You Need Decision Intelligence?

Perhaps you've heard one or more of these questions within your organization:

> "I think that our organization's decisions should be more evidence-based. What's the best way to do that?"

"I've heard that data and AI are transforming organizations, and I don't want to miss the boat. But where should I start?"

"I feel that we could do better when decision teams get together to make strategy decisions that impact us for many months or years. How can we effectively manage assumptions, uncertainty, and risk?"

"We track certain key performance indicators (KPIs) in our company, and that's a good start, but it leaves an open question: can't technology help us decide what to do when the KPIs show we're in trouble?"

If so, then you need DI. (We'll have more to say about assessing your particular decision for its fitness to DI in Chapter 2.)

What DI Does for You and Your Organization

In many ways, DI is like other new disciplines that have changed how we work together, like project management (*https://oreil.ly/p67Wa*), business process re-engineering (*https://oreil.ly/9jlZ3*), or data governance (*https://oreil.ly/h6h7W*). We know that you're probably overwhelmed with new technologies and methods, and we don't want to make your life even harder! We are, however, asking you to join us on a journey—and on a learning curve.

If you've been working within a medium-sized or large organization for a while, you might already have started to think about how to fix organizations at a *systems* level, rather than adding yet another technical silver bullet. DI is that systemic fix: not another gee-whiz, overhyped method, but rather a solidly designed discipline that builds on—instead of replacing—over a century of management innovation.

Most of this book walks you through the nine DI processes that we mentioned briefly in the Preface. Have no fear: they're not hard! You can learn them one step at a time, and by the end of the book you'll have one of the most powerful disciplines of the 21st century at your command.

Before we get to the processes, though, this chapter sets the table with some context. We'll give you an easy on-ramp into DI, describe how to motivate your organization to use DI, and give you a brief glimpse of the discipline's history and current status. It's no problem if you choose to skip this chapter and go straight into Chapter 2, where you can roll up your sleeves to get started.

From Data to Decisions

You've probably run into a "data-driven" or digital transformation initiative at some point in your career. At the very least, your organization has probably asked, "What can we do with all this data? Can it help us to reach our goals?" Most organizations don't fully understand how data fits into decision making. Often, data analysts make guesses about the decisions they'll be supporting without any clear understanding.

They apply sophisticated mathematical and AI techniques to gain insights and find patterns and trends, provide charts and graphs that they think will be helpful, and then throw it all "over the wall" to nontechnologists.

Imagine you're sitting at a restaurant and your waiter brings a bowl of water, a cup of flour, and a bowl of spices. This is how many nontechnologists feel when their data teams show them charts and graphs: this information is just not "cooked" into the form that is "digestible." Data, insights, even information: that's like those ingredients. To make the information "taste good," it needs to show how your actions lead to the outcomes you want. Because that's how nontechnical people think.

That's why the core focus of DI is finding the data that helps decision makers to connect actions to outcomes: this is what it means for data to be "well cooked," because action-to-outcome thinking is the "natural" thought process that decision makers use.

There are three specific gaps between data and decisions in most organizations.

First, we've found that many analysts and nontechnologists struggle to reach a shared understanding of how data will be used. What are you trying to achieve: sales, profit, customer retention, population health? What actions do you have available to reach your objective(s)? What can you measure that will help you understand the path from actions to outcomes?

Second, it's often hard to know where to begin with a new decision-making initiative. The decision context, available actions, and required outcomes are in the hands of the decision maker, who is often not a technical person. The data and models that inform the decision are in the hands of the analysts. How can nontechnologists communicate the decision's context to the analysts effectively so that the analysts can provide data that connects actions to outcomes?

Third, even when you have accurate data, it can be hard to use it well. To make a solid evidence-based decision, you need to know how your desired outcomes depend on the actions you can take and your external environment. Despite the finest AI techniques, typically your data doesn't answer the question, "If I take these actions, what will the outcomes be?"

DI is, then, the discipline of converting those "raw ingredients" into the right form. And this book is your recipe.

The Decision Complexity Ceiling

Organizational decision making has reached a *complexity ceiling*: the factors that come into play when making a major decision are so many and so complex that they exceed human decision makers' capacity to make the right choices.[1] Construction, software, finance, manufacturing, and many other disciplines have faced similar complexity ceilings as they've evolved: they all reached a point where the number of inputs, the interactions between them, and the time frames in which results had to be achieved overwhelmed the techniques of the day. Says DI entrepreneur Jazmine Cable-Whitehurst of CModel (*https://oreil.ly/AhE_L*), "Maybe back in the day, we didn't need to design decisions for a corner store. But now, businesses have a much greater reach, and they are affected in turn by global factors like climate change, diversity, race, planetary boundaries, and politics: all things that they need to be conscious of today that they didn't have to think about 50 years ago."

A 2021 Gartner survey (*https://oreil.ly/uiCqB*), for instance, found that 65% of organizational decisions are more complex—often involving more stakeholders or choices—than they were only two years earlier. And complexity is exacerbated by volatility: decision making can't keep up with a fast-changing context. This complexity might include:

Causal chain length and complexity
> The number of elements that make up the decisions, including choices of actions, desired results, dependencies between elements of the decision, peripheral (often unintended) consequences, and long cause-and-effect chains

Time variation
> Factors that change during the decision-making and execution process

Data
> Data that is only partially available, uncertain, incorrect, or difficult to obtain, manage, or interpret

Human factors
> Decision contributors' differing viewpoints, their levels of skill and experience, and the effects of political and social relationships, to name a few

You must consider so much information, so many choices, so many potential interactions between the two, and such serious potential consequences for bad decisions, that it can be overwhelming. For this reason, organizations end up taking big, unnecessary risks based on justifications that are often far from sound.

---

1 L. Pratt and Mark Zangari, "Overcoming the Decision Complexity Ceiling Through Design" (*https://oreil.ly/onbtO*), December 2008, Quantellia; L. Pratt and Mark Zangari, "High Performance Decision Making: A Global Study" (*https://oreil.ly/on-TZ*), January 2009, Quantellia.

In recent years, a knee-jerk answer to complexity has been to simply gather more data, create more models, hire statisticians, or ask the IT department to build an information architecture that allows greater sharing and collaboration. Although these approaches may sometimes be helpful, they are usually not enough, they often add complexity and cognitive overload, and they lack integration between people, processes, and technology. The result is that, in many organizations, systems, data, and human stakeholders are separated by culture, language, geographical distance, and time delays.

The stakes have become too high, and the game is now played too fast, for organizations to rely on intuition and luck. Decision makers need a system that gives them the best chance of winning. DI is a solution to this fundamental shift.

Fortunately, a very effective solution pattern has emerged. Disciplines like construction, software engineering, and systems engineering have overcome the complexity ceiling by developing and widely adopting a methodology that:

- Systematizes the tasks required for successful completion and makes them objective (like framing a house)
- Defines quality-control checks and balances for each set of tasks (like inspecting a house before occupancy)
- Defines a common formal nomenclature that removes ambiguity and facilitates sharing information and knowledge among groups with widely different skills and backgrounds (like having a standard way to draw a picture of a door on a blueprint)
- Is supported by tools (like blueprints and computer-assisted design tools)

DI applies these tried-and-true approaches to decision making.

Figure 1-1 shows a simple CDD for a decision: whether to buy regular coffee or bird-friendly, fair-trade coffee. As you can see there, the decision contains actions that lead to outcomes through a chain of events. Those events are defined by *intermediates*, the steps in the causal chain from actions to outcomes. They also depend on *externals*, or things beyond your control that affect the outcomes.

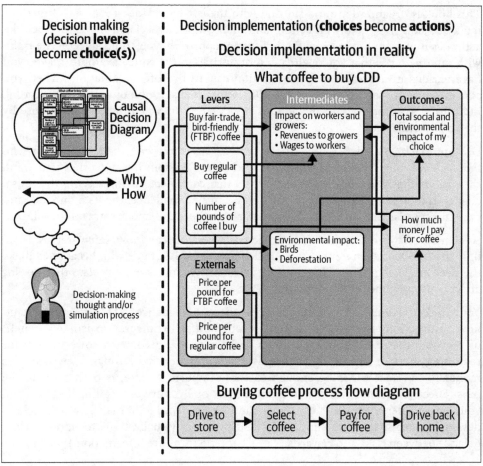

Figure 1-1. An overview of DI, from the point of view of a CDD, distinguishing the decision process from the action process, DI flows from process flows, and technology from nontechnology solutions.

There's a difference between the process of thinking about a decision (on the left-hand side of Figure 1-1) and the process of actually taking an action based on a decision (on the right). This figure also shows the difference between a process in which a decision is made (drive to the store, select coffee, etc.) and the action-to-outcome CDD (which also uses boxes and arrows, but does not show a process). The right-hand side is an abstraction or representation of the left-hand side. The distinction here is similar to the philosophical argument that "the map is not the territory" (*https://oreil.ly/yKRoF*).

This book is organized around starting with the left-hand side of Figure 1-1: design-ing a decision first, taking an action, and then using the decision model to track the action as it plays out over time. For a different approach, you could start on the right, with intermediates that you're already monitoring: in the coffee example, maybe you have various measures of the deforestation caused by coffee plantations. Then you can structure those measures into a CDD with a focus on the outcomes and leading indicators, working back to the actions over time. This will all make more sense by the end of the book.

DI's approach to evidence-based decision making *starts with the decision, not with the evidence.* First you need to understand your decision: the outcomes you want, the actions that you can take, the externals that can affect outcomes, and the causal chains from actions to outcomes. Then you can find evidence: the data, models, and human expertise that provide information about the boxes and arrows on the CDD.

A benefit of the decision-first approach is that you can now safely set aside all information that isn't relevant to your decision. This is a huge win, because to make the decision at hand, you don't need to cleanse, vet, or assess any data that doesn't affect your outcomes (*https://oreil.ly/_xPPx*).

Your CDD is a tool for integrating multiple pieces of evidence to help you understand how your actions lead to the outcomes you want. This integration is a key benefit of DI. With the addition of evidence, a decision model becomes a powerful tool for reasoning about or simulating your decision. Simply working through a few examples manually can sometimes be enough to show important patterns or illuminate the most effective actions. And when many dollars or lives are on the line and you and your stakeholders have difficulty understanding the decision, it may be worthwhile to develop in-depth software simulations and powerful visualizations to find the right balance between risks and rewards. (See Chapter 5 for more information.)

What Is DI?

In the Preface, we sketched how to design a decision, summarized the elements of the DI, and gave you a brief introduction to the nine DI processes. We'll tell you a little more here, to set the stage for the remaining chapters, but we expect you'll still have questions. Your understanding of what DI is and how to use it will deepen with each chapter.

DI is a methodology and set of processes and technologies for making better, more evidence-based decisions by helping decision makers understand how the actions they take today can affect their desired outcomes in the future.

The key concept of DI is the idea that you can *design* decisions (see Chapter 3). Importantly, a *decision,* as we treat it here, is a thought process about an action that, once made, leads to specific outcomes without any further intervention. (Contrast this to a process flow—if you're familiar with those—where you have control over each step.)

Just as organizations design cars, buildings, and airplanes before they build them using drawings and tools, it turns out that you can also design decisions. Much like a blueprint, a decision design helps align everyone involved in that decision—including stakeholders—around its rationale. If you think of creating decisions as a design problem, you can also bring many design best practices to bear, such as ideation, documentation, rendering, refinement, quality assurance (QA), and design thinking. You'll be documenting all this in a CDD, as we introduced in the Preface.

That might sound like a lot, but an important aspect of DI is that it's *easy* to do, at least the early processes.

DI begins and ends with the group or person making the decision. Rather than asking you to think about decisions in a new way, DI simply asks that you *document* the way that you think about decisions today. You'll find that just drawing that CDD picture of a decision—as we'll teach you to do—goes a long way.

Build Your First CDD, Right Now!

This is a long book, and we hope it will be an enjoyable read for you. But, if you're feeling impatient and want to get started doing DI *right now*, then you can focus on the simplified DI process shown here. This process is for building a CDD, like the ones in the Preface. We'll break it down in a lot more detail and give many more examples in the following chapters. But we'll be honest—and serious—if you just read and implement this one process, today, you'll be well on your way to better decisions in your organization. (We were surprised, too, when we first started doing it.)

Work by yourself if you are the sole decision maker, or assemble a decision team—ideally a diverse one that includes experts, stakeholders, and the person who will be responsible for the decision outcome. Then follow these steps:

1. Facilitate a brainstorming session to write down goals/outcomes for a decision (such as, for example, "launch a new product that will be profitable within two years"). (See Chapter 3.)

2. Select about three outcomes for initial focus. (You can add more in step 8 if you need to.) (See Chapter 3 for more on steps 2 through 8.)

3. Discuss those outcomes and ensure that the team agrees to them and that they're precise enough to measure.

4. Brainstorm actions that could lead to those outcomes (such as, for example, "launch a video course").

5. Select about three of those actions for initial focus. (Again, you can add more in step 8.)

6. Discuss the chains of events that might lead from actions to outcomes. Document them as boxes and arrows, working from left to right on a whiteboard. (While this looks like a flowchart, data flow, or process diagram, the boxes and arrows mean something quite different. We'll explain more in Chapter 3.)

7. Review the diagram to ensure everyone likes it.

8. Add more actions and outcomes to the original sets of three, one at a time, as you see fit. Stop when you think the diagram is complex enough to be valuable, but not overwhelming.

9. Clean up the diagram and publish it within your organization for review. (Maybe just hang it on the wall. You can even *send us a picture* if that's allowed—we'd love to see what you come up with!) Consider writing an explanatory narrative document as well.

10. Use the diagram to help to support decision conversations.

11. Send the diagram to your analytics team and ask them how they might provide data, ML models, or other technologies to refine your understanding of how the outlined actions lead to the desired outcomes (see Chapter 4).

12. Revisit the diagram from time to time to extend it, update it, and modify it as circumstances change.

You would be surprised at the number of decisions that are made without even getting to step 4. Simply aligning around the outcomes you want from your decisions has tremendous power (because—let's be clear—you make thousands of decisions a day, most of which will never be modeled, and a picture like this can help everyone to be better aligned).

The previously described process is a bridge to treating decisions as designed artifacts. Once you document decisions in this way, you can review, improve, and reuse them and treat them as a scaffold for integrating data, human knowledge, preexisting tools, and more. This process is a jumping-off point for the benefits you can achieve with a deeper understanding of DI, like the ability to make better evidence-based decisions, to better utilize your data stack and AI, and to understand how actions in one silo of your organization impact other silos. If you want practical steps to use this powerful new discipline to its maximum benefit, then this handbook is for you.

DI Is About Action-to-Outcome Decisions

If you've been involved in systems that involve decision making, especially if they're technology systems, then you might be feeling a bit confused about what we mean by the word *decision*. Not surprising, because this word has overlapping meanings, some of which may be unfamiliar to nontechnical readers. If so, don't worry about them. They are outside the scope of this book. For everyone else, it's important to zero in on what we mean by "decision" within DI. Consider the decision types shown in Figure 1-2 and summarized as follows:

Classification decisions

We sometimes call this "decisions that": for example, deciding *that* a particular picture shows a cat.

Regression decisions (predictions)

Another "decision that": for example, *that* there is a 20% chance of rain tomorrow.

Action-to-outcome decisions

Decisions to take one or more actions to achieve one or more outcomes.[2] Here, the actions we're choosing are *irrevocable allocations of resources*, as described by Google Chief Decision Scientist Dr. Cassie Kozyrkov (*https://oreil.ly/bD055*).

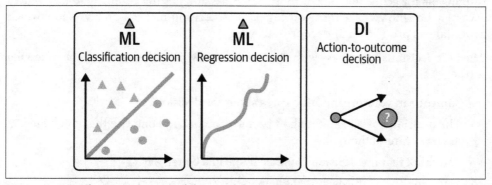

Figure 1-2. Different meanings of the word decision.

This book primarily covers the third category: decisions about actions that lead to outcomes. In the history of data, statistics, and AI, the first two categories—classification and regression decisions—have received the lion's share of attention while action-to-outcome decisions have received short shrift, despite how core they are to how people think. DI fills this gap.

Here are some examples that fit this actions-to-outcomes pattern:

- A teacher deciding whether to offer a course online or in person
- An employee deciding whether to travel to a conference or attend virtually

---

2 Note for experts: of course a choice to drive your car, take the bus, or walk to work is, strictly speaking, a classification decision. But we don't usually use statistical or ML regression or classification for this kind of choice. At heart, the difference is how we go about making that choice: using historical data (classification and regression) versus mechanistic reasoning and simulation, over an understanding of the world (DI's action-to-outcome decisions).

- A facilities manager deciding how and when to reopen an office building at the end of a pandemic work-from-home period
- A citizen deciding to which charity they should donate, along with when and how much
- A human resources department deciding on the details of a diversity hiring policy
- A farmer deciding on the best pest-management option for their crops
- A legislator deciding what elements to include in a bill that would ensure equitable access to broadband for all citizens
- A doctor comparing potential treatments for a patient

What all these examples have in common is that someone wants to achieve, or is responsible for achieving, one or more outcomes and has the authority to take one of several actions to achieve those outcomes. The decision maker wants to know which action(s) will produce their desired outcomes.

The best decisions to address with DI are ones for which at least one of the following is true:

- Someone in your organization cares about the decision.
- The decision has a big enough impact on you or someone else that you believe it deserves careful thought.
- You think that the decision could be made in a better way.
- You think that some data might help improve the decision.

Note that you are not required to have a lot of knowledge about the decision. Indeed, sometimes organizations are working "in the dark," making decisions about entirely new circumstances. These situations can be a good fit for DI, which helps to bring together the best minds and technology in novel situations. On the other hand, DI is not just for big, one-of-a-kind strategic decisions. DI delivers repeated value in tactical decisions, which are often the decisions at different steps in organizational business processes (*https://oreil.ly/S3uUc*).

DI Is About Human-in-the-Loop Decisions

Another dimension we use to classify decisions is the degree to which they involve humans, AI, or both: that is, *automated*, *hybrid*, or *manual* decisions.

The DI methodology described in this book applies to decisions made by people (usually with support from technology) to take one or more actions to achieve one or more outcomes. Fully automated decisions, such as Amazon's product recommender, are not core to this methodology—though it turns out that DI is very useful for them, too! Simply put, DI helps organizations to make better decisions by combining the best of human expertise with all sorts of technology.

The AI world doesn't always pay much attention to decisions that include a human in the loop: a person who consults some resource—maybe data charts and graphs—before making a decision. We think that's because a lot of the big AI "wins" over the years have been in fully automated use cases, such as Facebook and Google advertisements. This is another gap that DI fills. DI falls into the category of hybrid— also called *augmented*—decision-making methods, those that involve both humans and AI, which McKinsey notes (*https://oreil.ly/RUH_5*) constitute one of the most rapidly growing technology markets right now.[3]

You can have automated, hybrid, or manual decisions in each of the three decision categories: classification, regression, or action-to-outcome. This book, and our work, focuses on hybrid action-to-outcome decisions. Because other methods don't cover them, we've been asked to address hybrid action-to-outcome decisions over and over again.

AI models can make valuable single-link decisions, like what cross-sell item to suggest or what ad to display. DI lets you use multiple AI models together to inform a decision, and integrate AI and other technologies with human expertise and human judgment in your decision making. If you put action-to-outcome decisions together with human-in-the-loop decision making, you get a set of desperately needed capabilities that are new compared to standard AI and analytics methods. We hope the value this provides will motivate you to keep reading this book and to embrace DI in your work.

The core of DI is the idea that you can *design* these action-to-outcome decisions the way engineers design cars, buildings, and airplanes before building them using drawings or tools. Just as a blueprint helps many collaborators to build a skyscraper, a design of a decision helps to align everyone involved—including stakeholders— around its rationale. And if you treat decisions as a design problem, you can also bring to bear best practices from the field of design, such as ideation, documentation, rendering, refinement, QA, and design thinking. Under the hood, DI is all about integration and connecting human decision makers with data, AI, complex systems modeling, human behavior, and many other disciplines. Simply put, DI helps organizations to make better decisions by combining the best of human expertise with all sorts of technology.

---

3 Increasingly, even fully automated decision-making projects are using DI methods to align technical teams around decisions. Although it isn't the main focus of this book, there is substantial material to support fully automated use cases starting in Chapter 3. This is especially true on projects that need to combine multiple AI models in a process called AI orchestration (*https://oreil.ly/1ulTJ*).

Why Data-Driven Decision Makers Need DI

Many decision makers want to go beyond improving manual decision-making methods and learn to use data and technology more effectively. You might argue, even, that a modern organizational leader is behind the times if they're relying only on "gut instinct" in making important choices. This is why so many organizations strive to be "data-driven" and "evidence-based."

Time and again, we've seen technical analysts open a meeting on a new project by saying, "Here are the data and AI models we have for you." This approach is back-to-front: how can the analysts provide the right information before they know what their "customer" (from outside the analytics department) needs? Sorry to say, they are usually only guessing at how decision makers will use their data and information. They talk about what data and charts are "interesting" and where are the best "insights," without really understanding how any of it translates into actions and business outcomes. Without understanding the cause-and-effect chains that link actions to outcomes and what data informs those chains, technologists will usually gather and process more data than you actually need, as we described at the start of this chapter. Preparing data that is not useful is likely to take too long and entail a lot of unnecessary work.

There is a better way, and it begins by starting the conversation in the right direction. Consider a closely analogous situation. When an IT organization needs to create software that solves a problem, the first thing they are given is a list of customer requirements. The interaction between data science and analytics teams and their customers should begin the same way. The analytics customer should be able to say, "Here's what I need you to do for me" in a language that both technical and nontechnical people understand.

So why is there such a difference between data projects, where the tail seems to be wagging the dog, and software projects, where the deliverable is defined by those who have the problems that the software is intended to solve?

The reason is that software engineering has spent years, if not decades, recognizing that software is only successful when it meets end users' needs. The discipline thus developed formal and informal methodologies for eliciting requirements from users, stated in ways that nontechnical users can understand and that software developers can use to build systems that meet users' needs. This is the first stage of any software engineering project.

Decision makers need "requirements" tools to reap similar benefits. DI is starting to bring this same kind of maturity to the world of decision making. But software requirements alone won't cut it, because decisions are quite different than software applications. In Chapter 3, we show you how to design a decision so that you can see what data you need. Then, in Chapter 4, we show you how to link the data to your designed decision.

Erik Balodis, director of analytics and decision support for the Bank of Canada, illustrates in a Medium article why DI is needed (*https://oreil.ly/DXxP9*), pointing out "a recognition that investing in data to 'make better decisions' is too vague." He also describes a pattern he's perceived within organizations as:

> a desire to improve decision culture and to mitigate the risks inherent in unstructured or *ad hoc* decision-making based principally on heuristics; a desire to see decision intelligence (DI) as a unifying discipline, bringing together much-needed influence from a variety of social sciences, quantitative methods, and business concepts.

Balodis also mentions "a range of very business-sounding reasons," including "data and analytic investment optimization; optimized design and re-use of data, analytics, and decision products and artifacts; [and] driving focus in decision-support activities to enable business strategy and oversight."

DI offers a practical methodology that tackles two problems that are widespread in data-driven decision making.

Problem 1: How can you and your data science team identify the data you need to support your decisions?

You need to know how the outcomes you are trying to achieve depend on the actions you can take. But rarely is data available that directly relates actions to outcomes. While you can often determine this relationship from data, how can you know which data to use and how it relates to the decision you need to make?

DI gives you a systematic method for using a decision statement to derive requirements and specifications for the data science and analytic work required to support your decision. The core of DI is *decision modeling*, or creating a CDD (or "decision blueprint") and adding existing data and models to it. (See Chapters 3 and 4 for more details.)

Problem 2: How can you use your preexisting technology and human investments to find actions that lead to the outcomes you want?

Action-to-outcome decisions are based on this question: "If we take this course of action, what will the outcome be?" Historically, there have been a number of technologies to answer this question, including linear programming and the field of operations research. DI adds a new tool to the toolkit, *simulation*: the process of using your brain or a computer to see how different actions affect your outcomes. (We'll cover simulation much more in Chapter 5.)

Where DI Comes From

Unlike AI and data science, DI was born in the commercial world and takes a problem-first—not a solution-first—approach to bridging the gap from stakeholders to technology. DI begins and ends with the decision customer, starting from defining the problem or goals and ending with the solution, something that can be (but doesn't have to be) very sophisticated "under the hood."

Mark Zangari and L. Y. Pratt, a coauthor of this book, invented DI in 2008 based on hundreds of interviews with decision makers. We originally called it "decision engineering," but later renamed it "decision intelligence" to make it clear that DI is more than simply a technical field. While the term *decision intelligence* appeared in print as early as 1994 (*https://oreil.ly/Z9noS*), the DI methodology in this handbook originated with Pratt and Zangari's 2008 whitepaper (Pratt and Zangari were not aware of, nor did they build on, the previous meaning of this phrase).

Our 2008 research asked an ambitious question: "If technology should solve one problem for you that it doesn't solve today, what would it be?" Surprisingly, we heard a consistent answer: "Help me make better decisions, using data and other emerging technologies."

L. Y. Pratt's *Link: How Decision Intelligence Connects Data, Actions, and Outcomes for a Better World* (*https://oreil.ly/kINon*) was the first book on DI. It provides a beginner's introduction to DI best practices and describes how DI projects worldwide have saved and generated many hundreds of millions of dollars of value, as well as nonfinancial benefits. You don't need to read *Link* before this book, but you might find it an interesting and less technical overview of the field.

Link generated a new wave of interest in DI, with the Gartner Group including DI in its "Top Ten Trends" reports for 2020 (*https://oreil.ly/1RD26*), 2021 (*https://oreil.ly/ cLkv9*), and 2022 (*https://oreil.ly/_1pDz*). However, we have found that *Link* needs a practical guide as a companion volume. This handbook is that guide. It is loosely based on a source book we wrote in partnership with a G20 central bank as we implemented DI across that organization.

Another important DI thought leader is Dr. Cassie Kozyrkov, Google Cloud's chief decision scientist, who writes that DI is "a vital science for the AI era, covering the skills needed to lead AI projects responsibly and design objectives, metrics, and safety-nets for automation at scale." Kozyrkov defines DI (*https://oreil.ly/PE2Wi*) as a blend of behavioral economics and psychology, data science, statistics, and decision science. We agree with this multidisciplinary approach: Kozyrkov's "unified field" definition of DI correctly includes statistical rigor as well as both "hard" and "soft" decision-making factors.

DI is not the only discipline designed to support better decisions. Others include business intelligence (*https://oreil.ly/Y7LNG*), decision support (*https:// oreil.ly/6sGQX*), knowledge management (*https://oreil.ly/UaxtL*), balanced scorecards (*https://oreil.ly/-QjO4*), KPIs (*https://oreil.ly/jycwl*), data visualization (*https://oreil.ly/ wzKQ5*), data science (*https://oreil.ly/RiogO*), business process modeling,[4] and decision analysis.[5] Many organizations have found that these practices can be very helpful, but for decision making in complex circumstances, they don't go quite far enough. And DI builds on them; it doesn't replace them.

An analogy best illustrates what's happening. The world had effective airplane technology long before it had flight simulators. To learn to fly, you had to watch a pilot in real life, then take the controls yourself. That was dangerous! It's much better—and much safer for pilots and passengers alike—for student pilots to learn from challenging scenarios within flight simulators many times before taking the controls of a real airplane.

DI is like that: it introduces a "simulation" environment to decision making. It pulls other technologies together to fundamentally change the experience and safety of "flying"—making organizational decisions. You can try things out and "crash" in simulation instead of reality, which is a lot more cost-effective. This approach *integrates* effective preexisting data and AI technologies and makes using them easier and more natural for human decision makers. By doing so, it helps to solve complex, previously unsolvable problems.

---

4 S. Williams, "Business Process Modeling Improves Administrative Control," *Automation*, December, 1967, 44–50.

5 Ronald A. Howard and Ali E. Abbas, *Foundations of Decision Analysis, Global Edition* (Boston: Pearson, 2015).

Finally, DI is an approach to what some call *neurosymbolic computing*, which integrates the historical symbolic (words and logic) world of AI with more modern data-centric approaches. Those of us who have been around the AI block a few times aren't married to one or the other of these approaches, but rather see DI as an approach to integrating them for the best of both worlds. James Duez, CEO at Rainbird.AI (*https://oreil.ly/GZO_G*), says it best:

> Throughout the years, the field of AI has experienced remarkable shifts. While symbolic AI dominated the 1980s, today the focus has shifted considerably towards data science and machine learning, valuing predictions from data and insights over symbolic models of human knowledge. As we look ahead, the future of AI will be shaped by a balanced integration of these approaches, capitalising on the merits of both symbolic reasoning and data science and machine learning through decision intelligence.

What DI Is Not

There are a number of disciplines that are often confused with DI. Let's take a quick look at them to clear up the differences.

DI is not process modeling or project planning

Process modeling is the practice of agreeing to a sequence of steps to achieve some goal. A related area is project planning. Both often use boxes and arrows to represent tasks and dependencies, respectively.

Here's a way to understand the difference between process modeling/project planning and DI: think about the difference between choosing a price for a product and implementing that pricing in some software. These are fundamentally different tasks. Choosing the price depends on your model of the chain of events that leads to your revenues, such as the demand curve that determines how many people will buy your product, as well as external factors like the economic climate and your competitor's price.

In contrast, setting up your website to charge $20 per month for your product involves a very different set of activities that might be better captured in a process diagram or project plan. That sequence of steps might consist of updating two fields, changing a coupon, and then testing that the payment system still works. Each of these steps could be represented as a box in a diagram, with arrows between them to indicate their relative order. This is not DI, but it interacts with DI at the point where you choose to charge $20 per month.

DI is not a decision tree

A *decision tree* is a sequence of questions to ask to reach some conclusion. For instance, a doctor might use a decision tree to diagnose a patient with heart disease. The tree might start with "measure blood pressure," then "if the blood pressure is greater than 140 systolic, then give the patient a blood test," and so forth. At the end of the question sequence, the decision tree might say, "this patient does not have heart disease." Note that the decision tree leads the doctor through a series of questions and measurements. The decision tree determines which measurements to take in what order, but it does not show any cause and effect.

A decision tree is fundamentally different than a CDD, because the boxes in a CDD represent a cause-and-effect chain between actions and outcomes. It might tell you that "if you charge this price," combined with "if you market to this demographic," then "this many people will be interested in your product," which, in turn, might cause "this many people to buy your product," which, in turn, might cause "this amount of revenues in this fiscal year." As you can see, this is a representation of a chain of events set in motion by your action, not a list of tests or questions to answer to reach a decision.

DI is not data flow

You might also see lots of boxes and arrows in a *data flow diagram* (also called a *data pipeline*). There, depending on how you do things, the boxes might represent data in a particular format or location, and the arrows might then represent how that data is changed to a new format or location. Modeling how data flows is not the same as modeling how a nondata causal chain might play out in the world: data flow happens inside a computer, and causal chains happen outside a computer.

What can get confusing here is that you might use data flow to *simulate* events that happen outside of a computer, as we'll talk about in more detail in Chapter 5. The key difference is that data flow can be designed however you like, but causal flow should represent some noncomputer process: the computer is only a simulation of the flow from actions to outcomes, even though you might use some sort of data to simulate that.

DI is not about "decisions that"

Something to keep in mind: the word *decision* is a bit overloaded. We can use it to mean human or automated "decisions that" or predictions. For example, we might decide *that* a particular picture shows a cat (classification) or predict *that* there is a 20% chance that a user will click on a button (regression). In DI, the word *decision* has a third meaning: a choice to take an action with the intent to lead to an outcome.

DI is not operations research or linear programming

For some decisions, you can use math to determine the best action to lead to your outcomes. If so, then the mature and powerful discipline of operations research (*https://oreil.ly/Hrphx*) has great answers for you (formally, operations research focuses on *analytical* methods in contrast to DI's *numerical* focus). But the vast majority of decisions aren't amenable to this approach, so we need something different. If you've got some math that works for your decision, then we say to go for it! But if not (and especially if math is not your thing), then this book is for you.

DI is not decision analysis

Although they're closely related, DI and decision analysis (DA) are not the same. Here's how *Link* describes the difference:

> With an over-30-year history, the field of Decision Analysis (DA) covers the philosophy, methodology, and professional practice for formally addressing important decisions ... often in complex situations where there are multiple objectives and decisions must be made under uncertainty.
>
> DA has a considerable overlap with DI, but with a particular focus: providing tools and techniques for teams and leaders to formalize and structure high-value decisions in complex situations. It is less technology- and data-focused than decision support, business intelligence, and DI, all of which go beyond decision making to provide tools that are used continuously in an organization.

Although it was invented independently, you can think of DI as a natural descendent to the important discipline of DA. DI adds technology integration, simulation, data, and AI to the picture. It stands alone, but if you really want to be an expert decision maker, we recommend you take a look at a few DA books as well.

The Decision Framing process of Chapter 2 gives more details about how to decide if your decision is right for DI.

The DI Maturity Model

The DI Maturity Model in Figure 1-3 captures a number of trajectories by which organizations improve their adoption of DI over time.

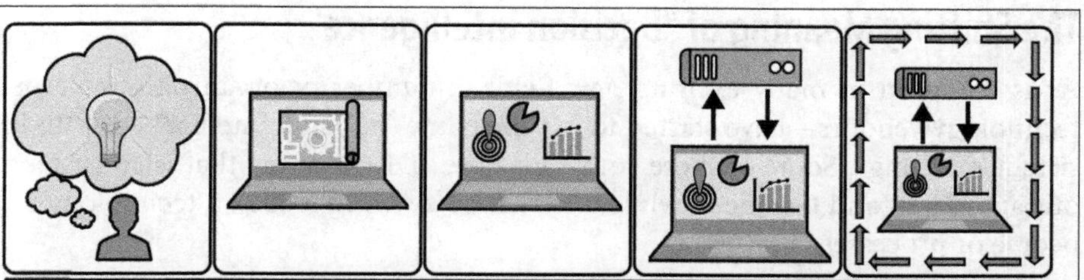

	Basic	Data-driven	Outcome-aware	Outcome-driven	Optimized
People	Focus on the need to use data to improve decision making.	Focus on data-driven insights.	Focus on how actions drive outcomes.	Embrace DI and focus on outcome assurance.	Focus on outcome optimization.
Process	Decision makers connect data to decisions in their heads.	Decision makers use BI dashboards to gain insights and mentally connect insights to outcomes.	Decision makers use CDDs and interactive simulations to explore actions to outcomes.	DI helps decision makers focus on outcomes at risk.	DI partners with decision makers and suggests optimizations.
Technology	Office tools.	Data, AI, and models drive insights on BI dashboards.	Decision model simulation for key decisions.	CDD simulations detect outcomes at risk.	CDD simulations find optimal actions to achieve best outcomes.
Data	Considering data governance.	Maturing data governance.	CDDs connect cause and effect to data governance.	Decision models fully integrated with data governance.	Decision-data integration powers optimization.

Figure 1-3. The Decision Intelligence Maturity Model, version 1.3.

Like Capability Maturity Model Integration (*https://oreil.ly/fhGDa*) for software or ISO/IEC 15504 (*https://oreil.ly/V90Yp*) for processes, the DI Maturity Model is a roadmap for improving how an organization does DI. It shows the attributes of organizations at different maturity levels. It does not, however, tell you how to "personalize" the maturity levels so that they work within your specific organizational context or how to recognize whether your organization is ready to start moving up a level. No book can do that! Look instead to the same HR, change management, or organizational development people who can help you communicate the value of DI. They can also help you bring your organization to a higher DI maturity level.

The Shifting Meaning of "Decision Intelligence"

As is common in many exciting new fields, a number of organizations—especially technology vendors—have started to use the name "decision intelligence" with inconsistent meanings. Some of these companies use "DI" in a way that is consistent with our approach (and Google's), while others have a strong focus on technology but not people or processes.

This handbook seeks to correct that imbalance. To realize the maximum benefit of this important new discipline, all three "legs of the stool" must be included: people, process, and technology.

Who Is Doing DI Today?

DI is being applied in many domains, including agriculture, telecommunications, government, health care, climate, space, energy, earth science, and venture investment. As covered extensively in *Link*, there is a growing DI community of practice: people and organizations who are passionate about DI and are working to improve the methodology and develop tooling. There is a vibrant market of DI vendors and organizations around the world, many of whom are graduates of DI courses (*https://oreil.ly/OyLOc*). Many of them fall into the Decision Intelligence Service Provider (DISP) category: experts within specific verticals/decisions that use DI to bring their products to market. Companies include Data Innovation.AI (*https://oreil.ly/eG_r7*), which uses DI to help buildings make decisions about employee health, CModel, IntelliPhi (recently acquired by a large management consulting firm), SatSure, and C-Plan.IT (*https://oreil.ly/dqo7v*); the Decision Intelligence Tokyo meetup group (*https://oreil.ly/pZqJf*); and companies like Astral Insights (*https://oreil.ly/0eFws*), Diwo (*https://oreil.ly/gBJSZ*), Pyramid Analytics (*https://oreil.ly/J2CQJ*), Tellius (*https://oreil.ly/Sgunq*), Peak (*https://oreil.ly/RZbvf*), Rainbird.AI (*https://oreil.ly/GZO_G*), and Aera (*https://oreil.ly/djJp0*). Decision Intelligence News (*https://oreil.ly/zgxW7*) covers the discipline as well. And Trillium Technologies (*https://oreil.ly/d3ZEV*) is working with Oxford University and the European Space Agency to bring DI to important problems of climate stewardship.

As any discipline matures, certifications (like the PMP for project managers (*https://oreil.ly/6aVfq*) or the Six Sigma belt system for quality managers (*https://oreil.ly/Jotfg*)) become important for recruiting and consulting. A number of DI certification programs are currently in development.

The Nine DI Processes

The core of this book is a nine-part DI process model, shown in Figure 1-4.

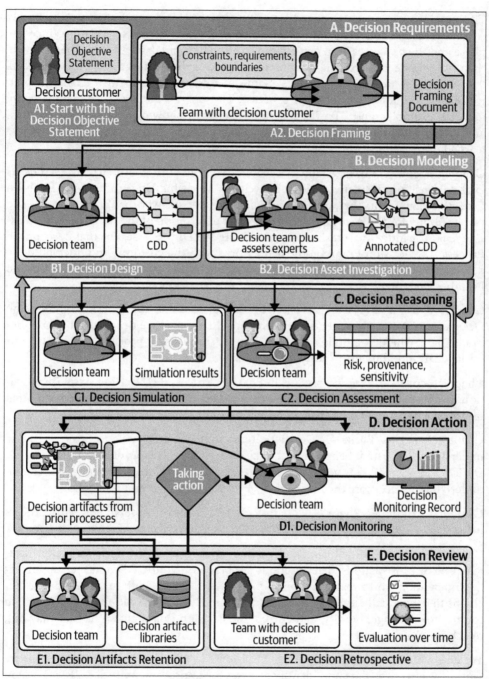

Figure 1-4. Overview of the nine DI processes.

The nine processes are organized into five phases, A through E, that group closely related processes together, with one or two processes per phase. We introduce the phase and the processes in it, explain the terminology and concepts, and then provide the tools you need to execute the processes: process descriptions and the worksheets that document process deliverables. Some phases are covered in a single chapter, while others require two (one per process). Throughout the book, we include many use-case examples and "Try It Yourself" exercises, showing you how to perform and document the processes in that phase and allowing you to practice what you've learned.

Chapter 2 covers Phase A, the Decision Requirements phase, which establishes expectations for the deliverables of Decision Modeling. In Process A1, Decision Objective Statement, the *decision customer* (the person who has the authority and responsibility for the decision) provides a brief description of the decision to the *decision team* (or individual) tasked with executing the DI processes for that decision. In Process A2, Decision Framing, the team works with the customer to understand the decision requirements and constraints and record them on a worksheet or Decision Framing Document.

Chapter 3 begins Phase B, Decision Modeling, focusing on Process B1, Decision Design. Decision requirements are a prerequisite to effective decision modeling, but modeling is where you build value. In the Decision Design process, you create your initial CDD, the "blueprint" for your decision.

Chapter 4 covers the second process in Phase B: Process B2, Decision Asset Investigation. In this process, you identify the existing data, models, and human expertise that inform the decision and add these *decision assets* to your CDD.

Chapter 5 begins Phase C, Decision Reasoning, where you'll use your CDD to understand the system behavior and risks associated with your decision. Process C1, Decision Simulation, lets you understand the behavior of the cause-and-effect system underlying the decision: the mechanisms by which actions lead to outcomes.

Chapter 6 continues Phase C with Process C2, Decision Assessment. This process helps you manage risk.

Chapter 7 covers Phase D, Decision Action, when you (or the decision maker) execute one or more actions. These actions are based on your CDD and the supporting documentation you created in prior processes. They set off the cause-and-effect chains that eventually lead to outcomes. Process D1, Decision Monitoring, allows you to monitor, manage, modify, and correct the decision causal chains as they play out, to achieve the outcomes you want.

We end with Chapter 8, on Phase E, Decision Review. This phase lets you improve your decisions over time and identify avenues for improvement. Process E1, Decision Artifacts Retention, preserves all the valuable information (or *decision artifacts*) from your well-documented decision so they can serve as starting points or reusable building blocks for future decisions. Process E2, Decision Retrospective, is the final process. It lets your team reflect on and learn from the current decision. Here, you'll ask whether your decision process was sound, then determine possible improvements to your process, information, knowledge, and/or model.

Conclusion

If you've taken the time to read through Chapter 1, you've got a good understanding of where DI comes from, how it fits in with other disciplines, and in particular what DI is not. By now, you're probably hungry for the details of how to *do* DI. Good, because that's the main point of the book. Let's start with Chapter 2, which guides you through the start of your DI journey.

CHAPTER 2

Decision Requirements

A subscription news service in the United Kingdom asked us to help it to come up to speed with using machine learning (ML).[1] This business was an insurgent in a crowded marketplace. It wanted to grow rapidly, our contact explained, while still retaining its long-standing reputation for excellent customer service. Could an ML strategy lower the cost of a high-touch relationship with the company's most important customers? We visited the news service in person twice—once for an AI strategy planning workshop and then a second time to teach its software engineers how to develop an ML model.

To set things up in advance of our ML training, we held a few phone calls to choose a project through which we could train the team while also helping the news service accomplish its goal. The company selected to build a *churn model*: a system that predicts which customers are most likely to close their accounts and switch to a competitor. ML-based churn models have been widely successful and can be applied in a broad range of situations: for instance, similar systems are used to predict who will vote in an election, who is likely to continue donating to a nonprofit, and more.

As we were preparing, the director of analytics invited us to a Zoom meeting with his boss, an executive and company owner who was skeptical of the project. The executive spoke frankly:

> I don't believe in machine learning for churn prediction. And here's why: *just predicting churn isn't enough.* Most companies just call whoever they think is going to leave and make some sort of offer or deal to retain them. But, for some of our customers, I think that if we call them on the phone, then this will *encourage* them to leave, not *discourage* them: quite the unintended consequence! Some of our customers will say, "Glad you called, I was planning to close my account and switch to a new provider—let's do it now."

---

1 This example, along with all others in this book, has been anonymized.

In the ensuing conversation, we learned that effective churn prediction was only *part* of what the news service wanted. It turned out that the company needed three separate ML systems, integrated through DI. The executive explained that the true goals were, in order:

1. To maintain the highest level of customer service, especially for our high-value customers, and to avoid the decrease in customer attentiveness that we've observed at the incumbent operators

2. To retain those high-value customers for their lifetimes

3. As one way to achieve these goals, to call those customers on the phone who are:

   - Likely to churn

   - Likely to respond in a positive way to our offer to retain them (as opposed to using the phone call to leave us)

   - Likely to be high-value customers for a long time

You may have faced a similar situation in your own organization: sometimes you only find out a project's true goals partway through. This is a well-known situation in software engineering, where overenthusiastic coders sometimes start building things before they fully understand exactly what is needed. The result is unnecessary rework once the true requirements are discovered.

Software engineers know to try to prevent this mistake through careful *requirements analysis*: ensuring that the frame of the problem is right. After all, it's about a hundred times cheaper to fix problems early on than to fix them after a project is delivered. "Measure twice, cut once," as carpenters and tailors like to say.

Fortunately, thanks to this news service's culture of transparency and plain speaking, we learned about the potential miscommunication early on and could refocus our efforts toward the real goals.

But most projects aren't so lucky. Time and again, we've seen statistics, ML, and other quantitative project teams *guess* at the structure of their decision—its goals, actions, and more—instead of following a structured process to ensure that the project starts off in the right direction. Sometimes they even get all the way to the end before they realize that their work has been fundamentally misdirected.

This bears repeating and emphasizing: *guessing at the decision is massively inefficient.* It means that you're gathering data, preparing and presenting it, converting it into models and software, and then delivering results to customers that don't match those customers' needs, in form or capabilities. For this reason more than any other, analytics projects often miss their marks—and that leads many senior executives to refuse to include "the data people" in their most important decisions.

"Using all the right math to answer the wrong question," as Google's Kozyrkov has put it, is known as a "Type III error."[2] Kozyrkov goes on to describe DI (*https://oreil.ly/mUhi5*) as "a cure for asking and answering the wrong question" and a way to "build up your immunity to Type III error and useless analytics."

The practices in this chapter will help you ensure that your project starts off on the right foot and remove a great deal of risk. But you're going to have to think in a new way. You'll be starting with the *business*, not the technology.

Decision Requirements (Phase A): Overview

Decision Requirements is the first DI phase. It contains two processes. Process A1 involves creating an initial description of the decision—called the *Decision Objective Statement*—and Process A2 is for developing the requirements for modeling the decision, called *Decision Framing*. Decision Framing includes a *decision verification* step, in which you ensure that the DI approach is the right one for this decision.

The purpose of the Decision Requirements phase is to set the stage for all subsequent DI processes, aligning your team around what decision is to be made and ensuring everyone understands the decision maker's scope of responsibility (such as outcomes, goals, and business objectives) and authority (available actions).

It can be tempting to skip Phase A, but beware: if you do, you could start off on the wrong track, which could limit the value of all downstream processes.

In this chapter, we'll give a brief overview of both processes in Phase A. Then we'll look at each in detail, explaining why they are important, briefly discussing their conceptual background, and providing use cases from two teams conducting Phase A processes, complete with process descriptions and worksheets.

Figure 2-1 shows Phase A in the context of the other process phases. You'll begin with a simple Decision Objective Statement, which is more of a trigger than a true process: it gets the ball rolling. Objective Statements are usually vague and need to be clarified before moving on to Process A2, Decision Framing. Once you have an Objective Statement, you'll convene your decision team.

---

2 Ian I. Mitroff and Abraham Silvers, *Dirty Rotten Strategies: How We Trick Ourselves and Others into Solving the Wrong Problems Precisely* (Stanford, CA: Stanford Business Books, 2009).

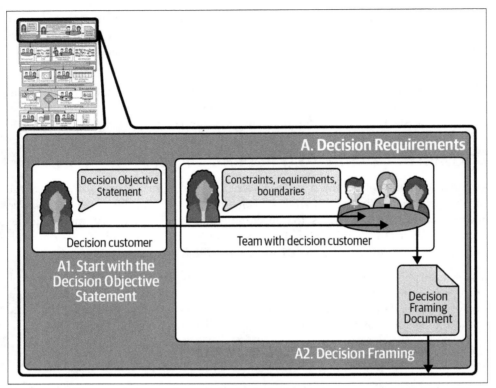

Figure 2-1. Phase A, Decision Requirements, includes two processes: A1, Decision Objective Statement, and A2, Decision Framing.

The purpose of Decision Framing is to clearly communicate the nonnegotiable "guard rails" of the decision-making process to the decision team. This process consists of agreeing to boundaries around the decision, such as what is in and out of scope, what the outcomes and objectives are, and what actions are available. This will help you to verify that the Decision Objective Statement represents a decision that is appropriate for DI, along with how you will work with the decision customer to understand the decision requirements and constraints. You'll record this information in a *Decision Framing Worksheet*, which is the deliverable from this process that's used in later processes.

Now, let's look at each process in more detail.

Process A1: The Decision Objective Statement

The Decision Objective Statement is not a true process but rather a trigger that creates the initiative within which the remaining eight processes are followed. It usually begins with an email or other communication that describes the decision to be made. Here are some examples:

> "Please help me to decide whether we should sell our company to our competitor."
>
> "Please help me to create a policy that will help our company reach net-zero greenhouse gas emissions by ten years from now by reducing our use of air travel."
>
> "Please help me to decide what demographic(s) to target with my new product."
>
> "I grow sweet potatoes in the face of changing weather patterns, and I have detected a pest in my field. Please help me decide what to do to maximize my profits in the next two years under these circumstances."
>
> "Please help me to decide which of the buildings on my corporate campus should be decommissioned and sold."

The Decision Objective Statement serves as an anchor for later decision making and keeps the team focused on the original request from the decision customer. It does not follow any formal structure. As you can see, however, it does follow a pattern, starting with "please help me to decide." Sometimes there's an unstated context, such as when the requester believes that there is some new resource that will help them make a better decision than in the past. One reason is that organizations are hearing about DI and decide to use it to help with decisions that, in the past, were made informally.[3]

A quick point from previous chapters bears repeating here: *all models—including decision models—are by necessity incomplete*. A decision model supports people's intuition, instead of replacing it. And DI is—by and large—an intelligence *augmentation*—aka *hybrid*—approach, where we're not handing off all automated decision making to a machine, but working with it in collaboration (the "CI" of Chapter 1). This is new, attractive, and exciting to many: it opens up a raft of new opportunities to use AI, data, and other technology. And, since DI can take advantage of an LLM (like ChatGPT) "copilot," we think that DI is a "killer app" (one that, all by itself, justifies the existence) for LLMs.

Back to the Decision Objective Statement. Sometimes it lists choices: for instance, whether to sell to a competitor or not. Sometimes it lists the goals but not the choices, such as in the sweet potato example that was given. Sometimes it lists a combination or subset of goals, actions, and externals. Again, there's no consistent pattern. Nor

---

3 Most of the decisions described in this book are made by organizations, not individuals. However, we believe that, as DI becomes better known and new tools emerge to support it, individuals will start to use DI as well.

should there be: the idea is to make it easy to get started by remaining in the natural language of decision makers.

In this chapter, you'll be working to fill in the gaps in these incomplete Objective Statements by identifying and answering unanswered questions about the frame of the decision.

As we get started, please note that, for each of the DI phases in this book, we provide a formal process description, along with worksheets that you can use to guide your work. You can find blank versions of the two worksheets for this chapter in the supplemental materials repository (*https://oreil.ly/DIH-supplemental*). Note that some processes contain optional steps that you may or may not need. Others contain sets of alternative tasks for decisions or teams with different characteristics.

We'll now turn to another Objective Statement use case, which we'll follow by giving some notes about what you might do to convene a decision team in response to it.

Decision Objective Statement: Net-Zero Emissions Program Use Case

We'll now show you an example of objective setting for an example DI project. We recently worked with a European federal government agency tasked with bringing its greenhouse gas (GHG) emissions down to net zero within 10 years, to achieve a strategic goal of reducing its overall climate impact.

Our point of contact was the VP of analytics, who had in the past been tasked with gathering data and creating dashboards to support this initiative. For three years, management had mandated that the agency as a whole should become more "data-driven." The load on this VP's data team was increasing steadily, as more and more projects asked for data to be collected, stored, and organized. The agency invested in data and analytics tooling—databases, BI tools, data warehouses, and more. But costs were rising without a commensurate improvement in decision making.

Before we were brought in, the project had focused on understanding the organization's historical GHG emissions. Our VP's team spent considerable effort identifying internal sources to answer questions about the emissions of each of the organization's buildings and of staff members' air travel. But all that data was not leading anyone to a better understanding of what actions could lead to achieving the actual organizational goals, like the net-zero initiative.

The senior executive sponsor of the effort then posed a question that captures the goal of using DI: "Even if we have the best data for the present and past, how can we use that data to inform decisions about the future?"

The VP read coauthor Pratt's previous book *Link* (*https://oreil.ly/kINon*) and reached out to our company, Quantellia, for help. He described his situation as a "last mile" problem: his data was great, but not enough. The organization needed to create a link from data to decisions.

We agreed to start a DI project in parallel to the data presentation effort that would focus only on the missing link between data and decisions—in particular, the "people" and "process" sides of the "people/process/technology" triad, since this was the greatest lack in the organization.

To narrow the scope of the initiative, the VP chose to begin by focusing specifically on the GHG impact of international air travel to conferences. He arrived at this Decision Objective Statement:

> What policy should we create regarding airline travel amongst our employees, so that we can reduce our GHGs while at the same time maintaining the benefits of travel (relationships, trust, reputation, learning, employee morale, and more)?

The agency asked Quantellia to provide an external team to facilitate the DI initiative. We began recruiting volunteers from multiple departments to form the decision team.

Interlude: Convening the Decision Team

After you have received the Objective Statement and before you start gathering the decision requirements, it's time to convene the decision team. It will be the decision team's job to shepherd the decision through the DI project phases, starting with Decision Framing, as is described later in this chapter.

The ideal decision team includes people with strong and diverse expertise about the decision at hand. To cover the most important dimensions of this diversity, we recommend ensuring that team members:

- Come from different parts of the organization (such as engineering, finance, and operations)
- Bring different life perspectives (such as genders, ages, races, and socioeconomic backgrounds)
- Work at different points in the value chain (such as technicians, policymakers, and stakeholders)

We have found that the ideal team size is 5 to 15 people. It is best to avoid including any two people with a supervisory relationship within the team, like a manager and subordinate, to avoid political issues.

Here are some examples of the people on decision teams we've worked with:

- Department heads from across an organization whose work was interdependent, but who had not previously worked together
- Experts looking to structure their knowledge and data with the eventual goal of embodying it in a software product
- A part-time, matrixed team tasked by a senior executive facing a particularly challenging and costly decision, chosen for their known access to data and/or knowledge to support that decision

It's helpful at this point to formalize the roles involved in the decision. First, the *decision maker* is the person (or group) who actually makes the decision and executes one or more of the actions. The decision maker has both authority and responsibility (*https://oreil.ly/Ap5-A*) for the decision. They may work alone through the DI processes, or delegate some or all of the DI processes to a group or individual. In both cases, we'll call these process-executors the *decision team* throughout the book. If the decision is delegated, the decision maker is sometimes called the *decision customer*, reflecting the decision team's service relationship to them.

Many organizations choose to tailor the decision-requirements DI processes to their particular needs. To achieve this, sometimes it is useful to appoint a disinterested party—a *facilitator*—who is a DI expert to do this tailoring and to lead the decision team through all or some of the DI processes. The facilitator may also train the team on DI processes as needed, which is what Quantellia did for the European agency.

Appointing a team leader is another helpful strategy. The responsibility of the DI team leader is to manage all or most of the DI processes and communication between the DI team and the larger organization, especially the decision customer. The team leader may also be responsible for ensuring that the team appropriately follows all organizational policies and non-DI processes.

Making Decisions at Multiple Organizational Levels

Many organizations make decisions about the same topic at multiple levels. For instance, in our net-zero emissions program example, executives want to create a policy that lowers the average number of trips per employee and thus reduces GHG emissions. This policy may result in each department being allocated an air travel budget. Each department head must then decide which travel requests to approve, in a way that complies with the policy created at a higher level of management. Then, at the next level down, individual travelers must decide what to request, again in compliance with higher-level decisions. Their sphere of influence is limited to their own travel.

Each of these decisions represents a different decision level, so when you're getting going with DI, it's important to be clear about the organizational level of your decision. The easiest way to do this is to identify the decision maker: a particular person or role.

If the decision is really several decisions at different organizational levels, framing can uncover that. Then your team can create separate Decision Framing Worksheets (and, ultimately, different but interlocking decision-making projects) for each decision at each level.

Balancing Information, Authority, and Responsibility

Most typically, authority and responsibility for the decision lie with the decision customer, and the decision team acts in an advisory capacity. A classic decision-making mistake is to cross the line from advising ("here is an action you might not have considered," "here is a consequence of that action that you might not have anticipated") to making a decision ("you should take action A") when you don't have that authority, nor responsibility for the outcome.

Occasionally, some decision customers do delegate decision authority to teams. This can be the right move, but if you do, be sure to clearly establish (and capture it in the Decision Framing materials) who has the authority to make the decision. Keep information, responsibility, and authority in balance to hold everyone accountable.

Delegating responsibility without authority is a recipe for sloppiness and mistakes, because there's no accountability for the result (this is called a *moral hazard*). On the flip side, when a team has information but no authority nor responsibility, it can be tempting for them to *take* that authority without going through proper channels.

DI helps with these imbalances. It allows all parties to better share information. Decision models make the data, models, and knowledge—along with the connections between them—explicit in a way that might otherwise not be apparent to a decision maker.

If the decision customer will ultimately be held responsible for the outcome of the associated decision, then the onus is on them to decide how much to use the model and how much to rely on their intuition. This will be especially challenging when their intuition and the decision model suggest different actions. Decision modeling, by its nature, does not address this challenge: that remains up to the person with the decision responsibility and authority to weigh these two sources of information. The decision model improves on—but does not replace—"invisible" intuition by helping the decision customer to understand situations with complex dynamics, like feedback effects and multiple links between actions and outcomes, and by providing a structure that helps them integrate knowledge from multiple sources.

Before moving on, let's be clear about the Process A1 deliverable. An Objective Statement is an imprecise, unrefined description of the decision in the decision maker's own words. It's a starting point. In each of the next five processes you'll build on it, make it more precise, and add information. By the end of Phase C, Decision Reasoning, in Chapter 6, you'll know quite a bit about the decision and be ready to act.

The next process in Phase A is Decision Framing, where you'll start by getting clear on what the decision maker wants to decide.

Process A2: Decision Framing

This section provides guidance on how to conduct the Decision Framing process. This is our first *true* formal process, since the Objective Statement is more of a trigger that starts everything than a process itself. Decision Framing builds a common understanding of all the decision requirements and the team's deliverable(s) between the customer and your team. A clear Decision Framing Worksheet ensures that any confusion is resolved at the beginning of this project. This has the effect of reducing the likelihood of rework downstream. Decision Framing also sets expectations for the deliverables of the DI processes (which are different from the outcomes of the decision itself).

Decision Verification

The first step of Decision Framing is called *decision verification*. Here, your decision team confirms that the Decision Objective Statement represents a decision that is appropriate for DI.

As you learned in Chapter 1, DI is used for human-in-the-loop action-to-outcome decisions. Fill out Phase A, Worksheet 1: Decision Verification, available in the supplemental materials repository (*https://oreil.ly/DIH-supplemental*), answering all of the questions thoroughly, to ensure that the decision at hand is best made using DI (see "Phase A, Worksheet 1: Decision Verification, tailored for the telecom use case" for an example). If it is *not* an actions-to-outcomes decision, consult with the decision customer to decide what to do next. If it is an action-to-outcomes decision, is it too simple for DI to be useful? For example, "If my customer signs off on the deliverable by noon tomorrow, I'll take a long lunch with my husband." If there are no causal chains because the data leads you directly to your action, DI may not be justified.

Next, you'll work with the decision customer to understand the decision requirements and constraints and to record them on Phase A, Worksheet 2: Decision Framing, as illustrated in the use cases that follow (see "Phase A, Worksheet 2: Decision Framing, tailored for the telecom use case" for an example).

But before you get to the decision, the first question you should ask is: "How is this decision (or ones similar to it) being made today?" The most common answer we hear to this is: "We talk about it, and often whoever tells the best story prevails." We call this the decision *baseline*.

The second question to ask is: "How can we measure the quality of today's decision?" Often the answer is: "We can't, really, but we're pretty confident that if our decision processes are better, our decision won't be worse"—with "better" meaning changes like using data and ensuring participation from a diverse group of experts.

The third question is: "How will we know if the new decision is better?" We often hear something like: "Well, we used data and more experts and we drew a CDD, so it seems pretty obvious that the decision is going to be better."

The worksheets mention three important DI elements: *actions*, *outcomes*, and *metrics*. For purposes of this framing step, the descriptions of these elements in the worksheets will suffice.

You should resist the temptation to teach anyone these terms' formal definitions at this point. Experts have a long tradition of speaking to *impress* more than to *communicate*, but your goal at this stage is to use the natural language of the decision maker for as long as possible. Keep your language plain and allow ambiguity (for now). Listen more than you talk. If you fill people's heads with new terminology and concepts, you'll reduce their ability to do the most important task right now, which is to think clearly and creatively about all of the actions available to them and all of the potential outcomes—intended and unintended.

Why Decision Framing Is Important

Many organizations skip Decision Framing. Others make an unspoken assumption that everyone shares the same understanding of the decision, without taking the time to document the framing. This is understandable; if your organization places great value on being nimble, then framing can feel like unnecessary baggage.

Yet decisions can live or die based on how well they're framed—even more so than on getting the right data, the right expertise, or even the right decision makers in the room. Indeed, researchers looking to understand the roots of bad decisions often trace them back to this very early process going awry: too often, the decision makers are simply trying to achieve different goals. Decision Framing is designed to prevent that.

In contrast to Decision Modeling (see Chapters 3 and 4), Decision Framing focuses on the "box": the boundaries, constraints, responsibilities, and authorities within which the decision team is allowed to work. You might call the "box" the "what" of the decision-making process, with the "how" of the process details located "inside the box."

As organizational complexity and volatility increase, it becomes more and more important to borrow best practices from engineering disciplines that build complex things, like airplanes and software. This "what" versus "how" distinction is one such best practice. It may seem simple, but it is widespread in engineering disciplines, where it is often described as the "principle of interface versus implementation." When you get too technical about the data, models, or terminology, you violate that important boundary.

Documenting the framing of the decision provides a formalized "contract" or "charter" between the inside of the box and the outside: in this case, between the decision customer and the decision team. This allows the team to maximize its latitude while working to meet the goal of its "what," without having to guess as to its responsibilities and authorities. Although crisp communication along these lines can feel onerous at first, it is essential.

Our treatment of Decision Framing follows Tversky and Kahneman (*https://oreil.ly/Sfjce*), who define a decision frame as "the decision-maker's conception of the acts, outcomes, and contingencies associated with a particular choice." They demonstrate rigorously that the choices teams make can vary radically if the frame changes, even when the expected outcomes are identical. A well-documented decision frame can go a long way to achieving better decisions.

Another perspective: if organizations are "decision factories," as Roger Martin writes (*https://oreil.ly/rqbeZ*), then clear interfaces between the "machines" of the factory (the people who make the decisions) are essential for efficient operations. This is the role of framing.

Indeed, simply following the framing process can have considerable value on its own—even before you take any other steps in this book. If you do choose to go further, then you will add value at every step—by designing your decision, by finding the right data and other technologies and models to support your decision, and by using that data and technology to simulate your decision. But take the time to fully understand the framing questions in the worksheets before you look at any data, talk to any resources, or do any decision analysis, as Google's Kozyrkov explains (*https://oreil.ly/0Q4x3*).

Take a moment to read through the formal process description. As a reminder, you can find blank versions of the two worksheets for this chapter in the supplemental materials repository (*https://oreil.ly/DIH-supplemental*).

Formal Process Description: Process A2, Decision Framing

Description

Documents the frame of the decision: any constraints, boundaries, and/or requirements that come from outside of the decision team

Prerequisites
- You have identified the decision customer, decision team, and decision team leader.
- You have documented a Decision Objective Statement.

Responsible role
Decision team leader

Steps
1. Read through this process and tailor it, as appropriate, to your organization. Choose which alternative to use for step 2.

    - Complete Phase A, Worksheet 1: Decision Verification and revise the statement, if necessary.

2. (Alternative 1) Complete Phase A, Worksheet 2: Decision Framing, if a brief form is appropriate.

    (Alternative 2) If extra effort is justified—such as for a highly impactful decision in terms of costs or benefits—then append the following additional sections to the Decision Framing Worksheet as appropriate:

    Motivation for the decision-making project
    Who will benefit from a rigorous treatment of this decision? What risks will be avoided? What goals—strategic, operational, and/or tactical—will be served?

    Background and context for the decision
    In particular, it can be very helpful to describe how the decision is being made today. If it hasn't been made before, then how are similar decisions made?

    Desired form of deliverables from the team
    This might be one or more of a CDD (specify appropriate level of detail for the stakeholders and decision maker), a decision tree, a document, a presentation, a research study, and/or software.

    Relevant resources
    Examples include research, data, statistical or ML models, human expertise, documents, and external publications.

    How you'll measure the success of the decision
    This might mean comparing the performance of different decisions, comparing your process to an external standard (such as the ISO standards) to ensure that you're following best practices in your field, or using another specific metric for what constitutes success.

3. If the decision involves several levels in the organization, explain in your worksheet or document whether you'll address them one at a time or all at once, and how they relate to each other.

4. Capture suggestions or ideas that come up regarding other decision elements (like datasets, budget approximations, or cause-and-effect links) for later use.

5. Establish a decision glossary to capture and define any ambiguous terms.

6. Obtain sign-off or agreement on the completed Decision Framing Worksheet as needed.

Deliverables
- A completed Phase A, Worksheet 1: Decision Verification

- A rewritten Decision Objective Statement, if appropriate

- A written and approved Phase A, Worksheet 2: Decision Framing

When the Decision Frame Is Wrong

Without the right decision framing, we have found that team members often focus too much on the "how" without making sure the team is aligned on the "what" (as mentioned, this is called a *Type III error*).[4] And, for complex decisions, *cognitive overload*—when your brain is "maxed out" with ideas and unable to take in any new information—is an important factor. You can mitigate cognitive overload by deferring any "how" discussions until the "what" is well understood.

Without an effective Decision Framing process, we've observed several problems that commonly arise, including:

The decision customer rejects the decision team's work.
When the decision customer's needs are not well documented, the team may build a decision model that is not useful to the customer or makes recommendations that contradict the customer's intent.

For example, if the CEO views Italy as a "must-have" country for a product launch but this requirement isn't captured, the team might present a recommendation that doesn't include Italy at all. The CEO might ultimately reject the recommendation, wasting significant resources.

---

4 Technologists are often rewarded for their ability to provide great *solutions* (the "how" of this paragraph). So much so, we have observed, that in many domains they've lost a connection to the *problems* that solutions are meant to solve. We've seen this in particular among data scientists, who are not typically taught how to communicate with their customers. DI fills this gap.

The decision team does not leverage all available expertise.
> If the decision team fails to document the guidance of all relevant experts within the organization, the decision maker could miss something important and make a suboptimal decision.

The decision process solves the wrong problem.
> When the decision isn't framed clearly, the team might do a lot of work to solve the wrong problem, spending considerable time and expense on data collection and governance only to have to start over.

The decision customer confuses "how" with "what."
> The framing needs to capture the *real* goals of the decision customer. If the CEO specifies that one of the countries to launch into in the next three years is Italy, ask why. If the CEO's real goal is simply to maximize revenues, the team can evaluate whether to launch in Italy based on how well it achieves that goal, rather than simply taking the request at face value.

There are unintended consequences.
> The framing DI process is the first time the decision team attempts to think of unintended (and often undesired) outcomes that a set of actions could cause. For instance, the European agency's net-zero emissions project turns some in-person relationships into remote relationships, which could weaken those relationships and thus make them less effective.

Now that you have a sense of how the framing process works, let's return to our net-zero emissions program use case to see how the team frames their decision. We'll then look at a hypothetical case so you can try out your decision-framing skills.

Verifying and Framing: Net-Zero Emissions Program Use Case

When we last left our European government agency, they had just convened the decision team, asking it to address this Decision Objective Statement:

> What policy should we create regarding airline travel amongst our employees, so that we can reduce our GHGs while at the same time maintaining the benefits of travel (relationships, trust, reputation, learning, employee morale, and more)?

Next, the team created a Decision Framing Worksheet (shown in "Example of a Decision Verification Worksheet"). They also tailored the process and worksheets in two ways: combining the verification and framing exercises into a single worksheet, and omitting questions from the template for which management did not provide answers.

Example of a Decision Verification Worksheet tailored for the net-zero emissions program use case, combining elements of Phase A, Worksheet 1 and Phase A, Worksheet 2

	**Decision Objective Statement:** What policy should we create regarding airline travel amongst our employees, so that we can reduce our GHGs while at the same time maintaining the benefits of travel (relationships, trust, reputation, learning, employee morale, and more)?
	**Decision Verification**
Item	**Answers and/or comments**
Is this a decision made by people (possibly with technology support)?	Yes, at the individual and executive levels.
Is this a decision to take action(s) that will lead to outcomes?	Yes, travel contributes to our carbon footprint and also provides the company certain benefits.
If not, can the objective be restated as a decision to take action(s) that will lead to outcomes?	Not applicable.
Are we sure that this is a decision and not a process?	Yes.
Have you identified at least one possibly vague outcome?	Yes, "reduce our GHGs."
Do you agree that there are actions that someone could take to create this outcome?	Yes, to create a policy.
Is this decision obvious given a specific piece of data? (If yes, this is not a good DI decision.)	No, this decision is complex, involving relationships, reputation, and GHGs.
	**Does the decision appear to be too simple for DI?** **If the answer to any of the following questions is "yes," then DI will be valuable.**
Is it possible that the team is not aligned around outcomes?	Possible, but unknown.
Do the outcomes include soft factors like brand?	Yes, "quality of relationships," so DI will be valuable.
Do actions or outcomes cross silos?	Yes, sustainability and HR and the travel department, at the very least.
Is there a high cost of error?	Yes, we could accidentally hurt our standing in the world and our relationships.
Are unintended consequences possible? (Note that unintended consequences will be explored further in later phases; this is just the first time we ask this question.)	Yes, reducing travel is a big change to how we've operated in the past, so there seem to be the likelihood of these kinds of "unknown unknowns."
Will the team use data, models, or other decision assets to make the decision?	The team notes that there may be existing technology assets that could support this decision: research about the impact of virtual meetings, data about the cost of carbon offsets, and more.
Is there a need to track the decision over time and make adjustments?	Yes, the rollout will take time, and feedback from our employees will be important to take into account.
Is this a recurring decision?	No.
Are we sure that this is a decision, and not a process?	Yes, once the decision has been made, that *may* trigger a process to implement a policy and/or internal communication plan regarding how to think about travel planning.
Based on the answers to the previous questions, have we decided that this is a good decision for DI?	Yes, this is a good decision for DI.

Do we have the right members on the decision team?	No, we don't have experts who have helped with net-zero decisions in the past.

Decision Framing	
Item	**Answers and/or comments**
Baseline: how do we make the decision today?	We don't have a policy for this at all; focusing on GHGs has not been on the radar for travel decisions; it's informal.
Role of the decision-making team: advisory or decision-making authority?	Advisory; the sustainability head will be making the decision.
Outcomes (potentially measurable things, for which the decision customer considers the team responsible)	• GHG emissions: measured by our agency, as well as by an industry body that tracks GHG emissions in our sector • Influence on our peers and the world • Teams (new and existing): cohesiveness, engagement, creativity, ability to learn from others in teams • Cost of travel
Actions (the choices that you can make). This could be a selection between a few alternatives or a range (for example, "number of people who travel" could be a range from 50 to 1,000).	• Number of people who travel • Means of travel allowed: air, rail, local public transportation, foot • Policy decisions regarding employee travel incentives, privileges, and expectations • Means of engagement: digital participation versus in-person • Which events held in a foreign country are people allowed to attend (if similar conferences are run regularly)? • Class of service (Economy class? Business class?) • Trip length • Aircraft type • Number of stops and routing • Supplier (airline) choice • Frequency of trips (Could we combine things and fly overseas every two weeks instead of every week?)
External factors that influence the decision outcome(s) but are not in our control	• Attitudes toward the pandemic, specifically whether we need to keep adapting to more virtual meetings for a long period of time • Price of airline travel • Price of gas (for when automobile travel is a possible alternative) • Mandatory travel: some things must be done in person, such as production faults that require on-site approvals, equipment downtime, quality issues. "Hop on a plane and go to Australia" • Overall agency budgets for travel
Known goals	• GHG net zero in 10 years • Nearer-term targets • Travel-specific targets may arise later
How much time, money, and energy are we willing to invest to achieve these outcomes/goals?	Staff years

How much detail do the decision maker and stakeholders want in their CDD? Select one.	• Low—actions and outcomes with very sketchy causal chains • **Medium—casual chains should show key KPIs and leading indicators for outcomes** • High—stakeholders are analysts; bring on the details
What risks are we willing to take to achieve these outcomes/goals?	(Not specified)
Do we want to include in our analysis any externalities, including intended and unintended consequences?	(Not specified)
Decision constraints/boundaries	Must retain important relationships despite a reduction in the use of air travel
Suggestions that arose during framing	(Not specified)
Glossary terms	(Not specified)

Once the team has filled out this worksheet, then you're ready to move on to Phase B, which begins in Chapter 3.

Try It Yourself: Decision Requirements for a Telecom Use Case

It's time to make things a little more concrete by giving you a use case illustrating how you might go about receiving an Objective Statement and framing a decision. We include a number of exercises in this section so you can "try it yourself."

We'll start by describing a decision for a fictitious mobile telecom provider.

Imagine you are a product manager for a mobile telecom company that currently charges its subscribers for each minute of talk time and gigabyte of data usage.[5] The company needs to find ways to increase customer satisfaction. The executives believe that one way to do this may be to launch an "unlimited" subscription service, where customers can use all the voice-call minutes and data they desire for a single monthly price. The executives want to explore a range of unlimited plan options and understand the advantages, disadvantages, and risks of each one. Their goal is to decide whether or not to offer such a plan and, if so, what its specific parameters should be in terms of price, minutes, gigabytes of data, and so on.

The CEO, Dr. Smith, asks you to form a decision team to advise the board and describes the decision objective in an email:

---

5 This example is a composite of telecommunications companies interviewed for "High Performance Decision Making: A Global Study" (*https://oreil.ly/on-TZ*). As presented in this book, this example is an extension of the treatment in *Link* and L. Y. Pratt and Mark Zangari, *Decision Engineering Primer: Simplifying Complexity Through Collaboration* (Quantellia, LLC, 2015).

The executives want to explore a range of unlimited plan options supported with advantages, disadvantages, and risks in order to make a decision whether or not to offer such a plan and, if so, what plan.

You review the Decision Framing process and the two worksheets it uses. You decide that for now you don't need to bring in a facilitator.

Exercise

Before you read further, take a moment to think about the job roles you want to include on your team and why. For instance, do you want to include someone from the finance team? Someone from the customer service team? A software engineer? Who from around the company will be affected by the decision? Write a list.

You recruit your team. It includes the key stakeholders: the product manager in charge of pricing plans, two customer-care representatives, a member of the CFO organization, and an external market analyst. It's a diverse group in terms of gender, age, and ethnicity.

The team's first task is to verify that the decision is indeed a good fit for DI. You introduce the team to the Decision Verification Worksheet and work together to fill it out.

Exercise

Before you look at the completed worksheet that follows, download a blank copy and work through it, filling it out based on your understanding of the use case. When you're done, keep reading to see how your version compares to ours.

Phase A, Worksheet 1: Decision Verification, tailored for the telecom use case

Decision Objective Statement: The company needs to find ways to increase customer satisfaction. The executives believe that one way to do this may be to launch an "unlimited" subscription service, where customers can use all the voice-call minutes and data they desire for a single monthly price. The executives want to explore a range of unlimited plan options supported with advantages, disadvantages, and risks in order to make a decision whether or not to offer such a plan and, if so, what plan.

Item	Answers and/or comments
Is this a decision made by people (possibly with technology support)?	Yes, this decision will be made by the CEO, based on the work done by the decision team.
Is this a decision to take action(s) that will lead to outcomes?	Yes, the team is advising the CEO whether to take an action—offer an unlimited plan.
If not, can the objective be restated as a decision to take action(s) that will lead to outcomes?	Not applicable

Are we sure that this is a decision, and not a process?	Yes, once the decision has been made, that *may* trigger a process to implement an unlimited plan.
Have you identified at least one possibly vague outcome?	Yes, "increase customer satisfaction."
Do you agree that there are actions that someone could take to create this outcome?	Yes, "launch an unlimited plan."
Is this decision obvious given a specific piece of data? (If yes, this is not a good DI decision.)	No, this decision will use several kinds of data and models.
Does the decision appear to be too simple for DI? **If the answer to any of the following questions is "yes," then DI will be valuable.**	
Is it possible that the team is not aligned around outcomes?	Possible, but unknown.
Do the outcomes include soft factors like brand?	Yes, "customer satisfaction," so DI will be valuable.
Do actions or outcomes cross silos?	Yes, we expect there will be financial as well as soft outcomes.
Is there a high cost of error?	Yes, we could reduce profits or become less competitive.
Are unintended consequences possible? (Unintended consequences will be explored further in later phases; this is just the first time we ask this question.)	None are expected at this time.
Will the team use data, models, or other decision assets to make the decision?	The team notes that there may be existing technology assets that could support this decision: data about costs and benefits as well as customer behavior models.
Is there a need to track the decision over time and make adjustments?	Yes, the rollout will take time.
Is this a recurring decision?	No.
Based on the answers to the previous questions, have we decided that this is a good decision for DI?	Yes, this is a good decision for DI.
Do we have the right members on the decision team?	No, there is no one representing the customer.

In response to the answer to the last item in the worksheet, you invite to the team two employees who are also subscribers to the current plan, and you change the answer to that item accordingly. You and your team agree that there are enough answers provided in the validation questions that it makes sense to proceed using DI and to continue framing the decision in the next meeting.

Framing the Decision

Your decision team invites the CEO, Dr. Smith, to its next meeting. You start by delineating roles and responsibilities. You agree that the team's role is to gather information, build a decision model, and make a recommendation. Smith will review the team's work, make a final decision, and be ultimately responsible for its outcome.

Smith begins by suggesting that $50 per month might be a good price to charge for such a service. Jumping straight to choices like this is typical! Fortunately, you're prepared to keep the meeting on track.

You ask, "Are you requiring that this be what we charge, or are you simply suggesting that number as one option?" They answer that $50 just seems like a good idea, based on their experience. In response, you write on the whiteboard:

Decision Framing
- Determine the following aspects of an unlimited usage plan:
  — Price of the new service

On another part of the whiteboard, you write:

Ideas for Later
- $50 might be a good price.

You explain to the CEO that their judgment is very valuable: the team is interested in their ideas for how to implement the unlimited usage plan, and you'll consider them as you weigh evidence for the right price to charge. However, you explain that the primary focus of this meeting is to clarify the authority, information, and responsibility framing for the project. You add that it's important to separate the "good ideas" from the "rules of engagement" for the team, so everyone understands what latitude the team has available to you.

Asking About Outcomes and Goals

The discussion then turns to the outcomes that Dr. Smith wishes to achieve with the plan.

> *You:* The Objective Statement simply asks whether this unlimited usage plan is "a good idea." Dr. Smith, could you please clarify "good idea"? Does this mean that the company would achieve higher net revenues with the plan than without it?
>
> *Smith:* The board and I are concerned that a competitor might launch a similar plan and steal market share from us.

Again, answering a different question than the one you asked is typical. Patience here is important!

> *You:* Would you like us to consider offering an unlimited plan even if a competitor does *not* launch one of their own?
>
> *Smith:* Yes. We need to be anticipating, not just reacting to our environment, so the team should consider this scenario as well.

Note that the competitor's behavior is neither an action the company can take nor an outcome. It is an *external*—something that can affect outcomes and that the organization cannot control, but might be able to observe or measure.

You: Dr. Smith, do you or the board have any thoughts about the risks involved in this new plan, or about how much money and time we should plan to invest in it?

Smith: Those factors have yet to come up in our discussions. I'm sure you'll make some good recommendations. Thanks for having me here. I'll leave you to it! (*Smith leaves.*)

Exercise

Before you look at the completed Decision Framing Worksheet that follows, try filling out the worksheet yourself. For sections whose contents haven't already been specified, please make a guess as to what the framing might be in the use case described here. Then compare your work with the example.

Completing the Decision Framing Worksheet

Your team goes on to complete the Decision Framing Worksheet, including a rewritten Objective Statement, through a series of drafts and reviews with Dr. Smith.

As you can see, the worksheet's language is relatively informal. There are still some ambiguities, and it is missing many components that will ultimately be part of the decision. This is typical: *the idea is to minimize the impact on the decision customer's time by capturing their thinking about the decision in a way that is natural for them, rather than asking them to go through a formal process.*

Unlike other mathematical methods for decision formalization, the most important criterion here is to maximize the cognitive "space" available to the customer to think about their situation. To do so, it's important to speak in their "native" language and to not overload them with new concepts or formalisms. Avoid the temptation to teach them DI, unless they explicitly ask for it.

Phase A, Worksheet 2: Decision Framing, tailored for the telecom use case

Decision Objective Statement: The company needs to find ways to increase customer satisfaction. The executives believe that one way to do this may be to launch an "unlimited" subscription service, where customers can use all the voice-call minutes and data they desire for a single monthly price. The executives want to explore a range of unlimited plan options supported with advantages, disadvantages, and risks in order to make a decision whether or not to offer such a plan and, if so, what plan.	
Item	**Answers and/or comments**
Baseline: how do we make the decision today?	Typically a meeting and discussion, after reviewing some charts and graphs
Role of the decision-making team: advisory or decision-making authority?	Advisory. The CEO will be making the decision.
Outcomes (potentially measurable things, for which the customer considers the team responsible)	• Avoid losing money to competitors • Avoid reducing net profits year-over-year • Grow profits on this plan

---

Actions (choices)	Determine the following aspects of a monthly unlimited mobile telephone service: • Pricing • Services included • Contract period • Inducements Analyze these choices to see if at least one combination of them is likely to achieve our outcomes.
Known goals or business objectives (tests against the outcomes)	(Not specified)
Known external factors that will influence the outcomes	The outcomes should be achieved whether or not our competitor launches a similar plan.
How much time, money, and energy are we willing to invest to achieve these outcomes/goals?	Three to six staff months
How much detail do the decision maker and stakeholders want in their CDD? Select one.	• Low—actions and outcomes with very sketchy causal chains • **Medium—casual chains should show key KPIs and leading indicators for outcomes** • High—stakeholders are analysts; bring on the details
What risks are we willing to take to achieve these outcomes/goals?	(Not specified)
Do we want to include in our analysis any externalities, including intended and unintended consequences?	(Not specified)
Decision constraints/boundaries	Do not launch to markets outside the USA.
Suggestions that arose during framing	$50 per month might be a good price.
Glossary terms	(Not specified)

This process is just a first step toward identifying the final decision frame. The Decision Modeling phase, which you'll learn in Chapters 3 and 4, often surfaces new questions and ideas about Decision Framing, and teams often loop back to update the Decision Framing Worksheet while they are working on decision design.

Conclusion

By completing the previous steps, you've avoided one of the most widespread sources of problems in decision-making projects, especially those that involve data or technology. You've established the initial communication process between diverse stakeholders, and you've begun setting expectations within your organization for continued collaboration between problem-solving technologists and subject matter experts. This initial process has been informal by necessity, because it seeks to maximize the contributions of nontechnical experts who are not accustomed to formal specifications. This approach avoids distracting or overloading them.

Sometimes Decision Framing raises a lot of questions without providing all the answers. You may feel like you have a lot of destinations but no map. This is normal. Framing is an early process in a series of many. It's common to feel frustrated or overwhelmed with information and complexity, and to do a lot of rework at this "fuzzy frontend," especially if your organization has never done DI before. You can mitigate this frustration by normalizing the "messy" feeling. No worries! The later processes will wrestle things into place.

CHAPTER 3

Decision Modeling:
The Decision Design Process

Moneyball, the 2011 movie adapted from Michael Lewis's book, tells the story of the struggling Oakland A's baseball team. In the film, coach Billy Beane (played by Brad Pitt) tries something radical: using statistics to decide what players to recruit. Beane faces massive opposition but ultimately succeeds, bringing the A's to the playoffs two years in a row on a much lower player budget than other teams.

Thanks to the film's success, you might have heard this story before. What you're less likely to know about is how our friend Dr. Erik Korem (*https://oreil.ly/W3b7s*), a sports scientist, has done much the same for US football. Korem, in his role as director of Sports Science and Football Operations at Florida State University, equipped his football players with GPS and measurement devices to generate data on their movements. He used these statistics to optimize the game and bring his team back to the top of their division, winning the Atlantic Coast Conference and an Orange Bowl championship.

Later, after being selected as a Presidential Leader Scholar, Korem transferred his collegiate sports experience to helping anyone with a wearable device enhance their mental and physical fitness. He founded a startup, envisioning a wellness app called AIM7 (*https://oreil.ly/YDKu8*) that would make daily recommendations to its users designed to help them achieve their goals.

As he was launching AIM7, Korem discovered coauthor Pratt's book *Link* (*https://oreil.ly/kINon*) at the library. He reached out to us to help bring DI to his startup effort, where he was toying with some ML work for his app prototype. Working with him, we learned a lot.

For one thing, on a project like this, you'd usually start with a big dataset. It's expensive and time-consuming to gather enough user data to build a full ML system, though, and that was an unnecessary barrier: AIM7 could go to market without that happening first.

Instead, Korem started the design process by building a decision model instead of an ML model, using his expertise as structured into a CDD. His AIM7 app asks users a few questions when they first use it, then tracks data about them over time. The early release of the product applied human expert knowledge from the field of sports medicine to make recommendations and then gathered data to find patterns as users provided more data. The AIM7 product development team used that to improve the app in later releases.

Erik told us, "We've accelerated our development timeline by taking a decision intelligence approach, which I estimate will save our company over a million dollars." And the AIM7 app is doing great. But they haven't made a movie about Erik Korem—yet.

Our work with AIM7 illustrates an important DI principle, which is that you can achieve a lot of benefits simply by structuring expert knowledge into a CDD, even before you add data to the picture.

But what does it mean to capture expert knowledge like Korem's knowledge about sports in a CDD? You'll be surprised to learn that it's not a very difficult process: we simply asked him a few questions, like:

- What outcomes are you trying to achieve with your recommendations to the users?
- What actions are you considering recommending?
- What do you know about your users' situations that would lead you to choose a particular recommendation?

While asking these questions, we collaboratively drew a CDD in an online whiteboard. Then we used that diagram to decide how to write computer code to capture Korem's and his team's expertise.

As shown in this example—and as you'll learn in more detail in this chapter—a CDD plays three important roles:

- The CDD represents human expert knowledge in everyday language, which helps technologists communicate with nontechnical experts. The CDD showed that Korem used Apple Watch data about each user, along with unchanging information like their gender and date of birth, to determine the recommendation to send to that user each day. This reflected how he'd advised his sports teams in the past: use some data, combine it with his expertise, and then recommend an action to lead to a particular outcome.

- The CDD helps to organize and structure expert knowledge in a way that's formal enough to be useful in building software. For Korem's AIM7 company, we realized that a fairly simple lookup system would be effective for a first release.

- The CDD shows where various technologies and data can be best used so that when it's time to include that technology, you'll know where. For AIM7, the CDD showed that an ML model could be used—down the road, after the system had gathered enough data—to provide an "early warning system" that could predict when a user was having an "off day" so that the system could tailor the user's recommendation.

Colin O'Neill, CEO of StrategicOps Consulting (*https://oreil.ly/5kGqa*), captures the essence of this idea: "Well-defined goals, strategies, and outcomes are the levers of successful executives and managers. Focusing on decision-based outcomes creates an environment within which frontline workers can innovate with maximum creativity to solve problems and develop solutions, all within the guardrails defined by clear goals and strategies."

The Decision Modeling Phase: Overview

Decision Modeling is DI Phase B, starting after the Decision Framing process is done. There are two Decision Modeling processes:

Decision Design
> This chapter addresses the first process in this phase, *B1: Decision Design*. Here you'll build your initial decision "blueprint," or CDD. In this chapter, you'll learn how to elicit a CDD with your team to capture the outcomes you want to achieve, identify the actions available to achieve those outcomes, discover things outside the decision maker's scope of control that affect the outcomes, and link up the causal chains that lead from actions to outcomes. We'll also show you how to help your team align around the CDD, the causal chains that lead from actions to outcomes.

Decision Asset Investigation
> The second process, *B2: Decision Asset Investigation*, presented in Chapter 4, helps you to work with your data team, analysts, and data scientists to identify *decision assets*—the data, models, and human knowledge that will inform your decision. You'll learn how to examine each cause-and-effect chain in your CDD to discover information sources, annotate your CDD to show all your decision assets, and document your decision assets properly. This process prepares you for the third DI phase, in which you'll simulate your CDD, assess its sensitivity to various assets, and assess assets' provenance, quality, and risks.

This chapter starts by looking at a sample CDD and explaining each of the elements that go into a decision. It describes the Decision Design process in detail, complete with a process description and worksheet. It then provides in-depth advice on CDD elicitation and why it's important. The chapter wraps up with two use cases: examples of these processes in action.

Figure 3-1 shows Phase B, Decision Modeling, in the context of the other process phases. Note that Process B2, Decision Asset Investigation, is grayed out because it is covered in the next chapter, not in this one.

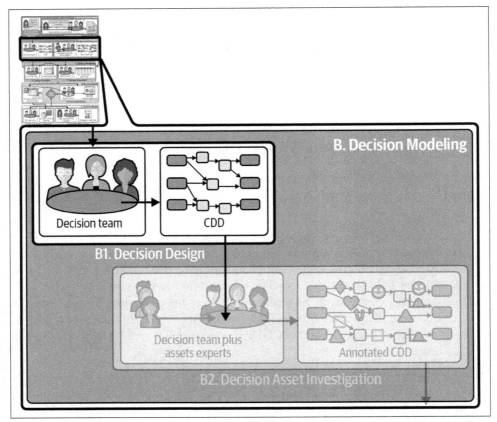

Figure 3-1. The Decision Modeling phase includes two processes: Decision Design and Decision Asset Investigation. This chapter addresses Decision Design.

When you're done with the Decision Modeling phase, you'll be much more confident that the decision makers, stakeholders, and the technology team(s) who will support the decision are aligned around a shared understanding of the causal chains that lead from actions to outcomes. This common understanding will later help your team identify evidence that can inform the decision.

Decision Elements

Before you look at the processes, you'll need to understand some terminology. Imagine you're standing at a shelf in a grocery store, looking at the coffee. You're deciding whether to pay more money for a coffee that claims to be fair trade and bird friendly. You're seriously considering doing it, because although you certainly care about the price of coffee, you also want to feel good about the impact that your purchase decisions have on the world around you.

Before we show you a CDD, we first want to show you another kind of very common diagram: a *process flow diagram*, which shows the order of steps involved in a process. People often confuse process flow diagrams with CDDs, so we want to illustrate the difference for you.

The process of buying coffee has four steps: drive to the store, select the coffee, pay for the coffee, and drive back home. In this kind of diagram, each box represents a step in the process. We could represent those steps with a diagram like the one in Figure 3-2.

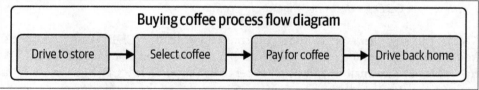

Figure 3-2. Process flow diagram for buying coffee.

While one of the steps in the process flow diagram involves a decision ("select coffee"), there's nothing here that tells us how to arrive at that decision. That's where the CDD comes in. The CDD helps us weigh various decision elements to arrive at a decision.

Take a look at the CDD in Figure 3-3, which takes us through the actual decision about what kind of coffee to buy. The boxes and arrows in this diagram are called *decision elements*.

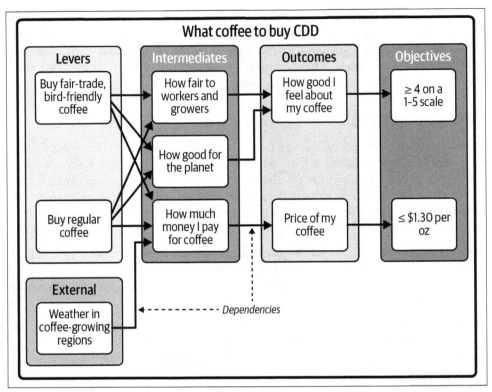

Figure 3-3. A CDD for deciding what kind of coffee to buy.

"Wait," you say, "here's something you should add to that CDD." Congratulations! You get it! CDD building is iterative. You can stop iterating at any point if the CDD has sufficient information and detail to serve its purpose. The CDD in Figure 3-3 is early in the iteration cycle. The CDD in Figure P-2 in the Preface or many of the CDDs later in this chapter have gone through more iterations. And at the end of this chapter, you'll have a chance to work through several iterations of a CDD.

It's very important to emphasize that the boxes and arrows the CDD shows are *not* steps in a process; rather, they are factors in a decision that you make at one step of the process. Since people often confuse CDDs for process diagrams, it's important to keep this distinction as crisp as possible. The boxes in a CDD are *not* steps that anyone takes. Rather, they are measurable consequences of actions that require no additional action on anyone's part. *Process steps* are things you can choose to do. *Decision model actions* are choices you make that lead to consequences that are outside of your control.[1] The boxes and arrows in Figure 3-3 thus represent *decision elements*. Let's break those elements down now, one by one:

Outcomes

Outcomes represent the results of a decision that you'll measure to determine if you've achieved what you desire. Each outcome should represent something measurable, such as "amount paid for coffee" or "degree of environmental impact." Note that just because it's hard to measure something doesn't make it any less of an outcome. "How good I feel about my coffee purchase," "employee morale," "brand reputation," and other "soft" factors are often essential desired outcomes from decisions, yet they're often left out of the picture. One of the most important aspects of DI is surfacing desired outcomes like these!

Objectives

Objectives are the target measurements for your outcomes. They let you know if your outcome achieves your desired goal or not. In this example, the objective for the price outcome is "$1.30 per ounce or less." You may or may not be able to achieve your objectives. And often, objectives work against each other: if you paid $100 for your coffee, you might really help the rainforest, but your wallet would take a big hit.

Levers

Levers are sets of choices that lead to actions and, ultimately, via intermediates and dependencies, to outcomes. In the coffee example, each lever is just a yes/no choice. But a lever may also be a set of numbers to choose among, such as the price of a product or the amount you'll invest in something. Levers in the CDD represent actions you might take in the real world. Making your decision (see Chapter 7) means that you select a set of lever choices and perform the corresponding real-world action(s), like changing the price of carrot cupcakes on the signboard outside your bakery, planting sweet potatoes, or electronically signing the contract to acquire a subsidiary.

Intermediates

Intermediates are things you can measure along cause-and-effect chains to show how "pulling" a lever (making a choice that leads to an action) leads, in turn, to an outcome. In this simple example, the causal chains are short, with only one intermediate. Longer (including much longer) chains are common, too, as you will see in the CDDs later in this chapter (or the CDD in Figure P-2 in the Preface).

---

1 Also note that this book uses the word *process* both for the nine DI steps and for the steps in a process like the one shown in Figure 3-2.

For example, why does buying fair-trade, bird-friendly coffee make me feel good? Because fair trade means that the coffee comes from small growers and that the workers involved were treated fairly. A bird-friendly habitat means that the coffee growers are protecting biodiversity (*https://oreil.ly/LWaRQ*). Each one of these elements—the degree to which small-grower workers are treated fairly, the degree of biodiversity protection—is an intermediate.

Dependencies

Dependencies tell us how one decision element relies on others: in this example, the price of coffee depends on the weather in coffee-growing regions, which, in turn, affects the harvest. In short, dependencies say, "When this thing to the left of the dependency arrow changes, I expect that this other thing will change, too." Sometimes there's a simple "when this goes up, this other thing goes up (or down)" relationship on a dependency. Sometimes it's a lot more complex, as we see when it's captured by computer code or a complex function. In a CDD, arrows representing dependencies connect the elements into a causal chain. When two arrows point to the same entity, then the value of that entity depends on two upstream elements, sometimes in a complicated way.

Externals

Externals are things that you (or the decision maker) can't control, but that nevertheless influence intermediates and/or outcomes. Examples of externals are the weather, how customers behave (outside of your influence), and what competitors do. You can observe and measure externals and even build models of how they influence intermediates or outcomes. For example, agricultural economists create models to predict how weather patterns will affect coffee prices. You can change externals in simulations, but not in reality.

Note that, if your situation and level of authority change over time, levers can become externals and vice versa.

Causal chain

You can trace at least one path through the CDD, following the dependency arrows from a lever through one or more intermediates to an outcome. This path is called a *causal chain*. Most CDDs contain many causal chains.

There are a few more useful concepts that will help you to build CDDs, covered later in this chapter.

Whether an element is an outcome, a lever, an intermediate, or an external depends on the scope and boundary of the decision. Figure 3-4 shows how to use your knowledge of your (or your decision maker's) authority and responsibility to ask, "Is this element an intermediate or an outcome?" and to use a series of "why" and "how" questions (the "why chain" and "how chain") to determine where the element goes in a CDD.

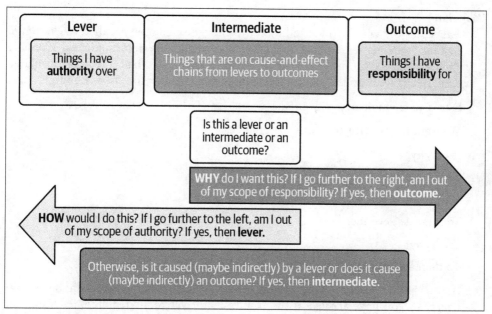

Figure 3-4. How you can determine if an element is a lever, an outcome, or an intermediate.

There are a number of important concepts represented in Figure 3-4:

Scope of authority and responsibility
   "Scope" refers to the decision maker's scope of authority (to take actions) and responsibility (for outcomes). See "Balancing Information, Authority, and Responsibility" on page 35.

Decision boundary
   The decision boundary is an imaginary line we can draw around the decision to decide what is or isn't external. The boundary can't be bigger than the limits of the decision maker's scope of authority and responsibility. Things the decision maker controls and things that are consequences of actions the decision maker can take are inside the boundary. They will be levers, intermediates, or outcomes in the CDD. Things outside the decision maker's control are externals. If you're a CEO, you have authority over things within your organization but not suppliers or competitors, although supplier or competitor actions may be important externals in your decisions. If you're a manager, actions by other departments are often externals. If HR doesn't complete a hire you need or Purchasing loses a purchase order so you run short of a critical part, those are externals, outside the boundaries of your decisions, although they are inside the boundaries of your CEO's decisions.

Why chain

The series of "whys" you asked to get to the true outcome is called a *why chain*. Asking "why" several times will help you to identify intermediates. If you're eliciting a CDD from a team and you have the sense that you haven't elicited enough elements on the right-hand side, asking "why" is one step you might take.

Here's an example of a why chain:

We want to improve customer experience.

- Why?

To drive more sales.

- Why?

To increase revenue.

- Why?

To increase profits next year.

At this point, further "whys" don't elicit any more elements down the causal chain, so you have arrived at the true (but not yet refined) outcome. Note that the elements to the left of "To increase profits next year" in the why chain will appear on the CDD as a causal chain of intermediates. Only the last element, "To increase profits next year," is, formally, an outcome. In Figure 3-4, you can see that following the why chain moves you down and to the right on the causal chain.

How chain

Just as you can ask "why?" to move from left to right along the causal chain to find outcomes and objectives, you can ask "how?" to move left along the causal chain to find levers.

Proxy outcome

Sometimes, as you go down the "why chain," you stop too early and reach what is known as a *proxy outcome*. A proxy outcome is an entity on the causal chain or why chain leading to the desired outcome that can be mistaken for an actual outcome. Proxies can be misleading (*https://oreil.ly/k_uSg*) if they're not identified as such.

In the previous example, if we only made decisions to improve customer experience without knowing why, then we might experience unintended consequences. For instance, we might invest more in customer experience than is justified by the revenues we obtain from those customers.

Scenario

A set of values for multiple externals, combined with a set of lever choices.

So how do you create one of these beautiful CDDs? This is one of the most important parts of this book, because—we'll be honest—magic happens when you get it right. There's a "lightbulb" moment when team members realize that, for the first time, they have a shared understanding of a complex decision (and they don't have to spend all their effort keeping it invisibly in their heads and talking through it to keep it matching others' understanding).

Decision Design Is Like Object-Oriented Software Modeling, but for Analytics and Decisions

If you ask software engineers to write a traditional software application, they'll review use cases and map out workflows to create a set of diagrams that they'll use to design and build software that meets the project's needs. Why isn't the Decision Design process that straightforward?

The answer is that software engineers have a mature, well-tested methodology for capturing and recording business requirements, and tools for implementing it. Data scientists and analysts have almost none of these. How can we equip data science with a systematic approach for capturing the needs of decision makers and, from these, specifying the deliverables they must create to meet these needs? Again, we can borrow from software engineering.

At the foundation of modern software engineering is the object-oriented programming (OOP) paradigm and its diagrammatic representation system, called the Universal Modeling Language (UML).[2] OOP is a set of principles for describing the elements (or "objects") in the domain within which a software application will work, how they behave, and how they relate to one another. In an industry where the shelf life of an idea is measured by the time it takes to develop the next idea that supersedes it, OOP has maintained its dominant position for more than three decades, and there is no sign of any change to this. Its long-lived success is grounded in four key characteristics:

- It matches the natural, intuitive way that nonengineers think about the needs the software must satisfy.

- It contains enough detail for programmers to create the solution in code.

- It organizes information in a way that can be translated into algorithms and therefore implemented on a computer.

---

2 To learn more, see Michael McMillan, *Object-Oriented Programming with Visual Basic .NET* (New York: Cambridge University Press, 2004); Russ Miles and Kim Hamilton, *Learning UML 2.0* (Sebastopol, CA: O'Reilly, 2006); Dan Pilone, *UML 2.0 Pocket Reference* (Sebastopol, CA: O'Reilly, 2006).

- It is represented diagrammatically, which facilitates clear, transparent communication between the end-user community and the developers, as well as among the developers themselves.

Let's apply these characteristics to decision making and data science in the Decision Modeling phase of DI:

- Decision Modeling defines a general way of representing decisions that corresponds to how decision makers intuitively think about them.
- A good decision model contains sufficient detail for data scientists and other analysts to develop any information assets the decision customer needs.
- A good decision model represents information in a way that can be translated into algorithms to facilitate computer modeling.
- Decision models are represented diagrammatically, in CDDs, which facilitates clear, transparent communication between the decision customer and the analysts, and among the analysts themselves.

In short, effective DI boils down to helping human decision makers (1) map the causal pathways between actions and their outcomes, (2) use this mapping to find the right data and knowledge to more accurately compute the expected outcomes corresponding to any set of actions, and then (3) use the computer to help find the best actions to take in a particular circumstance.

Decisions and Time

We are often asked about how to design decisions that happen over some time period. To get started in answering this question, it's first important to understand that there are three time periods in the use of a decision model:

Decision design time
   The period described in this chapter.

Decision reasoning time
   The period in which you use your decision model (whether it's a CDD or a computer simulation) to help you make a decision. This is described in Chapter 5.

Action time
   After you've made a decision, you'll take some action based on that decision. For instance, making the choice to charge a particular price is different than changing your systems to reflect that new price. Then the effect of that action will play out over time, hopefully in a similar way to how you predicted during the decision reasoning time. This is described in Chapter 7.

You can use your decision model during action time as a *tracking* mechanism: watch your *actual* intermediate values and compare them to the ones that you *predicted* during Decision Design and Reasoning. If they are different, then that's an indication that you might want to loop back to Decision Design and reconsider your choice, because it's not playing out as you'd expected. So now the decision model isn't just helping you to make a decision you've already realized is needed, it's also helping you to know *when to start a new decision-making process.*

You can think of these time phases as playing out in an observe-orient-decide-act (OODA) loop (*https://oreil.ly/l0n8i*). Invented in the 1970s by military strategist John Boyd (*https://oreil.ly/KelLz*), this concept reflects the cycle that people go through as they make multiple decisions over time. Indeed, we might think of DI as showing us how to do OODA loops when we have a computer to help us to reason.

In addition to the previous three distinctions, you can also have levers and outcomes that represent time. You might have a lever that says "how much I'll invest in 2030" and another that says "how much I'll invest in 2031," a different time period. You might also have an outcome that says "net profits in 2033" and one that says "net profits in 2034."

Chapter 5 will have more to say about how computers can help us to understand how decisions play out over time.

Process B1: Decision Design

Decision Design is the process of drawing a CDD. In this section, you'll learn how stakeholders from different parts of the organization collaborate to do so. You'll learn about the importance of managing cognitive fatigue during CDD design, how to move effectively between styles of thinking, how to handle disagreements, how to collect out-of-context ideas respectfully so that they can be added at the appropriate time, and how to decide when the initial CDD is sufficiently complete to move on to the next process.

The rest of this chapter gives you a lot of help with this process. It includes a detailed, formal process description, some guidance through the tricky bits, and a chance to try it yourself.

But first, a bit of terminology. *CDD elicitation* means leading a team through the process of creating a CDD, often done by a *facilitator*—a disinterested person outside the team charged with making the decision—who understands the DI processes and can lead the decision team through them and provide explanations and assistance as needed.

Next, we'll show you the formal Decision Design process. After that, you will find more details about CDD design, including details of each step, common mistakes, guidelines, and best practices.

Formal Process Description: Process B1: Decision Design

Description

Elicit information from the decision team and stakeholders in one or more joint and/or offline exercises to create a first-draft CDD.

Prerequisites

- The Decision Framing process has been completed, and the decision customer has approved the Decision Framing Document.

- The first meeting to develop the CDD has been scheduled and all attendees notified. You can send the process description to the attendees if you like, but sometimes this can cause unnecessary concern. Most participants do fine when we say, "No preparation needed."

Responsible role

Decision facilitator

Notes

There are two kinds of activities interleaved in this process for building a CDD: joint activities and offline ones. Much of the tailoring you'll do for this process involves deciding how best to interleave them. The process also includes a step to assess team expertise and provides for gathering any necessary additional knowledge and information.

Joint team activities

These activities take place during team meetings. They include eliciting and reviewing the CDD.

Offline activities

These activities take place outside the meetings and include refining and cleaning up the CDD, as well as gathering new information from outside the decision team, if needed (see steps 12 to 14).

Steps

1. Prepare for the meeting:

   - Study the Decision Design process by reading the formal process description and, ideally, the rest of this chapter, so you understand its purpose and steps.

   - Tailor the process for your organization as you see fit.

   - Schedule the Decision Design meeting(s) and reserve a room or online meeting tool (see Figure 3-5 on page 67).

- Inform participants of the meeting and provide appropriate messaging from the decision customer or other executives about the importance and purpose of the meeting. If the DI methodology is new to the team, provide a short explanation of DI and a brief overview of CDD concepts, as described in Chapter 1.

- If possible, arrange for the decision customer to attend the first few minutes of the meeting to motivate the team and add any new context.

- Arrange for drinks, snacks, and/or lunch for in-person participants.

- Reserve any physical equipment you need, such as whiteboards or flip charts, markers, sticky notes, or a projector and screen.

- Select a collaboration tool if you'll be working online. Ideally it would allow multiple people to simultaneously create, move, and label boxes on a screen (ideally each person's boxes are different colors), and to connect them with arrows. It should be easy to learn and to use.

- If using a collaboration tool, learn to use it proficiently and create working boards or templates as appropriate.

- Identify someone to assist the facilitator with moving items around the collaboration tool, taking notes, arranging elements of the presentation, and the like.

2. Begin the CDD elicitation meeting, as scheduled.

3. Review the Decision Framing Document, as needed, with meeting participants.

4. Write the Decision Objective Statement down and post it somewhere everyone can refer to it easily.

5. Ensure all meeting participants are comfortable with any meeting tools you're using, such as an online whiteboard.

6. Brainstorm outcomes and vote on the top three to work with initially.

7. Brainstorm levers and vote on the top three to work with initially.

8. Work with the team to draw some intermediates along causal chains from actions to outcomes.

9. Capture externals if they come up.

10. Capture all process steps in which this decision will be embedded if they come up.

11. Capture any known information about dependencies. Your team may have described the high-level direction of dependencies (arrows where the thing on the left leads to a larger or smaller thing on the right), created sketch graphs (sketches of relationships between two elements, made by a human expert),

and listed existing decision assets. The process for obtaining details on these is covered in Process B2, Decision Asset Investigation.

12. **Checkpoint:** At this point, the whiteboard or collaboration tool screen can look messy. If you have not taken "cleanup breaks" between earlier steps in the process, it is often best to break off joint work at this point to allow the facilitator or decision team leader to do some offline work, such as:

    - **Refine:** Clean up the draft CDD by refining levers, outcomes, and externals.

    - **Assess framing:** If you have uncovered significant issues with the Decision Framing Document or worksheet, suspend Decision Design work and return to Process A2, Decision Framing.

    - **Assess expertise:** Does the decision team need outside expertise to complete the CDD? If so, once you've exhausted their expertise, then use the following steps. As the team acquires the information needed, you can complete the Decision Design process iteratively.

        a. Create a list of missing information and issues that need to be resolved to complete the CDD. See Phase B, Worksheet 1, Decision Modeling Research, available in the supplemental materials repository (*https://oreil.ly/DIH-supplemental*).

        b. If this investigation reveals issues with the Decision Framing Document (such as its scope, its constraints, or the decision customer's authority and responsibility), reopen Process A2, Decision Framing, to resolve them.

        c. Rank the priority of each item on the list from step 1. Initially, focus on a small number of the top-priority items.

        d. For each top-priority item, determine and document how you'll resolve it: for example, adding an expert to the team, interviewing an expert, or finding a written source.

        e. Acquire and record the information.

        f. Incorporate it into the CDD.

        g. Repeat the previous steps until Decision Modeling can continue.

13. **Internal refinement and review cycle:** Usually there is a point where the CDD is complex enough that it's best to move to offline work combined with review meetings. (See "How Do You Know When to Stop Decision Modeling?" on page 83.) This refinement may include:

    - Adding more outcomes and levers

    - Clarifying outcomes until they are measurable

    - Identifying more objectives

- Analyzing for why chains
- Identifying proxy outcomes
- Paring back outcomes to the system boundary
- Drawing new dependencies
- Eliciting externals
- Documenting assumptions about externals
- Writing a narrative document describing your CDD

It's also a good idea to revisit the Decision Framing Document and to reassess the team's expertise from time to time as you review the CDD.

14. **Refine and review outside the team:** Publish the CDD to the decision customer. Review and revise it until the decision team and decision customer agree.

Deliverable

A CDD showing how possible decision actions and externals lead to outcomes.

You might find this process a little overwhelming. No fear! Two things are worth repeating. First, the very simple approach to decision modeling shown in Chapter 1 shows that you can learn the basics in just a few minutes: it's a tiny fraction of the complete process shown here. This example process is for more advanced practitioners who want to become experts at decision facilitation: you definitely don't have to learn all this to get value from DI.

If the decision is very complex, the stakes are high, or the team has strong differences of opinion, expect the DI processes to take longer (see Figure 3-5). Plan on at least three or four sessions of 60 to 90 minutes each to complete a moderately complex CDD with a well-aligned team that has substantial expertise around the decision. If the decision is simple, the team is well aligned (especially around outcomes), and its members have all of the subject matter expertise you'll need, it might go more quickly.

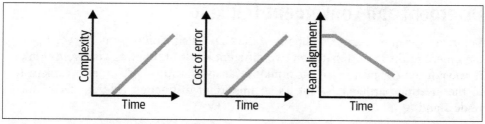

Figure 3-5. How complexity, cost of error, and team alignment affect the time needed to create a CDD. Complexity and the cost of error tend to lengthen the DI processes, but a well-aligned team can complete them more quickly.

If your team needs expertise, knowledge, information, or models created outside of your team to complete the CDD, then you should plan for research time to locate experts and onboard them to the team, interview experts, and/or conduct desk research.

CDD elicitation can take hours, days, or even weeks. The schedule needs to include many breaks, preferably every hour, because the exercise takes a lot of brainpower! You can use whiteboards, flip charts and markers, or a collaboration tool.

Why is the first CDD elicitation conducted in a "live" joint meeting? Because we've seen—time and again—that big breakthroughs in shared understanding happen when you do this, even if the CDD is pretty messy during the meeting. In particular, discussing the CDD surfaces discrepancies in language or mental model that can be resolved quickly and that otherwise can create unnecessary miscommunication. You'll typically work together in the first elicitation meeting to create a first CDD, refine it offline, and then review it in one or more cycles. The facilitator can use breaks and downtime to clean up the notes and diagrams. If you're meeting virtually, it's best to schedule smaller time chunks, no more than 60 to 90 minutes, since people tire faster when attending virtual meetings (this is sometimes known as "Zoom fatigue" (*https://oreil.ly/mpvM7*)).

An alternative—which only became possible just as this book was going to press—is to use a Large Language Model (LLM) like ChatGPT to help to create the decision model. See coauthor Pratt's "ChatGPT Does Decision Intelligence for Net Zero" (*https://oreil.ly/fK-QK*) for the net zero example of this book, assisted by ChatGPT. There's lots of value here, and DI may even be a "killer app" for LLMs.

Now that you have the basics, though, let's look at the details.

With the previous process in hand, the following sections will give you more information about CDD elicitation, including best practices, common mistakes, and more details about how to get it right.

Divergent and Convergent Thinking

Before we get into the nuts and bolts of the CDD elicitation session, it's worth taking a moment to distinguish between two different kinds of thinking: *divergent* thinking (brainstorming), and *convergent* thinking (analysis). You don't have to explain this to the meeting participants, but it's an important distinction for your facilitator to understand.

An example of divergent thinking might be to start by saying, "Please write all the outcomes associated with our decision on sticky notes and put them on the whiteboard." The goal of divergent thinking is to generate as many ideas as possible. Because people will be suggesting all sorts of ideas, it is essential to create a safe, collaborative environment, and to explain—and model—that "there are no bad ideas." This part of the process is particularly valuable for drawing out *intangible outcomes*: those that are harder to measure, like employees' happiness.

Your goal here is not to obtain "good" decision elements: "success" at this stage is just to capture all of the decision element ideas that come to people's minds, a process that can be inhibited by assessment or analysis. This is a subtle but essential point, because so many people are in the habit of assessing the quality of ideas when they're presented. Try to gently reemphasize that "we need all ideas right now, good and bad, please."

Convergent thinking comes after divergent thinking and is about evaluating the ideas you've all generated. If someone says, "I think that this is a good idea" or "I disagree with this idea," that's convergent thinking. Those are fine things to say, just not when you're brainstorming! Criticism has a chilling effect on creativity, so you need to keep it out of the divergent thinking stage. This takes practice and tact, because it sometimes means you'll need to be assertive with opinionated people.

Brain research (*https://oreil.ly/EZW6o*) shows that these two kinds of thought use different parts of the brain, and that blood sloshes from one to the other when switching. You'll maximize your team members' effectiveness if you don't try to do both kinds at once. In fact, it hurts our brains when we're asked to switch from one to the other too fast! And you'll see what we've observed is a big cause of decision failure: a too-narrow focus on just certain actions and certain outcomes.

So one of the most important aspects of the decision facilitator's job is to clearly separate the divergent from the convergent parts of the process.

The CDD Elicitation Meeting

In a CDD elicitation meeting, a decision facilitator gathers the decision-making team members in a physical or virtual room to draw out information and create the first draft of the CDD.

Over the years, we've tried a number of approaches to what to show to a team that has never elicited a decision before. We've oscillated between a 20-minute "What is DI?" lesson and—the other end of the spectrum—no background at all, we just plunge straight into outcomes. We've found that a middle ground is best. We describe the goals of our project, show one or two simulated decision models in less than five minutes, and then say, "You're going to help us to build one of these." We then show a CDD example, with levers, outcomes, externals, and intermediates labeled clearly, and say, "This is what we're going to build first; it will help to capture your understanding of this important decision." Up to about seven minutes of up-front explanation seems to be about the right amount.

Another way you'll need to tailor the process is to decide who will write down (or otherwise capture) the CDD elements during the meeting. Some facilitators choose to do the writing—that is, create the CDD—alone or with their assistant(s), based on verbal input from other participants. Others invite everyone to join in, using different colors to write down CDD elements all at once. Use your judgment: this can get chaotic, but it can also get the team's creativity flowing!

If your participants will be asked to use a tool, you'll want to take a few minutes to teach them how: either an online tool or just Post-it notes on a whiteboard.

Next, write down the Objective Statement as created during Decision Framing. When we do this in an online workshop, we just write, "Objective Statement:" on the online whiteboard. Usually there won't be any discussion at this stage because people have either agreed to the objective or it has been assigned to them in advance of the meeting,

Divergent Thinking: Eliciting Outcomes and Objectives

As you can read in the previous process, one of the first important steps you'll do in the meeting is to elicit outcomes and objectives. Your goal is to get as many great ideas "on the table" as possible. This is where you're doing divergent thinking. You'll refine everything later.

At this point, we usually say, "Please enter some silly or stupid ideas for outcomes onto the whiteboard." We explain that the reason for this is that it helps to get the conversation going, and it helps to remove reluctance that people may otherwise feel to participate. If you've already entered something stupid or funny, you'll be more creative!

Sometimes people will enter actions instead of outcomes. For example, they might say, "Buy all employees ice cream." You may want to use this as a teaching moment by replying, "Why?" You might also want to illustrate this distinction yourself, by entering, say, "Grow to a billion-dollar company by next week," or "Drive revenues by popularizing a new cuisine based on sweet potato parasites." Stay in divergent thinking—no judgments. Just keep the ideas flowing.

You may choose to elicit objectives as well: certainly capture them if someone states their outcome in objective terms. Note that you may choose to use the word *goal* during initial CDD elicitation instead of *objective* if that's a more comfortable word for your audience. Again, you're trying to make this as easy for them as possible! But if nobody states an objective, that's OK for now, and you can move on. You're trying to get the "skeleton" of the decision model out of people's heads, not all the details.

Capturing Out-of-Context Decision Elements in a "Parking Lot"

During CDD elicitation, participants will often mention decision elements that are outside the scope of the current step: for example, during outcomes brainstorming, someone might bring up a lever, an intermediate, or an external. Sometimes element types are ambiguous! If a suggestion is clearly not what you're eliciting at that moment, it's still important to capture it. To avoid disrupting the brainstorming, you might write them down in a "parking lot": someplace where you can set them aside for later consideration, like a designated corner of the whiteboard. Explain respectfully that the suggestion is not part of the current step, and then return to the task at hand.

You might also discover an existing model or dataset that provides information about dependencies or externals and can help you complete or add information to the CDD. Examples include an econometric model that calculates the cost of something, an ML model that predicts a value of an external, or even another CDD that was developed in another part of the organization. These models and data are decision assets and are covered in more detail in Process B2, Decision Asset Investigation, in the next chapter. As with out-of-context comments, the best practice is to capture them quickly and then return to the task at hand.

Especially during the divergent thinking stages of creating a CDD, it's important not to analyze, overthink, or expect precision. But if you want your decision model to be reusable and suitable for more rigorous contexts, you need to refine it in subsequent convergent thinking stages. You will often work back and forth in the CDD, refining individual elements and then reworking the diagram until you reach the level of precision you want.

Convergent Thinking: Refining ("Cleaning Up") Outcomes and Objectives

After you've elicited some outcomes, we've found that it's a good idea to ask participants to vote for the top three outcomes that best match the Decision Objective Statement. Focusing on only a few outcomes at a time in this way helps to reduce cognitive overload. And of course, you will come back later and consider the remaining outcomes a few at a time. Be sure to explain that to your participants.

When we elicit outcomes in a collaborative session, we strive to not introduce distinctions that make it hard for the participants—we need to keep them in "creative mode" and focused on their decision, not on the method or on analysis. During these sessions, we don't typically insist on hard-and-fast rules like separating objectives from outcomes or ensuring that outcomes are measurable, and more. That's asking too much of typical decision makers.

Some teams are so misaligned around important outcomes and objectives—and care about it so much—that it takes many sessions over many days to get on the same page. Sometimes they're misaligned but they're willing to focus on just a few outcomes—not completely refined for now—and move on to actions. It's as much an art as a science to figure out how to organize things.

If you take a break between eliciting outcomes and eliciting levers, consider using the offline time to refine the first three outcomes in particular. This kind of offline convergent thinking work, which facilitators do behind the scenes alone or with a few modeling-oriented colleagues, can make the rest of the elicitation sessions more effective.

If you move directly to eliciting levers without a break, that's fine, too. You can refine outcomes whenever there is time to think between elicitation sessions.

Whenever you choose to refine outcomes, you can use this checklist. For each outcome, check that these statements are true:

The outcome is within the scope of your decision maker's responsibilities.

The outcome is related to the Decision Objective Statement.

The outcome is measurable.
> Here's how to think about that: if you made a bet about this outcome, you'd have enough information to determine if you won the bet. If the outcome is "Revenue," for example, you might refine it to "Gross revenue as reported on our tax return for next year." "Morale" could similarly be refined to "Morale score as measured on the M2 survey in May of this year."

The outcome is separated from its corresponding objective.
> Often, the outcomes produced during brainstorming aren't explicit about their corresponding objectives. State the two separately. (If an outcome doesn't already have an associated objective, you can discover it in later refinement stages.) For instance, if your measurable outcome is "Gross revenue as reported on our tax return for next year," the associated objective might be "Ten percent growth in gross revenue as measured against our tax return revenue from this year." Likewise, the outcome "Morale score as measured on the M2 survey in May of this year" could have the objective "Morale measured on M2 instruments is 20 points higher than the score measured in May of last year."

The outcome doesn't specify a direction, such as lowering the number of complaints or increasing sales.
> Any such direction should be part of the objective. You'll usually do a lot of converting elements like "Increase morale" to statements like "Morale as measured on the M2 instrument." Remove all verbs (like *increase, grow, decrease, shorten, raise*) from elements and change them to measurable nouns.

The outcome is not a process step.

The outcome shouldn't specify an action or tell you to "do something." If you find that process steps have come out of the elicitation session, restate them as outcomes if possible, or capture them in a separate process diagram.

The outcomes are not redundant.

Each outcome should stand on its own. If two or more of the outcomes the team has chosen to start with overlap, it's a good idea to merge them. If that leaves you with fewer than three outcomes, add the outcome with the next highest number of votes, so that you start lever elicitation with three clear and distinct outcomes.

Partially overlapping "outcomes" like profit, revenue, and cost often can be separated into intermediates and outcomes, as shown in Figure 3-6.

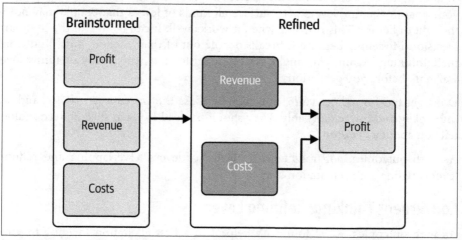

Figure 3-6. Separating overlapping "outcomes" into two intermediates (Revenue and Costs) and one outcome (Profit).

The outcome is not a proxy outcome.

As you saw earlier in this chapter, a proxy outcome is an element on the causal chain leading to the real desired outcome. How far you go to the right on the why chain depends on the decision maker's role. For example, for a customer care manager, "improve customer experience" might be a real outcome because the customer care manager is not accountable for revenue or profit. For a CEO, however, it might be a proxy outcome.

If the outcome *is* a proxy outcome, categorize it as an intermediate, and then you can elicit the real outcome.

Note, in addition, that outcomes may partially *conflict* with other outcomes. This often occurs in cross-functional decisions, where managers at the same level are responsible for a set of interacting and partially conflicting KPIs (outcomes). It may, for example, be impossible to maximize customer experience while remaining profitable. You'll have to find a balance between them. This kind of conflict may indicate productive collaboration, and its lack may even indicate that key stakeholders are missing: you may wish to not only include KPIs from other groups as externals but also include representatives from those departments on your decision team.

Divergent Thinking: Eliciting Levers

You may choose to elicit levers just after you've voted on a few "top three" outcomes, or after many days of outcome discussion, as previously described. As with outcomes, your goal in eliciting levers is to surface all kinds of levers that people may not have thought of before. This is magic when it works well. It can be one of the best parts of Decision Modeling, because it breaks people out of their mental "ruts" and expands their thinking. Again, you might ask the team to start with a silly or funny lever to warm up before you get serious.

Don't get too formal: let your team members use the words *lever, choice,* and *action* informally and interchangeably. They shouldn't need to learn specific terminology to tell you about a decision.

As with outcomes, you might get a big list of levers. Overlapping and redundant levers are fine at the elicitation stage.

Convergent Thinking: Refining Levers

As with outcomes, we've found it's helpful in a first elicitation meeting to vote on the top three levers that your participants think will be helpful in leading to the outcomes. Focusing on only a few levers at a time in this way helps to reduce cognitive overload. And of course, you will come back later and consider the remaining levers a few at a time. Be sure to explain that to your participants.

As with the break between outcomes and levers, you might also create a break between levers and intermediates, and do some lever refinement. Alternatively, you might refine levers as part of a full-CDD refinement exercise, after your CDD elicitation team has given you a (usually very messy) CDD, complete with unrefined levers, intermediates, outcomes, and possibly also some externals and dependencies.

Whenever you choose to refine your levers, it's helpful to keep in mind their distinctions from related decision elements, which are summarized in Table 3-1.

Table 3-1. Levers, choices, decisions, and actions

Decision element	Function	Example
Lever	A well-structured question that captures a set of choices	"Budget for air travel in the coming year?"
Choice	One of the lever settings	"We will spend $100,000 on air travel in the coming year."
Decision	A set of one or more choices that are expected to lead to a set of outcomes	"We will spend $100,000 on air travel in the coming year, we will allocate $20,000 to the virtual tools budget, and we will task the HR group with maximizing the value of virtual meetings."
Action	The actual event that follows from making the choice	The act of disbursing $100,000 to the air-travel budget in the financial system

If you have the time, you might also want to reread the documents you generated during Decision Framing, so you're clear about the scope of authority and responsibility for this decision, which will help you to place the decision elements into the right categories.

The checklist for levers is similar to the one for outcomes. Check that each of the following statements is true for each one:

The lever is something that can be directly controlled.
That is, it's within your scope of control and thus is not an external. As with outcomes, whether an element is a lever or an external may depend on the decision maker's role and accountability boundary.

The lever is not an intermediate.
During elicitation, people often identify "levers" that they can influence but not control or over which the decision maker does not have authority. The system boundary should reflect the scope of the decision maker's authority.

The lever is not redundant and does not overlap with other levers.
Teams often suggest several overlapping "levers," such as "amount we spend on customer service," "amount we spend on the call center," and "amount we spend on the self-service chatbot." When you follow the how chain (Figure 3-7), you can see that the latter two are "hows" to the former, making "amount we spend on customer service" an intermediate.

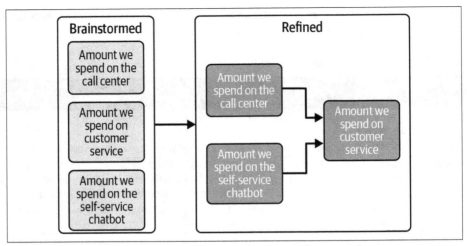

Figure 3-7. Refining overlapping "levers" into levers and intermediates.

If the lever specifies a range of values, then the range is one that everyone agrees to.
> For instance, you may have a lever that lets you choose a range of prices for a product, from $4 to $8.

If the lever specifies a set of choices, then check that all choices are listed.
> For instance, a lever may have two radio buttons, labeled "plant peanuts" and "plant sweet potatoes."

Before moving on to intermediates, take a final look at your three outcomes and your three levers. Identify outcomes that could be *proxies* and so may need *why chains* or other refinements. Then identify "levers" that may actually be intermediates because they need *how chains* or other refinements.

Divergent Thinking: Eliciting Intermediates (Causal Chains)

Before you begin intermediates elicitation, prepare your whiteboard or other surface by placing your three levers on the left and your three outcomes on the right, with some space in between where you'll add causal chains. As with the earlier divergent thinking sessions, ensure that you create a creative, accepting atmosphere. We don't usually ask for "stupid or funny" intermediates, because there is a bit of convergent thinking in this exercise: we're going to be puzzling about how the choices might lead to the outcomes.

We've found it's helpful for the facilitator to draw the first set of connections—with dependency arrows and intermediates—from actions to outcomes. As you do, give a running commentary of your thinking: "Hmm, I think that this choice to invest in marketing might...hmm...help people to like us more, which helps people to recommend us more, which leads to more customers, which leads to more people who can recommend…. Hey, that's a feedback loop, cool!"

Once you've done one chain like this, invite others to do the same. The best meetings—we had one with a group of sweet potato growers—are those where everyone is drawing chains at once in a shared whiteboard and we've got a great first-draft CDD in just a few minutes.

Keep in mind that you might not know much about the nature of the causal connection; you might only know that there *is* a connection, or that as one value goes up, another goes down.

When the discussion slows down, there are a few ways to keep ideas flowing:

- Keep asking "how," to elicit a *how chain* (or "why," to go in the opposite direction).
- Look at the "parking lot."
- Consider using KPIs that were identified elsewhere in the company as intermediates.
- Suggest that intermediates may be leading indicators.

Work iteratively, building causal chains one at a time. Some chains might not have intermediates, since some levers directly affect the outcomes. You might also have some outcomes that don't connect all the way back to levers; that's OK because it tells you there's an opportunity to research a new action that could have an impact on something important.

Note that LLMs like ChatGPT can be valuable DI research assistants (*https://oreil.ly/vT-Ij*). You can tell an LLM your list of outcomes and then ask, "What actions might help us achieve these outcomes?" Of course, you are still responsible for evaluating the suggestions you get from an LLM. The information you get might not be relevant to your decision and in some cases could be completely wrong. But we've found that their benefits far outweigh these costs, as long as you're careful to curate.

"Causal-ish"

Any scientist reading this book will recognize that when we use the term *causal* to describe the chains in a CDD, we're stretching the definition a bit. Some dependency arrows represent leading indicator relationships. Others might be just a bit of math, like Profit = Revenue – Cost. Does the cost "cause" the profit to have a particular value? And some might be correlations that are not causation.

So CDDs—especially the early and messy ones that get created during CDD elicitation—are only "causal" in the most informal sense of the word. We know that correlation is definitely different than causation, but in the context of CDD elicitation, this blurring of the definition is usually the lesser of two evils. Brainstorming takes a lot of creative thinking. If we ask nonscientists to learn, understand, and apply a sophisticated concept like the correlation–causation fallacy during CDD elicitation *while also brainstorming,* that's a recipe for cognitive overload!

That doesn't mean we're ignoring the issue: we *will* be looking for false causation as we refine the CDD. But even the most refined CDDs end up with a mix of components, not all of which represent—in the strictest formal sense—causation.

Just to be clear about correlation and causation (*https://oreil.ly/lTnbU*), there's a common fallacy, or thinking mistake, in which people assume that, because A and B happen together, A must have caused B—but in fact, A and B might both be caused by a third thing, or it might just be a coincidence. Does eating breakfast actually *cause* you to be healthier, or do very health-conscious people tend to eat breakfast? This kind of mistake can find its way into CDDs! As you elicit causal chains from people during Decision Design, there's no reason that they should be immune from this kind of mistake.

When CDD elicitation participants disagree

We've found that CDDs substantially reduce disagreements that might otherwise arise during decision making. But disagreements still occur, sometimes about the structure of the diagram and sometimes about language. Facilitating CDD disagreements is as much an art as a science. One of the most important contributions of the CDD is to allow disagreements about its parts to happen one at a time, in a structured way. This keeps everyone focused on collaboratively creating the best diagram possible and avoids cognitive overload. You can't remember every path from actions to outcomes without a picture. And if you've ever worked in an organizational setting where decision making is mostly about competitively disagreeing about the right actions to take, you know why that's best avoided.

Sometimes a disagreement doesn't have much impact on the outcome. Being able to see the flow of a decision can help you avoid spending unnecessary time and effort coming to agreement about irrelevant details. For example, the CDD may help the team to realize that it doesn't matter whether a competitor charges $10 or $15, because you will make the same decision either way.

Convergent Thinking: Refining Intermediates

As with outcomes and levers, after the initial elicitation, it's worth your time to refine intermediates. Seek to ensure that your intermediates are not levers or outcomes. Remember: everything in a "how chain," except the final lever, is an intermediate. Everything in a "why chain," except the final outcome, is an intermediate.

Make sure that intermediates are not redundant. During the elicitation, sometimes several people suggest variations on the same intermediate, like "Number of customers who recommend us" and "Percentage of customers who recommend us." Choose one as your intermediate and reconnect the CDD. People may also suggest overlapping intermediates, like "Performance on standardized tests" and "SAT scores." Once again, choose the most appropriate one for your CDD. Remember that the dependency arrows between intermediates represent cause and effect, not decomposition, so in a CDD you should never see something like "Scores on standardized tests" followed by two arrows to "SAT scores" and "ACT scores."

Make sure that your intermediates are measurable. Sometimes you will discover the range of allowable values for an intermediate during elicitation. If so, you can note it like this:

> Percent of customers who recommend us (Target 20–25).

Finally, check that your intermediates represent a consistent *level of aggregation,* or level of decision-making authority and responsibility. A CDD should represent a single level of aggregation, like the CEO, a department, or an individual.

Divergent Thinking: Eliciting Externals

As with outcome and lever elicitation, you may wish to elicit externals in the same or different meetings, depending on the complexity of the decision. An external could be the weather, a competitor's pricing, attitudes toward your industry, or anything else that you might be able to measure, but not control, and which interacts with your decisions to lead to outcomes.

To get people to start thinking about externals, ask if there are any elements outside your decision maker's control that affect the outcomes. You may find externals among elements you initially identified as actions or intermediates.

The decision maker's accountability boundary often determines whether an element is a lever or an external. If you're told that you won't have the chance to change the price of a product, then that's an external. Later on, you may be asked to make a price recommendation, in which case it becomes a lever. You may also have interrelated decisions, where the decision made using one CDD may create an external in another. A decision model of choices made by a competitor can be an external in your CDD, or an executive's choices may create externals to a departmental CDD.

By the time you've built a few causal chains, chances are that someone has already mentioned an external. If you placed it in your "parking lot," draw boxes and arrows to pull it into your diagram. Build a few connections to externals yourself to demonstrate how to do it, and again, think out loud. For instance, as you draw a box labeled "competitor price" and an arrow from "competitor price" to "units purchased," you might say, "Hmm, this competitor's pricing might affect demand for our product."

Another way to think about externals is to start with objectives and ask, "What else could I measure that would help me know if I'm going to achieve my objectives?" This is especially useful to organizations who are just starting their data journey, not having used data much in their business. They often start with the end in mind: their business objectives. Working backward from objectives, you might find externals, levers, and/or intermediates that have a big impact. You will probably care the most about externals that are (a) highly volatile and (b) have a big potential impact on outcomes. Identifying ways to measure these high-risk environmental factors as early and as accurately as possible often goes a long way. Drawing a CDD backward from outcomes to these externals can help you with this tracking.

Convergent Thinking: Refining Externals

After you elicit externals, you will want to step back and refine them, just as you refined outcomes, levers, and intermediates. The key to refining externals is to understand the *system boundary* for your decision—where does the decision maker's scope of control end? If the decision maker can control it and has the authority to control it, it's a lever, not an external. If it's a causal consequence of something the decision maker can control, it's an intermediate. While some elements like the weather are clearly not controllable by anyone, other elements like "Budget for customer service salaries" may be either levers, intermediates, or externals depending on whether the CEO or a department manager is making the decision.

Ensure that your externals are measurable and note any information you have about the time frame for measuring them. Are they unchanging over the time period of the decision model (such as the diameter of the earth), predictions about things you cannot change (such as predicted rainfall for the next 12 months), or information from a single point in time (like a competitor's current price)? Document any assumptions—and your uncertainty about these assumptions—that you discovered during elicitation.

Convergent Thinking: Refining Decision Elements

This is also a good time to ensure that all decision elements are measurable. We've described how to ensure that your outcomes are measurable, but this is important for intermediates and externals, too. Wording things in a measurable way does not necessarily imply that you *will* measure them. It's valuable to simply understand and agree to the simplest of causal flows: "If we do more of this, then we'll get more of that."

Table 3-2 gives some examples of measurability. As you can see, often we see both directionality and imprecision in the CDD as it's initially elicited. You can add measurement later or not at all, but thinking in these terms can be helpful in making clear, understandable CDDs, and those that can be used to build simulations later on.

Table 3-2. Examples of measurable elements and clear causal statements

Lever to the left of the causal dependency link	Nonmeasurable intermediate	Measurable intermediate on the right side of a dependency	Causal statement relating the two sides of the dependency
Number of flights to visit our suppliers in person	Worse relationships	Quality of our relationships with our suppliers, on a score of 1–10, as measured on the XYZ survey	If we visit suppliers more, we'll get better relationships with them.
Numbers of flights not taken due to replacing in-person attendance with virtual attendance	Reduce GHGs	Average GHG emissions for a flight	If we reduce the number of flights we take, we can decrease our GHG emissions.
Amount of money spent on a marketing campaign	Obtain new customers	Number of new customers signed in the 30 days after the marketing campaign	If we spend more on marketing, we increase new sales.

Refining and Expanding Your CDD

After eliciting and refining outcomes, objectives, levers, intermediates, and externals, you have an initial CDD. Even refined CDDs can look messy, which can put people off. But we like to say, "Imagine if you had to keep all of this in your head; isn't it better if the reality is this messy that at least we've written it down?" (A side note: as you read this section, you might want to refer to one or the other CDD pictures you've seen so far, just to keep the difference between actions, outcomes, externals, intermediates, and causal chains straight in your head. We're writing this assuming you've got that picture in front of you. Otherwise, this material can get overwhelming! And note that you'll have a chance to practice all this in the "Try It Yourself" section that follows.)

At this point, you might have what you need! Or you might decide to go further, either adding important CDD elements, or moving on to finding technical assets that augment your CDD, as described in the next chapter. If you do choose to go further with your CDD, you'll work incrementally, adding and refining elements until you are satisfied.

Make sure to check with all potential stakeholders to ensure the levers, outcomes, and externals they consider most important are reflected. You might not add them all, but it's a good idea to make explicit decisions about what to include or leave out.

Here are a few more questions to ask as you refine your CDD:

- Have you eliminated redundancy and overlapping elements?
- Are any of your intermediates really process steps? If so, can you reword them to show cause and effect?
- Have you considered intangible ("soft") outcomes, like brand, reputation, and happiness, as appropriate?

- Have you correctly identified the system boundary and the scope of the decision maker's authority and responsibility?

- Do you have any evidence that what looks like causation in a CDD is actually correlation? On a CDD, this would look like two values linked to each other, where the underlying reality is that they are both caused by some unknown, upstream element, which you haven't captured yet. (Recall the breakfast example: are breakfast eaters healthier *because* they eat breakfast, or because a hidden element that might be labeled "degree of belief in a healthy lifestyle" causes both breakfast eating and health, so they tend to be observed together, despite the fact that one doesn't cause the other?

- Do the outcomes on the CDD reflect the time frame in which you will want to measure them to see if you've achieved your goal? (For example, "Have we turned a profit after 12 months?")

- Is the CDD's aggregation level consistent? For example, we've seen unrefined CDDs for which one lever is about a choice that one employee makes and another lever is about a policy decision that covers all employees. The CDD should be consistent in looking at organizations, departments, or individuals, rather than a mixture.

- Have you considered using an LLM like ChatGPT to uncover actions, outcomes (including unintended consequences), and/or externals that the team missed?

Often, when you review your CDDs, you'll find that elements you initially identified as outcomes or externals turn out to be intermediates, or vice versa. This is a normal consequence of starting with open-ended brainstorming and then analyzing and refining the CDD. For example, you may think at first that the price of the product you're selling is an external. Later, let's say your manager tells you that you're free to suggest different pricing, if you can effectively argue that this would increase overall revenues. In that case, price is under your control, so it is now a lever, not an external.

Sometimes your decision team doesn't have all the information they need to complete the CDD. In this circumstance, complete Phase B, Worksheet 1, Decision Modeling Research, as described in step 12.

Levels of Modeling Detail

It's important to understand how much detail the decision maker and other stakeholders want to see in a CDD.

At one end of the spectrum, some groups of stakeholders have very little appetite for detail: they only want to see lists of actions and outcomes and leave the causal chains to more technical people. These stakeholders will usually re-engage with the CDD later if you show them causality via a simple simulation, as will be described in Chapter 5.

Other stakeholders want many details and are comfortable with CDDs with dozens of complex causal chains. In particular, analysts and data scientists usually appreciate a very detailed CDD to help them prepare data and models to support the decision. They may add more CDD elements during Decision Asset Investigation, as described in Chapter 4.

What this means is that, by the time you're done, you may end up with a few versions of your CDD at varying levels of detail.

How Do You Know When to Stop Decision Modeling?

The last step in the Decision Design process is, in essence, "repeat until done." When to stop is always a judgment call, and it is different in every circumstance. Some decision customers are happy with a very simple CDD. Some want a very detailed one. Some want a full CDD simulation implemented in code. Some want a pilot version of that software. You should have obtained an initial sense of what "done" looks like for the first iteration of your Decision Design exercise during Decision Framing. Then check with your customer and let them be the judge of when and how to continue.

One caveat: we've seen many people wait too long to use their decision models—especially those that are part of a data project. Even very low-fidelity decision models can have a lot of value. One of our customers told us that just a CDD was worth $10 million per year in improving the effectiveness of his program!

Here are some ideas that will help you decide what "done" means.

Decision models are never perfect and complete.
> Even if—by some miracle—you could create a perfect CDD, it would lose its fidelity the moment the situation changed. So don't let the perfect be the enemy of the "good enough" or fall for "the curse of overthinking": your goal is to support the decision maker in making a better decision than they otherwise would have.
>
> This can be a hard pill to swallow for some more technically minded people. They'll be surprised and skeptical at first to know that great decision improvement can come from low-fidelity decision models. Remind them of the baseline to compare against: many decisions that we model are currently being done in people's heads without any structure at all, and this leads to lots of inefficiencies. Just drawing a CDD—even if it's imperfect—is better than these "invisible and inconsistent" mental CDDs.
>
> So, for technical people like this, "done" may happen way earlier than they'd otherwise want, sometimes before there's any data or any computerization at all! This does not diminish the value of later processes that add the right data to the

CDD and use it for simulation and monitoring. While every process adds value, for some decisions, later processes do not add enough value to justify their effort.

As the statistician George Box famously put it (*https://oreil.ly/aGSpH*): "All models are wrong, but some are useful." Because your decision model can never be perfect and complete, it will always omit certain aspects of a decision and its influencing factors that are not captured on the CDD, recorded on a worksheet, or captured during Decision Design. For instance, a CDD model to launch a new product might include pricing and the expected market, based on research, but exclude an expert's "gut instinct" as to the value of the product.

It's unreasonable to expect full consensus on the decision.
All team members won't always be on the same page about what to include. If you build the decision model collaboratively, using existing decision assets as inputs in an unbiased way, the decision maker will be better informed and will probably do a better job of making good decisions and avoiding unintended consequences. But even with this degree of care, the decision model will never perfectly match the decision maker's mental model. For this reason, they may want to take a different action than it recommends. This is fine: their "gut instinct" *should* be part of the decision-making process, given the necessary imperfection of any model.

Decision models are advisory, not absolute.
Some people criticize decision models on the grounds that they cannot possibly capture all the details of a situation. That is not their purpose. A decision model and all its related decision assets and artifacts are advisory tools to aid the decision customer. The goal is simply to do better than has been done in the past; to present the decision maker with information they might not otherwise take into account, in a structured way; and to drive their intuition about key dynamics of the decision. Using a documented and shared decision model, including a shared understanding of outcomes and key cause-and-effect flows, helps a team pull together toward that common goal.

Perhaps an analogy will help to understand this better. Like CDDs, Gantt charts (*https://oreil.ly/LCdwG*) take something that used to be invisible and make it visible (tasks and dependencies), and are widely accepted planning diagrams. When project managers use them, it's generally understood that the chart doesn't show every single activity the team performs. The cost of documenting and maintaining that level of detail would not be justified by the benefit of doing so. The same is true of decision models: like Gantt charts, they strike a balance between fidelity and usefulness to drive organizational success.

What if the decision makers' judgment says, "The actions produced by this decision model are wrong"? It's possible that their gut instinct—and internal mental model of the situation, conscious and/or unconscious—is a better guide than the diagram or computer. And it's also possible that their gut instincts were "trained" in a situation that is so fundamentally different than the current one, or a cognitive bias is in play, that they're just plain wrong. What should they do?

Part of the answer lies in the responsibility/authority/information balance we introduced in Chapter 2: if the decision maker retains responsibility for the decision, then they can consider the model an information source. The consequences of making the wrong decision will fall on them (responsibility), and so they'll be incentivized toward a careful consideration of the opposing information. In a sense, this is nothing different than consulting an article or a colleague to help make a decision: it's a source of opinion that needs to be blended with other sources.

This is the essence of the "hybrid" nature of DI. As you might imagine, there's a lot more to say on this topic of how humans work hand in hand with AI (and LLMs like ChatGPT place this question into starker relief than ever before). Maybe our next book!

Now that you're familiar with the Decision Design process, the rest of the chapter presents two use cases. The first describes a project we worked on, while the second offers you the opportunity to try it yourself.

Decision Design Use Case: Governmental Net-Zero Project

For this use case, we'll return to the European government agency you met in Chapter 2. As you may recall, the agency's decision team began with this Decision Objective Statement:

> What policy should we create regarding airline travel amongst our employees, so that we can reduce our GHGs while at the same time maintaining the benefits of travel (relationships, trust, reputation, learning, employee morale, and more)?

Chapter 2 showed the agency's Decision Framing Document, which included the Decision Objective Statement and described the outcomes of lowering costs, of achieving net-zero GHG emissions by a particular date, and of retaining important relationships despite a reduction in the use of air travel. The primary lever was a travel policy that included guidance about whether to fly or drive and about whether airline travelers should use business or economy class.

Before its CDD elicitation meeting, the agency team drew the "mind map" diagram shown in Figure 3-8. It reflects team members' initial view of the connections between the agency's strategic goals and its net-zero aspirations. This diagram is typical of pre-CDD mental models: although it shows careful thought, it is not in a format that allows for integrating data, it does not include intermediates, and it mixes different levels of aggregation.

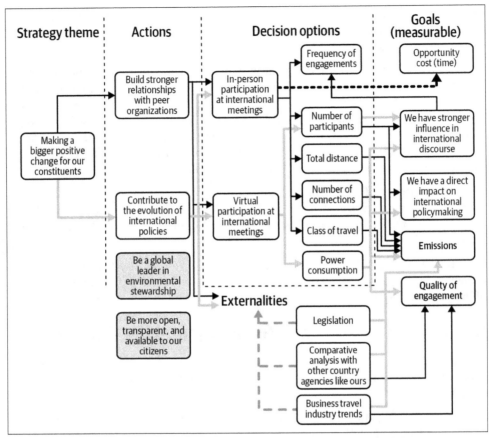

Figure 3-8. "Mind map" created in advance of the CDD elicitation meeting.

We worked with the team to create a first-draft CDD, using both online meetings as well as offline work. Figure 3-9 shows the result. Here, you can see clear actions, intermediates, outcomes, and externals. Actions here represent choices that executives can make about travel budget for particular categories of travel.

However, we see two major issues with this first-draft CDD. First, the intermediates are not well formed, nor are many of them measurable values. Second, most of the externals reflect the circumstances of particular travelers, but the CDD actions and outcomes fit a policy decision made at the executive level: an aggregation-level mismatch.

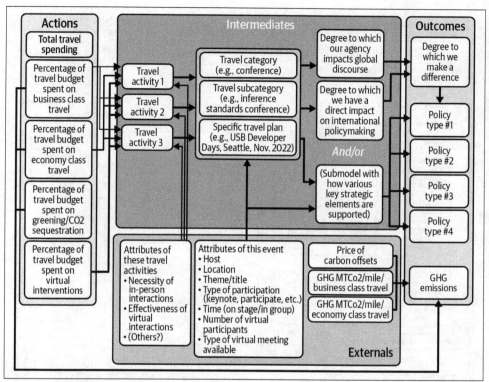

Figure 3-9. The agency's first-draft CDD.

We addressed these issues in our refinements. Along the way, we learned that our decision team didn't initially know everything required to build a good CDD, so they conducted some additional research (reading some articles and conducting interviews) about travel policies and completed the Decision Modeling Research Worksheet (in step 12).

Our final deliverable turned out to be several CDDs designed for different travel purposes, such as conferences, recruitment, and operations. Figure 3-10 shows an example: the CDD for conferences and external speaking engagements.

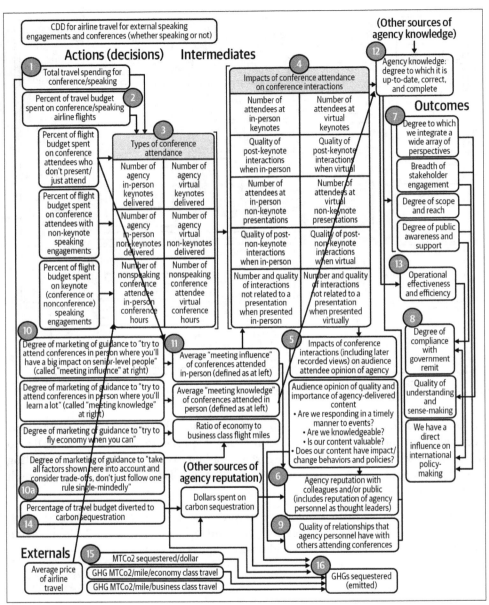

Figure 3-10. Net-zero final CDD example.

You'll notice a few things about this CDD. First, it contains a *lot* of details. And even so, it's not the full level of detail: not every dependency line is shown here. Indeed, we grouped several intermediates into tables to aid communication. To see all the details more clearly, please download the PDF version from the supplemental materials repository (*https://oreil.ly/DIH-supplemental*).

While this level of detail can feel overwhelming, the alternative would have been attempting to communicate about this level of complexity verbally, *without* a drawing. Imagine trying to communicate about a complex engineering project like a skyscraper without a blueprint—just by talking! It's no wonder that decision making in large organizations is so challenging. That's why the CDD represents a big opportunity to make it better, before you even get to the data.

You'll notice some circled numbers, 1 through 16, on the diagram. We delivered a document that described each numbered element, so this CDD was essentially a "map" to a policy justification document.

In this CDD, most elements are now measurable and well formed, except for the final outcomes. We left the original wording of the final outcomes because we wanted to convey the CDD's connection to a strategy document that used this language.

This CDD was the final deliverable from our involvement with the project. The agency found the diagram alone very helpful in its policy development and is now well on its way to its goals.

In Figures 3-8 through 3-10, you'll notice a progression as the CDD evolves from an initial set of concepts into a detailed, specific diagram that can guide policy.

Try It Yourself: Decision Design for a Telecom Use Case

Now it's your turn. In Chapter 2, you worked through the Decision Framing process for the telecom use case. In this section, you will complete the Decision Design process and create a CDD for the same use case.

Exercise

Before you look at the CDD in Figure 3-11, review the Decision Design formal process description. You'll be working through it step by step. Set up a workspace to build your CDD, such as a physical or virtual whiteboard (PowerPoint works well in some cases). Optionally, recruit a team of colleagues to work with you.

You will not be tailoring the process in this exercise, so you can skip step 1.

Your assignment: Please brainstorm outcomes for the telecom use case. List several on the right-hand side of your workspace before you continue reading. You might want to mark the top three for initial focus with a star.

Brainstorming Outcomes

Here's how your exercise might have proceeded.

You convene your team for an in-person CDD elicitation meeting (step 2 in the Decision Design process). (If you've convened a real team to work through the exercise, we encourage you to act this out!) You start by reviewing the Decision Framing Document (step 3) and the telecom CEO's suggestions. You copy out the Decision Objective Statement on the whiteboard (step 4):

> The company needs to find ways to increase customer satisfaction. The executives believe that one way to do this may be to launch an "unlimited" subscription service, where customers can use all the voice-call minutes and data they desire for a single monthly price. The executives want to explore a range of unlimited plan options supported with advantages, disadvantages, and risks in order to make a decision whether or not to offer such a plan and, if so, what plan.

You give each team member a pile of sticky notes and explain that they'll be contributing ideas on the whiteboard by posting them under the headings listed there, starting with "Outcomes" (step 5). You then explain the rules of brainstorming and ask the team to think of outcomes that fit the Objective Statement (step 6).

To get things moving, you ask the team to post some notes with a few playful ideas, like "Make every employee a billionaire." Once the ice is broken, you move the funny outcomes to the side and ask the team to get serious. They come up with two outcomes:

- Improve customer experience
- Launch the product successfully

To see if you can elicit some more outcomes, you then suggest that they consider intangible outcomes—like morale, trust, and happiness (*https://oreil.ly/ii77n*). You explain that, although intangibles are often overlooked in business decision making, they often drive decisions in ways that are hard to anticipate unless they are explicitly discussed.

The team adds:

- Fit within our environmental-impact policy constraints
- Create positive social benefit
- Help to reduce income inequality worldwide

Then, one of your team members—who has ChatGPT open on their computer—says, "Here's a new outcome: what about increasing employee morale?"

You let the team brainstorm until they are no longer adding new items.

A few comments come up that are out of the CDD's scope. The database expert mentions that she has a table of information about employee morale. A marketer suggests improving social goals by marketing to low-income households at initial product launch. And after someone lists "Using diverse resources within the company," a call center expert suggests using his team of retrained coal miners to help launch the product. Although these are all great ideas, none of them are about outcomes: they are externals (including new decision assets) and levers. It is natural for such ideas to arise during brainstorming. You note them in the "parking lot" section of your whiteboard, re-explain that they are not outcomes, and return to the task at hand.

At this point, the whiteboard looks a little messy. There are dozens of outcome Post-its, including many duplicates, plus the "parking lot." You take a few minutes to organize the ideas by topic and move duplicates off to the side. Then you create a poll so each team member can vote for their top three outcomes. They choose:

1. Improve customer experience
2. Launch the product successfully
3. Maintain employee morale

You leave space on the left side to add levers later. Then, to keep the initial CDD work manageable, you move all but the top three outcomes to the side.

Note that these outcomes are not well formed or refined. That's fine. Recall that your goal is to capture how people are thinking, not to get in their way with too much analysis or correction.

Exercise

Compare the outcomes you brainstormed to the ones the telecom team produced. What similarities and differences do you notice?

Now it's your turn to brainstorm some levers. Try to list levers that might affect the team's top three outcomes. Then continue reading.

Brainstorming Levers

You start the lever elicitation session (step 7) by listing the levers from the Decision Framing Worksheet:

- Pricing
- Services included

- Contract period
- Inducements

Your team then adds to the list:

- Marketing/advertising
- Competitive marketing/advertising ("we have this, the others don't")
- Encouraging customers to recommend the service to their friends (this is called likelihood-to-recommend, or L2R)
- Competitor offers same product, but at a higher rate
- Better customer experience

You poll the team for their top three levers, then list them on the left side of the whiteboard, next to the outcomes:

1. Pricing
2. Better customer experience
3. Marketing/advertising

Exercise

Check your levers now. Are they similar to the team's list?

Pick one of the levers and one of the outcomes in these lists. Can you design a chain of dependency arrows and intermediates to connect them?

Wiring Known Dependencies Together

Now that you have your top three levers and outcomes on the whiteboard, someone points out that "Marketing/advertising" and "Competitive marketing" are probably the same thing, so you delete the second one. Then you quickly sketch a causal chain from a lever to an outcome (step 8) to give the team a sense of where they are going (Figure 3-11). At this point, you realize that the team is very tired, so you choose to take a break and to work on remaining causal chains either offline or in a future meeting.

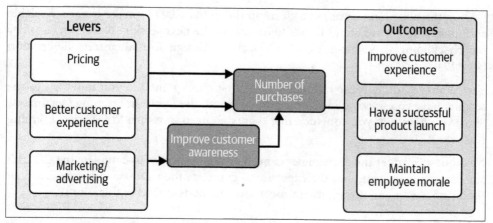

Figure 3-11. The team's draft CDD after initial cleanup.

You reflect on the CDD as the team is leaving the room. This CDD is a first draft; it's incomplete and inconsistent. It only shows the top three levers and outcomes, which don't cover everything. And it seems the team is not sure yet whether "improve customer experience" is a lever, an outcome, or something else. You've captured some "parking lot" externals already (step 9), and nobody has talked about process steps or known dependency information (steps 10 and 11).

Exercise

Does your causal chain look anything like the one in Figure 3-11? There are many possible correct answers!

Note that the outcomes in Figure 3-11 aren't measurable, and the intermediate "Improve customer awareness" includes a direction, which shouldn't be part of a well-formed intermediate.

Next, analyze the levers in the team's CDD. See if you can identify:

- Two redundant levers that could be collapsed into one
- One "lever" that is actually an external
- One "lever" that could be refined using a how chain

To stay synchronized with this exercise, we recommend that you proceed using the team's CDD from Figure 3-11.

During the hour-long break, you clean up the initial CDD to make it more readable and make a few notes about things to discuss in the next session. Next, you consider the checkpoint assessments from the Decision Design formal process description (step 12).

You've already done some refinement (the first checkpoint), so you move on to the second: have you uncovered significant issues with the Decision Framing Document? Since you have not, you conclude that there's no need to return to Decision Framing (Process A2).

Next question: does the decision team need outside expertise to complete the CDD? It appears that your team has the expertise to complete the CDD, so you conclude that there's no need to do the additional asset assessment described in this step 12.

Initial Refinement

Your meeting participants return from their break. At this point in the process (step 13), you have a choice: move offline and continue to refine the CDD yourself, or refine it in a collaborative team setting. Your team is pretty experienced; everyone wants to continue the meeting.

Refining levers

You and the team begin to review the levers, starting with the top three.

Identifying an external
You ask the team whether "Competitor offers same product" is really a lever: do you or the decision maker have control over it? The team agrees that this is an external—something you cannot control—so you move it to a new list for later.

Using a "how chain"
You now ask whether "Better customer experience" is really a lever, because you can't influence it directly. So you lead the team through a "how chain" exercise: adding elements to its left on the diagram, upstream on the causal chain. You ask: "*How* can we achieve a better customer experience?" The team makes two suggestions:

- Invest in call center training
- Invest in more call center personnel

You ask "how" again, and everyone agrees that these elements are as far to the left as could be possible, so you add them to the levers list.

Next, you add a link from these two items to an intermediate you call "Customer experience." A section of your whiteboard now looks like Figure 3-12.

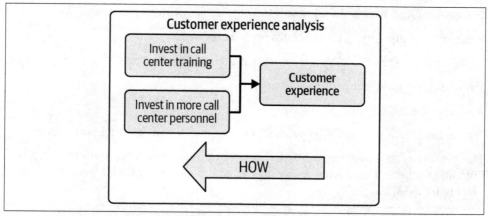

Figure 3-12. Working right to left to identify actual levers by asking, "How?"

Refining outcomes

You notice that "Customer experience" is mentioned in the list of outcomes as well as the list of levers and the intermediate, so you ask the team if they think it's really an outcome. One person replies, "I know how you can improve customer experience—just write every customer a check for a thousand dollars!" Everyone laughs, and they continue: "So, no, I don't think that customer experience improvement is an end outcome. It's probably more complicated than that."

Using a "why chain"

You decide to follow the why chain. Asking "why" is a way to elicit elements that belong to the right of an existing element (closer to the outcomes).

You ask, "*Why* is customer experience important?"

Another team member responds: "To ensure a successful product launch."

You clarify: "And how will we know if the product launch was successful?"[3]

Someone else pipes up: "If it generates positive revenues."

Back to the why chain: "Why is it important to improve revenues?"

"So we can improve our profits."

And, again, why?

"So we can provide shareholder value and keep the company growing and successful."

The process of repeatedly asking "why" questions has moved your team from a proxy outcome to the real one. After following the why chain, part of your workspace looks like Figure 3-13.

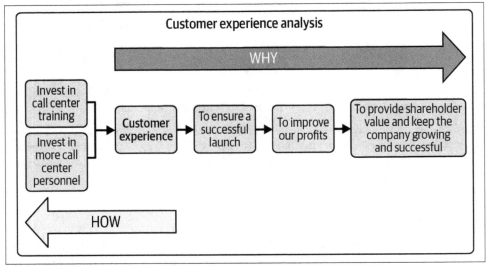

Figure 3-13. Adding the customer experience "why chain."

Adjusting the decision boundary

Sometimes the why chain leads you to outcomes that lie outside the scope of your current decision. When that happens, you might need to revisit the decision scope in the Decision Framing Document. You need to decide where the boundary is—what is in scope and what is external.

---

3 This particular *how* carries the sense of "how to measure it," not a "how to accomplish it." That's why it's not part of the why/how chain mechanism. Yes, it's confusing: the English language isn't quite up to this.

In this example, your team decides that "Provide shareholder value and keep the company growing and successful" is outside the scope of the current decision. So you pare the why chain back to end with "To improve our profits." You make a note to verify that Dr. Smith agrees with this adjustment to the scope.

Exercise

Were you able to build a why chain to profits or shareholder value? Where did you draw your decision boundary?

Before you continue reading, refine the outcome "To improve our profits" to be measurable. Suggest an appropriate objective for this outcome.

Making elements measurable and removing directions

Next, you ask your team to clarify the element "To improve our profits." It doesn't seem precise enough to be measurable, and it has a verb in it, "improve," indicating directionality, which is a checklist item. You ask, "How can we make this something measurable, and precise enough that if you and I placed a bet on it, we'd all know who won the bet?"

The team isn't sure. Someone asks, "What do you mean by *profits*?"

Another person replies: "And what do you mean by *improve*?"

One team member suggests that "improve profits" means "to maximize the net revenues we bring in after subtracting capital costs." Another amends this to subtract capital *and* operational costs. Everyone agrees that this is still too ambiguous and doesn't pass the "I'd bet on it" test. It also still has that verb, "improve."

Even though you know what capital and operational costs are, you ask the team to define these terms. Misunderstandings about outcomes can create big inefficiencies, so it's well worth the time to ensure everyone is on the same page. People make thousands of decisions every day, only a small fraction of which will ever make it into a CDD. But if the team is aligned around their "true north" outcomes, they're more likely to achieve them than if they're pulling in different directions.

Your team decides that *capital costs*, in this context, refers to the one-time costs required to get the new pricing plan out the door. They define *operational costs* as the ongoing monthly costs required to keep the plan going, such as customer care, technical systems that allow unlimited data, and advertising.

Should you include both in your understanding of profit? While you're at it, what does *maximize* mean, exactly? And *when* should you measure profit? After a couple of hours of debate, a call to Dr. Smith, and a few breaks for side conversions, your team decides on the following refined outcome:

> Achieve 2% net profit (after the costs of capital investment) after 18 months on this new product.

But there's one more thing to refine. This statement doesn't clearly distinguish the outcome (the value to be measured, in this case net profit) from the objective, which is the value of the outcome that is acceptable—in this case, 2%. This kind of distinction is sometimes worth bringing up, sometimes not. The team might agree to the outcome but debate whether to aim for 4% instead of 2%, for instance.

At this point, the customer experience how and why chains look like Figure 3-14. Among other things, you can see there that "Profit net of capital investment" (the outcome) is now separate from "2% improvement after 18 months" (the objective).

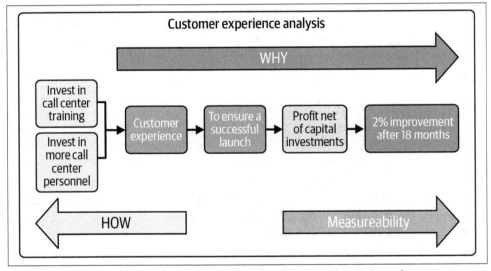

Figure 3-14. How and why chains showing how to measure the quality of customer experience.

Exercise

Of course, your answer will be different, but compare it and ask:

- Is your outcome measurable?
- Did you clearly define *profit*?

- Did you separate what you're measuring (the outcome) from the target value of the measurement (the objective)?
- Does your objective include an amount and a time frame for measuring?

Before you continue reading, see if you can draw a causal chain showing several intermediates that affect profit and sketch part of a CDD showing them.

Drawing more causal chains from actions to outcomes

When it's time to draw causal chains, many people ask us: is it better to dive down into the details ("depth first"), or build chains from decisions to outcomes ("breadth first")?

If you choose a depth-first approach, you might diagram a submodel that splits out the different components of startup costs. Working breadth-first, you might ask, "What chain of events from actions to outcomes will have the biggest impact on our objectives?"

In general, it's better to go breadth-first. The big picture—the one that crosses multiple decision models—is usually harder to understand than concrete details, like elements of startup costs. The great value of the initial Decision Design process is that it helps different departments understand their interdependencies.

You ask the breadth-first question: "What chain of events from actions to outcomes will have the biggest impact on our objectives?"

The first reply is: "Well, our operating margin depends on our costs and our revenues." You draw some intermediates to capture this (Figure 3-15).

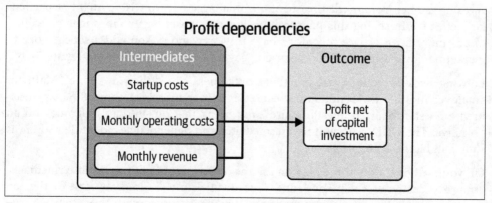

Figure 3-15. Enhancing the CDD by adding intermediates to show profit dependencies.

Next, you ask: "What is the most influential chain of events from levers to outcomes?" After some discussion, the team decides that offering an unlimited plan would substantially reduce operational costs by eliminating the need to track minutes of use, roll minutes over to the next month, and cut off service to customers who run out of minutes—all of which requires technological systems that must be maintained.

Because this cost reduction will be a benefit no matter what other choices you make about the unlimited plan, you decide to add a new lever called "Choose unlimited plan" to the left side of the diagram. You draw an arrow from it to the intermediate "Monthly operating costs." Check out how Figure 3-16 shows this change.

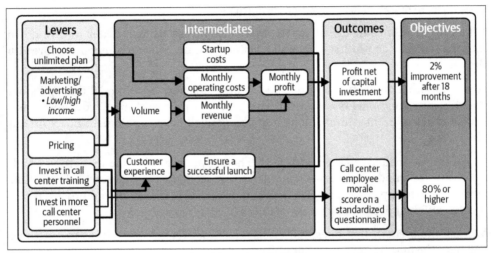

Figure 3-16. CDD showing the refined levers and all the intermediates and dependencies discussed so far.

A team member from marketing mentions that targeted advertising might be particularly effective in selling this plan to high-income subscribers, who might be willing to pay more for a service they don't have to worry about. You add a subcategory to marketing/advertising and link the pricing lever to volume, as shown in Figure 3-16.

Looking back at your initial top three outcomes, you decide to refine "Maintain employee morale" to "Maintain call center employee morale at above 80%, as measured on a standardized questionnaire." You break that out into an outcome and an objective. The CDD, with all the intermediates and dependencies identified so far, is shown in Figure 3-16.

Of your original top three outcomes, the team identified two as intermediates: "Improve customer experience" and "Successful launch." Similarly, one of the top three levers, "Better customer experience," has now merged with the "Improve customer experience" intermediate. During lever analysis, the team added three new levers and refined "Marketing/advertising."

Brainstorming externals and documenting assumptions

Your database person has been waiting patiently all this time. She asks now, "Is it time to talk about externals that I might help to support?" You wholeheartedly agree: the initial refinement didn't hit on any externals. So you ask the team, "What factors from outside of our organization might influence how our decisions lead to outcomes?"

They suggest several, including:

- Competitor behavior
- Macroeconomic shifts
- Demand from the target market

You discuss whether a major competitor might or might not also launch an unlimited pricing plan. This kind of discussion can become heated and sometimes even counterproductive, since it is based on the expertise and experience of the team members, which by definition vary.

Before attempting to resolve such a difference, make sure it's worth resolving: it may be that the outcomes don't depend much on this external factor. If it is, then respectfully record the team's range of opinions about competitor behavior in the model. Later, you can explore or run the model using different sets of assumptions about the externals and see how it behaves. You don't have to come to agreement now. It's worth emphasizing the power of this solution: it removes the need to resolve all differences of opinion.

In Decision Design, an *assumption* is information about an external factor about which you have some uncertainty. An assumption about an external can be uncertainty regarding a specific point in time or a prediction over time (such as, for instance, the global domestic product [GDP] of India for the next five years).

Your team now talks about how the economy will affect demand for your product. One team member says she's read a paper predicting that consumer spending in the UK economy will continue to decrease for the next 18 months. If consumer spending is low overall, will customers be less likely to purchase the unlimited plan? Another team member says, "Hey, can we re-invest our profit back into improving our call center?" You draw a feedback loop arrow from profit back to the lever box to show this connection.

You update the CDD, adding the externals and drawing causal chains from them (Figure 3-17).

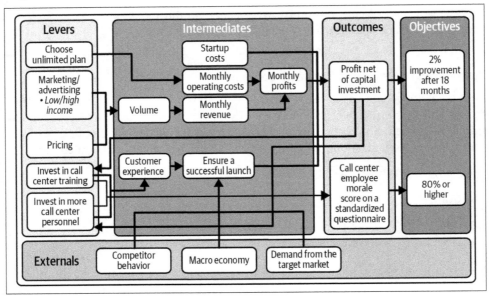

Figure 3-17. The team's CDD with externals added.

Exercise

Does your CDD look somewhat like Figure 3-17? What differences do you see?

Save the workspace you used for this exercise. You will need it again when you try Decision Asset Investigation in Chapter 4.

Iterating On and Publishing the CDD

Clean the CDD up so that it is well organized and readable, and publish it to the team. Is this CDD done for now? That's up to you and your team to decide. If not, you might lead the team in iterating over the prior steps until everyone agrees that the CDD is complete, incorporates all the necessary outcomes, actions, externals, and causal chains from actions and externals to outcomes, or agrees to document disagreements and move on. If you're satisfied with it, you can move forward. (See "How Do You Know When to Stop Decision Modeling?" on page 83.)

You can now publish the CDD to the decision customer. This kicks off another iterative round of review and revision, until the decision team and decision customer agree that the CDD is sufficiently complete and correct. Congratulations on learning and completing the Decision Design process!

Conclusion

By creating the CDD, you have aligned your team around the outcomes you want. You know what actions you can take to achieve those outcomes. You have identified some externals that also affect your outcomes, and you've mapped some causal chains that lead from your actions and the externals to your outcomes. Congratulations, you have designed your decision! It's no longer many models in many heads, it's one written model that represents the work of the entire team. It's a valuable asset.

For some decisions, alignment around the CDD may be enough. You might be ready to make your decision. For other decisions, completing your initial CDD means you're ready for the "data-driven" or "evidenced-based" part of decision making. You're ready to move on to the next chapter, where we'll talk about how to investigate technology assets that will help you to go from an "on-paper" CDD to using it to build a computer simulation. This is when a computer really starts to help us "think together," becoming an important new member of our decision-making team!

CHAPTER 4

Decision Modeling: The Decision Asset Investigation Process

Are we drowning in data? The world is now creating more than 100 zettabytes (ZB) (*https://oreil.ly/zbJFa*)[1] of data every year, "roughly equivalent to every human generating an entire copy of the Library of Congress each year," according to Marc Warner in *Computer Weekly*. But is it really helping us? "If data-driven decision making was right," Warner adds, "this growth should lead to vastly improved organizational performance.... Has that happened? Clearly not." What's going on?

Data can only help us think or do something more efficiently if it's the right data, in the right form, at the right time. Zettabytes of the wrong data in the wrong form don't help us meet our objectives; in fact, data can get in the way. This is why so many decision makers routinely say things like, "Please don't send me any data. I'm simply not interested."

Decision intelligence fixes this problem by changing your data into a more usable form. The Decision Asset Investigation process (Process B2, illustrated in Figure 4-1) is the first step on the path to building software simulation of the path(s) from actions to outcomes, to help you determine the best actions to take. The CDD serves as a "scaffold" that shows you where data supports that simulation. Decision Asset Investigation starts with your initial CDD and uses it as a guide to your investigation to find multiple assets that can be used to inform evidence-based decision making. In particular, this is where you'll ask, "If I change the element(s) on the left of this dependency, what happens to the element on the right?"

---

1 This is a really, really big number (*https://oreil.ly/JZYSm*): 1,000,000,000,000,000,000,000 (10^{21}) bytes.

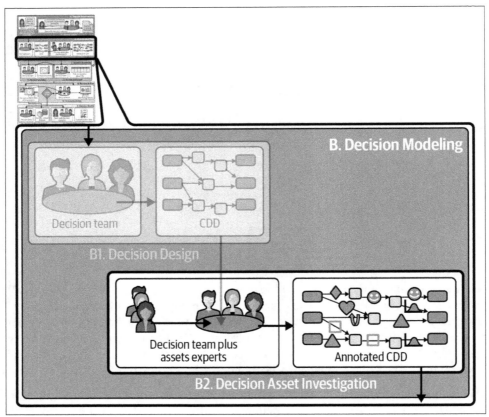

Figure 4-1. How Decision Asset Investigation relates to other processes in this book.

As you learned in Chapter 3, Process B1, Decision Design, focuses on aligning around the outcomes, identifying levers that can produce those outcomes, understanding externals that influence those outcomes, and building the causal chains from levers and externals to outcomes. Process B2, Decision Asset Investigation, in contrast, focuses on identifying the assets that will ultimately help you to implement those causal chains in software. Ultimately, you'll have a tool that allows you to say, "If I make these lever choices and these assumptions about externals, here is what I expect to measure for this outcome."

This chapter takes you step by step through the process of using and annotating your CDD to identify decision assets—data and other kinds of technology—that can support the simulation you'll build in Chapter 5 and facilitate your conversation with your data team. This is a very different conversation from the more common "back-to-front" decision conversations. This work transforms your "decision blueprint" into a "decision digital twin" specification, ready for simulation.

Deciding to Go Digital

When is it worth the time to go beyond a CDD and to model a decision in software? The simple answer is that it depends on your expected return on investment (ROI) from this exercise. You might find—as have some of our customers—that the CDD alone is a giant benefit, and that your organization isn't yet ready to take the next step. Or you might find, after you've had a chance to work with the CDD a bit, that either (a) your decision customers just aren't "getting it" or (b) the decision is so complex and valuable that you think that it's going to be worth building a simulation for it. If people's livelihoods and/or large amounts of money depend on a decision, then our clients have found that investing in decision-software implementation can be worth the effort. And you can "dip your toe in the water" with a simple—sometimes called "low-fidelity"—simulation if you'd like before bringing in all the data and analytics bells and whistles.

If you choose to move forward, you'll find a lot of variety in the levels of effort required to identify decision assets. Sometimes your decision asset is very simple—it's just the knowledge that, if the element on the left goes up, then the one on the right goes up (or down). Other times, you can identify a decision asset like a statistical model; an ML model; a behavioral, cognitive, and/or mathematical model; or human expertise that can provide detailed information about a certain dependency. In fact, one of the most important questions you'll answer in Decision Asset Investigation is: "Where is the model that informs this dependency arrow?"

Introduction to Process B2: Decision Asset Investigation

This chapter shows how decision teams can work with analysts to identify decision assets. You'll learn how to use the Decision Asset Investigation process and maintain a *Decision Asset Register*, in which you'll record the assets and the people responsible for them. In the "Try It Yourself" use case at the end of the chapter, you'll practice identifying assets, attaching them to a CDD, and entering them on the register.

You might like to take a look at the Appendix for a complete list of how data can be used both during decision reasoning as well as while the decision is playing out in reality. You don't need this full list to start collecting decision assets, however; feel free to get started without it. Basically, it says that data can inform many of the decision elements: providing predictions or assumptions about externals, providing expected ranges for intermediates, and (most important) driving the models that inform dependency arrows. This data is useful during decision reasoning and as the decision action plays out over time.

This process has two purposes. First, it guides you in documenting the *decision assets* (such as data, knowledge, and submodels) that will later inform your simulation. Second, it helps you identify missing assets so you can prioritize finding those assets or creating them by preparing and gathering new data, modeling, and/or researching initiatives.

It's common for people to realize, as this process unfolds, that they've forgotten important elements in their CDD, such as an external that determines the value of an intermediate. Don't hesitate to add those—effectively looping back to Decision Design from the last chapter—whenever you find them. If your organization has been doing DI for a while, you may find that someone else has modeled—and even simulated—part of your CDD, so you can see what data and models they used. The more you use DI and keep all the artifacts you create (see Chapter 8), the more you can build on the work of others and the easier it becomes.

From Simple to Sophisticated Assets

As you document your assets, you'll probably find that their degrees of precision are all over the map. Maybe all you know is that "as this element goes up, this other one goes down." Or—one level more sophisticated—maybe you can draw a simple X/Y graph (*sketch graph*) showing how the two are related. At the extreme end of sophistication, you could have a library of 30 research papers that bear on an asset—for instance, how nematodes respond to various treatments in different soil and weather conditions. You might have some software that calculates the dependency, or a simple or complicated mathematical function. Figure 4-2 illustrates assets at different levels of modeling sophistication. Table 4-2 on page 109 lists icons for many types of sophisticated models.

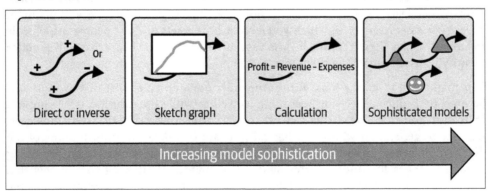

Figure 4-2. A few different levels of sophistication of assets that can inform dependencies.

Documenting Decision Assets

As you identify decision assets, we recommend listing them in a *Decision Asset Register*. You can find a template (Phase B, Worksheet 2: Decision Asset Register) in the supplemental materials repository (*https://oreil.ly/DIH-supplemental*). Table 4-1 shows an example of a Decision Asset Register.

Table 4-1. Decision Asset Register template

Decision element	Decision asset	Asset type	Asset source and contact
<Here, enter either a description of the associated decision element, e.g., "Dependency from Pricing to Volume," or you can label the CDD with numbers, and just include that number here, e.g., "(1)">	<Name or description of the decision asset to be used, e.g., "Price/Volume curve" or "Model named PV_33B in the data warehouse">	<This may be one of many types of assets, including a sketch graph, dataset, econometric model, observation, human knowledge, and many more>	<Who is responsible for maintaining/ providing this asset? >
<include as many rows in the table as there are assets to track>			

CDD annotations

As you fill out the asset register, it's a good idea to annotate your CDD to indicate the different kinds of assets that you're bringing to bear. For visual impact, and to avoid cluttering the diagram too much, you might want to draw an icon indicating the nature of the asset. Table 4-2 provides examples of icons we have used before, and Figure 4-3 shows part of a decision model annotated with icons for a few different kinds of assets.

Table 4-2. Icons that represent different types of decision assets on a CDD

Symbol	Type of decision asset
▢	Mathematical model (financial or econometric)
⇐	Mathematical model (not financial or econometric)
△	ML model
▮▮▮	Statistical model
☺	Behavioral or psychological model
⇒	Knowledge graph / inference model
♥	Medical model
⬠	Digital-twin model (human or nonhuman expertise in a domain)
◺	Sketch graph incorporating human expertise
☺	Human expertise not incorporated into a model or sketch graph

Symbol	Type of decision asset
📁	Data source for data not incorporated into a model or sketch graph
💻	Information source for information not incorporated into a model or sketch graph
⬧	Agent-based human movement model
👁	Observation, data capture, measurement, or monitoring system
🛑	Constraint
🧩	Assumption (usually based on human knowledge, intuition, or an information source)
⎱⎰	Decision submodel

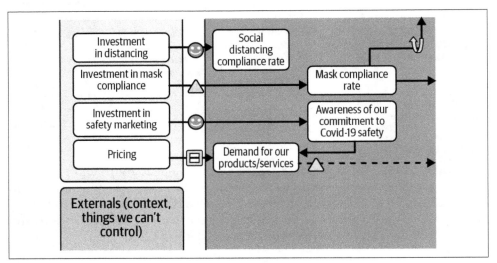

Figure 4-3. Subset of a CDD, showing several different kinds of the data and technology assets that inform its structure. This behavioral model predicts how investing in a marketing program to promote social distancing will affect the social-distancing compliance. The econometric model shows how pricing leads to demand, and the ML model predicts how investing in a marketing program will affect the mask compliance. Please see the full decision model in Figure P-2 or the supplemental materials repository (https://oreil.ly/ DIH-supplemental).

With all this in mind, please see "Formal Process Description: Process B2: Decision Asset Investigation" on page 111 (including filling out the register and annotating the CDD), followed by some guidance on how to do this. Note that this process is different from step 12, which involves assessing expertise, from Process B1, Decision Design (Chapter 3), because it assumes a complete CDD as input to the process. It's also about discovering technical elements that bridge the CDD from a diagram to a computerized model, not investigating new elements for the CDD. Both processes enhance the CDD, just in different ways.

Recording the decision assets

You need to record more information about each decision asset than you can show on a CDD. How you record it depends on how your organization manages data and knowledge. If you manage data and knowledge at the departmental level, you might use a spreadsheet or table like Table 4-3 on page 124 as a Decision Asset Register to record the locations and owners of the assets associated with your CDD elements.

On the other hand, if you have a mature data governance architecture, your lexicon can precisely define each data term and document the authoritative source for obtaining or computing its value. You can reference lexicon entries in a spreadsheet, but as you create CDDs, you might consider building a *dependency lexicon* that documents elements that appear as intermediates or outcomes and their dependencies, the arrows into them and the elements on the left sides of those arrows with ties to your data lexicon for the data that informs those dependencies. This makes the dependencies easily available for future CDDs.

If you choose to take this more formal route, then a dependency lexicon will let you answer questions like, "Which organizational outcomes does this piece of data drive?" as well as the question addressed by Decision Asset Investigation, "Which data and knowledge affects this outcome?" If your organization has mature knowledge management (KM) systems, standards, and/or processes, you can similarly link your dependency lexicon to it for dependencies informed by human knowledge.

You might also think about investigating how LLMs like ChatGPT and/or semantic search tools can help you to locate elements within your formal lexicon: this may be the future of KM, which can now treat decision models as a valuable corporate asset to store and continuously improve. You might use LLMs and semantic search to identify decision elements stored within your knowledge base.

Formal Process Description: Process B2: Decision Asset Investigation

Description
> Identify and document existing and missing data, information, human knowledge, and other technology that inform *decision elements* on the CDD, in preparation for integrating these assets into a computerized decision model.

Prerequisites
- The CDD created during Decision Design.
- A mandate (usually from the decision customer) to create an automated simulation based on the CDD.
- Guidance regarding the time, effort, and fidelity required for this process.
- Consider reading the Appendix.

- Create a blank Decision Asset Register in which to record your findings, or use Phase B, Worksheet 2: Decision Asset Register, available in the supplemental materials repository (*https://oreil.ly/DIH-supplemental*), or understand how to use any organizational tools that link CDDs to your data governance system and your knowledge management system.

Responsible role

Decision team leader. They will be assisted by people within and outside the decision team who can provide data, information, models, documents, or other forms of human knowledge related to the CDD.

Steps

1. Read through this process and tailor it, as appropriate, to your team.

2. Examine the CDD you created during Decision Design as a first step:

   - Start by documenting the "low-hanging fruit": the decision assets you've already identified during CDD elicitation (maybe you captured them in a "parking lot"). Add them to the Decision Asset Register.

   - Ask your team to look at the CDD again and identify the causal chains they think will have the biggest impact on the outcomes. Document them, including levers, externals, intermediates, and/or outcomes. As you did with outcomes and levers, you might also ask for what they think are the "top three" chains that make a difference.

3. For each intermediate and outcome, especially those along the "top three" causal chains, investigate whether there is some model or function that informs how it depends on the immediately preceding element(s). What data does each element supply to the model or function? Are any externals, levers, or intermediates missing?

4. For each intermediate, ask:

   - Are there any constraints on its allowed values? These will inform your simulation as well as how you monitor the decision as it plays out over time.

   - Are there systems that observe or measure that intermediate (such as a BI tool)?

   Add your answers to the Decision Asset Register, and annotate the CDD so that you have a clear connection between each asset and the location within the CDD that it applies to.

5. For each external, document its:

   - Assumed value(s)

   - Constraints

   - Relevant datasets

- Observations
- Measurement or monitoring systems
- Models (such as a predictive model for the GDP in India for the next five years)

6. Document where you think there are missing assets that are needed but not yet obtained.

Deliverables
- An annotated CDD
- A first-draft Decision Asset Register
- Documentation describing which decision assets are needed but missing

Decision Asset Investigation: A Sweet Potato CDD Drives Data Gathering and Research

As explained previously, the Decision Asset Investigation process has two purposes: to identify existing assets and to prioritize new data gathering or model building. Here's a story about how this played out in a recent project.

A few years back, sweet potato growers in the United States were facing a new species of soilborne agricultural pest called a *nematode*. It's basically an ugly sort of worm. Retail consumers tend to prefer unblemished produce, but nematodes cosmetically make them look unattractive. Even though the potatoes are perfectly edible, this "ugly" produce is unsuitable for sale to consumers and must be sold at a far lower price to canneries or pet-food manufacturers—a substantial financial blow to growers.

Growers can control nematodes in a number of ways. The most common methods are to rotate the crop (that is, to plant a different crop, like peanuts, in a nematode-heavy field for one season), apply pesticides, or both. These two approaches both have associated costs, and the rotation crops are substantially less profitable than sweet potato crops. Choosing the best step to take constitutes a complex decision in a volatile environment, and the decision can have a big financial impact.

As part of a United States Department of Agriculture (USDA) project to help sweet potato growers make better decisions using DI, we developed a decision model for this problem. Working with a group of sweet potato experts led by Dr. David Roberts and Dr. Michael Kudenov, along with plant pathologist Dr. Adrienne Gorny, we elicited outcomes, levers, and externals; wired up the CDD; and iterated a few times to make sure we hadn't missed anything important. The result was the CDD shown in Figure 4-4.

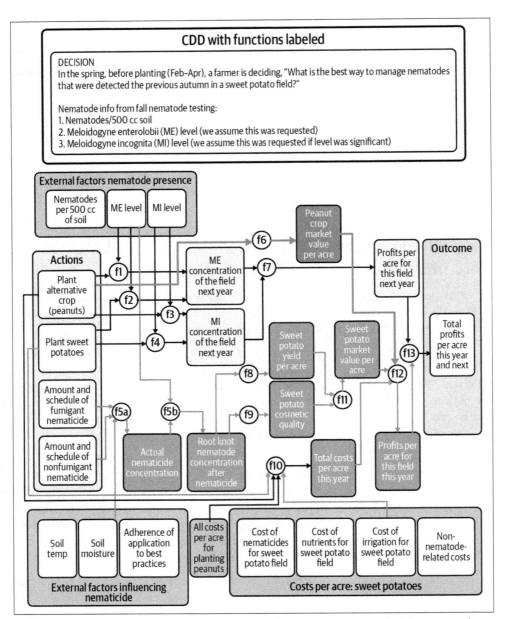

Figure 4-4. The sweet potato nematodes model, with functions indicated (courtesy of USDA Agriculture and Food Research Initiative-funded DECIDE-SMARTER project (https://oreil.ly/dJ0pF), reproduced with permission).

After the Decision Design process, we moved on to Decision Asset Investigation. Our experts sent us several lists of data sources. We matched them to the CDD and found, to our great surprise, that there was a lot of research and data to support one part of the CDD, but no research at all to support some other parts. In particular, the nematicide concentration link (marked f5a in Figure 4-4) and the yield, price, and profit links (marked f6 through f13) were well researched, but the remaining links had very little research to support them.

As it turned out, without the CDD to visually show the decision-making structure, researchers hadn't previously realized that they were only building data and conducting research to support some of it!

If you haven't faced this situation before, then you might be surprised that it happened. We were surprised, too: with so much data out there, how could it not inform the entire decision model, and how could there be such big gaps between what's needed by decision makers and what's been investigated? But we've seen this pattern play out again and again: today's data systems are designed to answer questions and provide insights, but not to connect actions to outcomes. Lacking the action/outcome perspective, they often fall short of what's needed.

So, returning to the process at hand: the previous example shows that CDD analysis can tell you not only when you *do* have assets to support a decision, but can also point you to when you *don't*: you'll need to consider some new research, find a new data source, and/or use the CDD as a low-fidelity model for now.

Data for Externals

Previously, you learned how to investigate data that might help to inform dependencies. Externals need data as well. You can think of externals in four categories:

- Things that never change, like the diameter of the earth
- Single changing values that you can measure, like the current temperature
- Values that will change in the future, and which you can predict, like tomorrow's high temperature
- Sets of values that you can predict for the future, like the daily high temperature for the next six months

We often call values that will change in the future and that you can predict for the future "assumptions" or "predictions." Note that the English language also uses these words for intermediates and outcomes, for example, "We predict that our company will grow by 20% revenue next month." But you know, as a decision modeler, that it's really helpful to distinguish between things that you can influence through your actions (outcomes) and things over which you have no control (externals). So we recommend that you teach your teams to use the more unambiguous "intermediates" (or "leading indicator" or "key process indicator") language instead of "assumption" or "prediction," to avoid confusion.

But back to predictions about externals. Often, analysts and statisticians use information about the past which they extrapolate into the future to make these kinds of predictions. Sometimes this works, and sometimes it doesn't.

To take just one famous example, toilet paper manufacturers had years of very stable data about consumer demand versus business demand (*https://oreil.ly/tGcZE*). They had made years of data-driven decisions about production lines and distribution channels. They used their existing data to make predictions about what toilet paper supply and demand would be in 2020. Because of the Covid-19 pandemic, however, it would be hard to argue that 2020 was "just like" 2019! And because lots of decisions made in 2019 were playing out during 2020, lots of things changed—including a 40% increase in consumer demand versus commercial demand for toilet paper, not to mention panic buying and hoarding (*https://oreil.ly/8fWre*). The just-in-time retail distribution chains that toilet paper manufacturers rely on to get their product to consumers could not handle the increased load, and the system broke. The lesson is that big, stable datasets are only "hard data" if you're discussing the past. In discussing the future, we can only make predictions.

Closely related to the idea of a prediction is the concept of an external *assumption*. An assumption is a guess about the value of an external that you're uncertain about, either because it relates to an uncertain future, or because you're not confident in your ability to accurately measure it in the present. For example, our sweet potato farmers may wish to assume that every field has some concentration of nematodes, because they decide that the cost of actually doing the testing isn't worth it. All predictions are assumptions, but not all assumptions are predictions.

Here are some kinds of data you might find to help you with external assumptions:

- Specific values or ranges of values, such as "Greenhouse gas emissions are assumed to be between 60 and 70 grams per revenue passenger kilometer"
- Predictions and models, including predicted numerical values or probability distributions from mathematical or ML models
- Datasets, such as the daily high and low temperatures for a specific location for the last 100 years

You may also find it useful to document *constraints* on externals: ranges or values that you believe will make it impossible to achieve your outcomes. For instance, "If the temperature goes outside the range of 0 degrees Celsius to 40 degrees Celsius for more than one hour, this plant will die."

The Puzzle Toy Use Case: The Decision Asset Conversation

Congratulations! Your company's new executive desk-toy product—a three-dimensional puzzle—is ready to launch! After you and your team celebrate meeting that milestone, you need to decide how to take your shiny new puzzle to market.

You've got a few decisions to make:

- How much should you charge for each puzzle?
- How many units should you order for the first production run?
- How big an investment should you make in marketing the puzzle?

You need to submit your decisions to the senior management team for approval, and you know they'll want hard evidence that your plan will be profitable and that your decisions won't expose the company to unacceptable risks.

Luckily, you have access to your organization's top-shelf analytics and data science team and state-of-the-art BI software. You call a "war room" meeting with your analyst team to explain the three decisions and start figuring it out. The analysts begin filling your whiteboard with diagrams of data lakes. They tell you about the AI algorithm they're going to use and open their laptops to show you a spreadsheet with 20 worksheets, their amazing analytics tools, and the even more terrific insights they deliver. Over the next week, they put their best information together to create the dashboard in Figure 4-5.

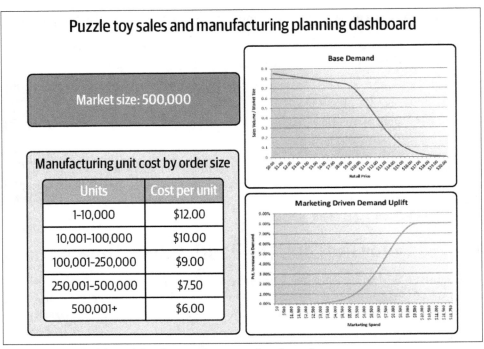

Figure 4-5. A dashboard for the puzzle toy product launch.

It's pretty impressive, but you have to ask: "How does this dashboard answer my three questions?" The data scientists look confused. Since the company's never launched a product like this before, they don't have any charts that can connect your three decision choices to the outcome you are measuring—profit.

The data scientists are puzzled and a bit frustrated. The company has spent a lot of money to collect, prepare, and manage a vast collection of data. After all, "Your decision is only as good as your data," right? Surely *somewhere*, in all that tech, lie the answers to these seemingly simple questions. But where?

Fortunately, at the very start of the project, you used a CDD to decide what kind of toy to build. Now you realize that a new CDD can address your questions. The three questions suggest three things you control, your three levers: sales price, production order size, and marketing spend as a percent of profit. The outcome is easy: profit. Your objective is to maximize that profit. With a little help from your team, you quickly sketch the CDD shown in Figure 4-6.

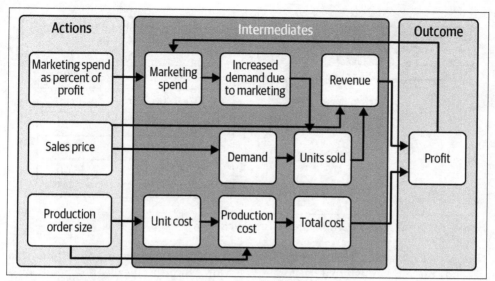

Figure 4-6. The product launch CDD ready for Decision Asset Investigation.

Now you are ready to look at the dependency arrows and search for data and models that inform them. You quickly observe that unit cost is inversely related to production order size; the more you buy, the cheaper each unit is. You also realize that you don't have control over production cost. That's controlled by manufacturing, a different department within your company. So you have a new external: unit cost versus number produced. And your analytics team has manufacturing data that predicts cost versus number for other desktop toy products. In fact, it's right there on the dashboard they gave you. So now you have added an external and its associated dataset to the CDD, as shown in Figure 4-7.

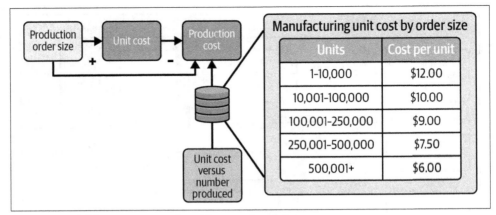

Figure 4-7. Adding an external and its associated data.

Next you look at the relationship between sales price and units sold. Units sold depends on another external, customer behavior. More specifically, it depends on a specific component of customer behavior, demand versus price. Your analytics team has an ML model that predicts demand for similar products, and they represented it on the dashboard graphically as Base Demand, a curve showing market penetration rate (*https://oreil.ly/nd8Mo*) versus sales price. Market penetration rate is units sold divided by market size. So, to understand the relationship between sales price and units sold, you need one more external, market size. The analytics team found marketing information that estimates your market size at 500,000 units. The "sales price to units sold" part of the CDD now looks like Figure 4-8.

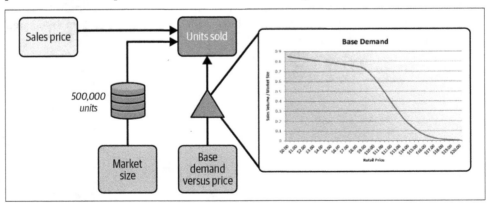

Figure 4-8. Adding externals and data that show the relationship between sales price and units sold.

You realize that marketing spend will also drive demand, and you turn to the causal chain that starts with marketing spend as a percent of profit. You need one more external: increased demand versus marketing spend. The analytics team has provided a predictive function, represented on the dashboard by the "Marketing-Driven Demand Uplift" graph. It shows percent increase in demand as a function of market spend. Adding that produces the CDD shown in Figure 4-9.

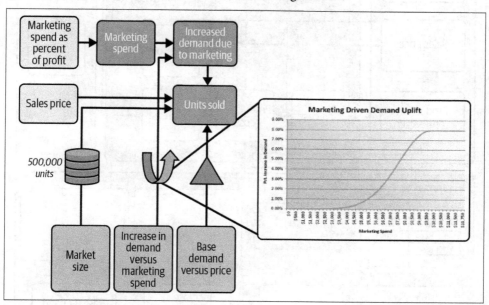

Figure 4-9. Adding the marketing uplift external.

Refining the CDD to show every place where the data is needed produces the annotated CDD in Figure 4-10.

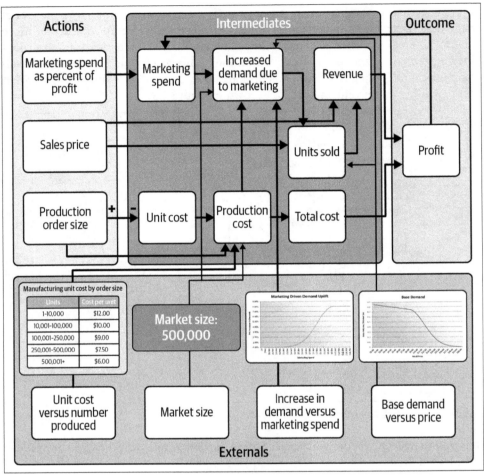

Figure 4-10. The CDD at the end of Decision Asset Investigation.

Try It Yourself: Decision Asset Investigation for the Telecom Use Case

You built a CDD in "Try It Yourself: Decision Design for a Telecom Use Case" on page 89. In this section, you will complete a small Decision Asset Investigation process for that use case.

Exercise

Before you continue reading, review the telecom use case CDD from Chapter 3. Inspect the dependencies and, as a beginning exercise in identifying assets, label any *inverse dependencies* (in which, if one value changes, the other changes in the opposite direction). Label them with a "+" at the tail end of the arrow and a "–" at the head, to visually convey "When the left-hand element goes up, the right-hand one goes down."

We'll start with a very simple approach to identifying assets, which is to "find" knowledge inside your own brain about the directions of some dependencies.

In your next meeting, you lead the telecom decision team in reading through the Decision Asset Investigation process description together. As your first step in reviewing the CDD, you decide to look at the dependency arrows. You note that for most of the dependencies in this diagram, when the element on the left increases, the element on the right also increases (these are called *direct dependencies*). You ask the team to look for exceptions: are there any *inverse* dependencies, where the changes go in opposite directions? The team quickly identifies the arrow from "pricing" to "volume" as an inverse dependency and marks it in the CDD, as shown in Figure 4-11. The team then finds two additional inverse dependencies and marks them on the CDD.

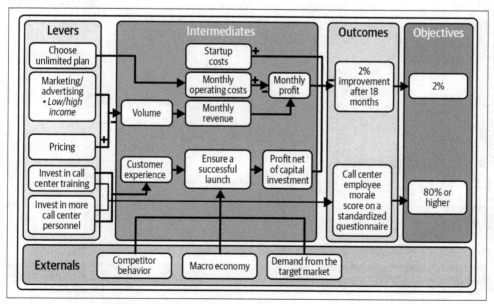

Figure 4-11. The unlimited usage plan CDD with inverse dependencies annotated.

Exercise

Compare your inverse dependencies to the labels in Figure 4-11. Did you find the three inverse dependencies that are marked in the figure?

Before you continue reading, see if you can annotate some places on this CDD where data, human expertise, or a model might inform a dependency. You may want to use some of the icons from Table 4-2.

Note that there is no single right answer to this exercise. Every team will find different assets for the same kinds of information. We will show you one possibility, along with our thought process.

You may hear some disagreement about how certain dependencies work, such as the shape of the sketch graph. Depending on the type of link, resolving them will require different approaches: a link based on a simple formula may mean talking to experts in the finance department, while a link based on ML may require building a new model. You may also want to capture different sets of assets in two different lists so you can try them both to see if they lead to different decisions.

You ask the team if they know of existing assets that would provide more information about any of the dependencies in their CDD. A product manager points out that the relationship of price to volume is seldom a simple straight line. To illustrate, he creates a quick sketch graph like the one in Figure 4-12. You make a corresponding entry in row 1 of the Decision Asset Register, as shown in Table 4-3.

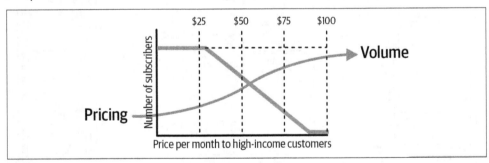

Figure 4-12. A sketch graph showing how price affects demand.

Table 4-3. Decision Asset Register for the unlimited usage plan

Decision element	Decision asset	Asset type	Asset source and contact
Dependency from pricing to volume	Price/volume curve	Sketch graph	Joe Smith, Product Mgr., Marketing
Dependency from pricing to volume	Consumer price testing results	ML model, based on a dataset	Mary Brown, Sr. Data Scientist, ML Group

Decision element	Decision asset	Asset type	Asset source and contact
Marketing/advertising lever	Historical advertising effectiveness	Human knowledge	Shanice Johnson, Advertising Manager, Marketing
Macro economy external	Econ. Dept. Model 1042	Econometric model	Prof. Sara García, Econ. Dept., UXY
Competitor behavior external	Competitive intelligence	Observation	John Wu, Sr. Research Analyst, Marketing

The team's ML expert responds, speaking up for the first time: "I have a dataset from a similar product where we price-tested different pricing levels on several thousand prospects with different characteristics. It shows that price to volume isn't a simple straight line. In fact, I bet I could use that dataset to give you an initial model of how different pricing decisions would change product demand—kind of a machine-learning-based precision demand estimator." The team is happy to identify an existing dataset that might be useful for the decision, and you label the dependency to show that, as shown in Figure 4-13, while making a corresponding entry in the Decision Asset Register, as shown in the second row of Table 4-3.

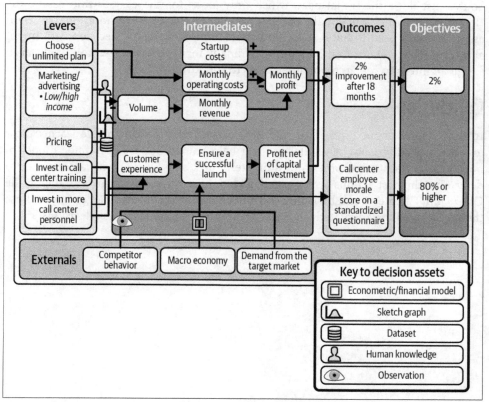

Figure 4-13. The unlimited usage plan CDD, annotated with decision assets.

The product manager speaks again, explaining that he's just texted a colleague in the advertising department and asked her to drop in and join the group. When she arrives, she explains that it is "common knowledge" that a targeted advertising campaign will convince about 2% of potential customers to move to the company running the campaign. You annotate this piece of human expertise in the CDD and add the third row to the Decision Asset Register.

You now move on to looking at externals. You ask the team to identify assumptions in your externals, and to think of any assets that might support those assumptions. A data scientist recommends a publicly available macroeconomic model from a nearby university (row 4 of the Decision Asset Register); someone from marketing explains that their department includes a competitive research group that knows immediately whenever a competitor launches a similar product (row 5 of the Decision Asset Register). This is an observation you can use to track competitor behavior.

You add the assets to the CDD as shown in Figure 4-13 and congratulate the team on their work, but you note that they did not find every possible decision asset. You've just done the initial pass, which only looks for the easy-to-find assets: the "low-hanging fruit." You'll make another pass later to look for any additional decision assets that you need to build a decision simulation or make the decision; you might also send the CDD out to others in the company for their expertise. You might even assign an intern to research potential assets to support the CDD.

Conclusion

In this chapter about Process B2, Decision Asset Investigation, you've learned how to start collecting a list of assets that will help you to build a computer model of how actions lead to outcomes and ultimately work side by side with a computer to determine the best actions to choose. You've captured those assets by annotating the CDD from Chapter 3 and by listing them in an asset register. In Chapter 5, you'll use the register and the annotated CDD to help you to simulate and track decisions.

CHAPTER 5

Decision Reasoning: The Decision Simulation Process

With AI there are two chasms to cross in turning data into useful insight. The first is whether we can trust machine learning (ML) systems, and that's increasingly solved. The second challenge is how to go about turning ML predictions into actions—crossing the "knowledge-action" gap. This is why decision intelligence is a critical emerging discipline. DI is every bit as nuanced and challenging as ML was in the first place. It requires integrative approaches, systems thinking, human factors, user interface design, and often multiple ML pipelines working in concert, as well as advanced ML pipeline management, active learning, MLOps, uncertainty identification, AI ethics, and all the other hygiene factors that should always accompany mature AI.

For this reason, DI is hugely transdisciplinary; we don't yet produce data scientists who are able to navigate the whole stack from data to decisions, and this is why at FDL.ai we always say this process is a "team sport."

—James Parr, Founder, Frontier Development Lab (FDL.ai), SpaceML, and Trillium Technologies

Using a computer simulation can help you to explore many combinations of lever choices and external assumptions to find the right set of actions. This is where "the rubber meets the road": in addition to using LLMs (including ChatGPT) to help you to build the CDD in the first place, it's a second place where DI becomes a true collaboration between computers and humans to make the best decisions in complex environments—or what the Gartner Group calls *decision augmentation* (*https://oreil.ly/qByTL*).

In Phase C, the *Decision Reasoning* phase described in this chapter, you'll use your CDD and the assets you discovered in the earlier phases to explore how various actions, within the context of various externals, affect outcomes. The phase contains two processes: Process C1, Decision Simulation, and Process C2, Decision Assessment. Since these are complex processes, we've split the Decision Reasoning phase into two chapters. This chapter covers Decision Simulation, and Chapter 6 covers Decision Assessment.

We'll start this chapter with a brief overview of the Decision Reasoning phase and its place in DI, then zoom in to get an overview of the Decision Simulation process. We'll explain a bit more about when and why simulation is helpful, present a formal process description, and then show you some best practices for implementing it (including how to treat the decision elements, what level of fidelity to use, and your technological options). We'll start with simple scenarios, examining different choices for actions and different assumptions for externals. Then we'll show you how to incorporate data and models into the simulations, look for feedback loops and long- and short-term effects, perform a sensitivity analysis, and optimize your simulation.

We'll then see how this plays out in the net-zero GHG use case from previous chapters, and at the end of the chapter, you can try it yourself by creating a simulation for our telecom use case.

Decision Reasoning: Phase Overview

In the Decision Simulation process, you create a "digital twin" of your CDD, using the decision model to determine how actions lead to outcomes or to find the best actions to achieve some objectives.[1] In contrast to the static, unmoving nature of a CDD, a simulation is dynamic.

Decision simulation can be done using a computer, "in your head," or using pencil and paper. It's like a video game: you try different combinations of actions to find the one that will "score" the best values for your outcomes. Along the way, you'll discover patterns and feedback loops, including virtuous and vicious cycles. Their behavior often dominates decision outcomes, sometimes more so than the data.

Airline pilots and astronauts train in simulators for a good reason: in a simulator, when you're testing actions and run into a disaster, you can simply start over and try something else. This activity drives a deep understanding of complex and otherwise dangerous systems, and it radically reduces the chances of failure in the real world.

You can simulate a simple, low-fidelity decision manually and qualitatively (more on this in a few pages). More complex decisions warrant a higher-fidelity, more quantitative simulation. Either can be supported by software. We'll show you both, and then you'll have a chance to try it yourself with a simple simulation that you can hand-calculate or implement quickly in software.

---

1 The term *decision model,* as used in this book, refers to either a CDD or the part of a software system that implements the CDD.

The second process in this phase, *Decision Assessment,* covered in the next chapter, lets you review your decision and its assets as a whole to decide what to do next. You'll look at factors like the provenance of your data, models, and human expertise. And yes, there will be implicit or explicit uncertainty, bias, and other elements of concern. There are no perfect data sources, datasets, models, or human expert judgments. This is where you'll ask questions like, "How good is the evidence I'm basing this decision on?"

Figure 5-1 shows the Decision Reasoning phase in the context of the other process phases. Note that Process C2, Decision Assessment, is grayed out because it is covered in the next chapter, not in this one.

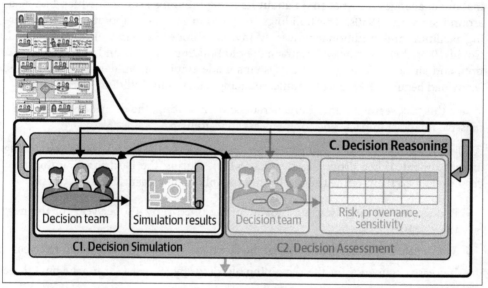

Figure 5-1. The Decision Reasoning phase includes Process C1, Decision Simulation (this chapter), and Process C2, Decision Assessment (Chapter 6).

When you're done with the Decision Reasoning phase, you'll be ready to take action in the real world (Chapter 7).

Decision Simulation Process Overview

Not everyone likes a CDD. Some end users need to see more: they prefer elements that move, and to have a chance to interact with a tool, not to study a diagram. As this section describes in more detail, one customer of ours was very cool on every CDD we showed them. But when we rendered it into a very simple simulation, it was like a lightbulb went on: "*Now* I understand!" The challenge is that it's not always obvious in advance who likes what.

An *automated decision simulation* is a computer-supported system that helps you to determine the most likely outcomes from a set of actions and/or the best actions to achieve certain objectives. When we want to determine likely outcomes, we often build an interactive visualization that lets users set up a specific scenario by selecting levers and external assumptions, then observe the results. Interactive visualizations are very helpful in demonstrating decision dynamics quickly. (See Quantellia's Live Model Gallery (*https://oreil.ly/0b7zu*) for some examples; also Microsoft Excel's Solver technology (*https://oreil.ly/8dUmA*) addresses this task for simple decisions that are small enough to be solved on a desktop computer.)

Our experience working with a big US company is a case in point. Its decision-making challenge was what to do about its aging buildings, some of which had been around since the 1950s. The buildings in question included laboratories, engineering facilities, and traditional offices. Many were underused and undermaintained. Covid-19 further complicated matters: the old buildings' layouts and heating, ventilation, and air-conditioning (HVAC) systems made employees vulnerable to the virus. Many had begun working from home, reducing demand for building space.

While this task seemed rather bureaucratic and unexciting, the decision would have a massive financial impact. The company asked us to help.

At the project's start—as is often standard practice—the decision makers were using an assortment of key process indicators (KPIs). During the Decision Framing process, we helped them refine their KPIs into the following measurable objectives:

- Reduce annual operations and maintenance (O&M) by 4% per year for the next three years
- Sell or otherwise dispose of 10% of the facilities on a specific list within five years
- Increase occupancy for the remaining buildings by 5% per year for the next three years
- Reduce total maintenance backlog by 3% in the next year
- Bring total O&M spend, including to reduce maintenance backlog, within budget within three years

If you look at these objectives carefully, you'll notice that they are interdependent—and partially conflicting. As you learned from the Decision Requirements phase, however, this is common at the start of a project and isn't a problem. This list captures the objectives "as is," without imposing a specific format.

Our next goal was to ask the decision team to prioritize these objectives, but internal politics became a roadblock: different departments were accountable for different objectives, and nobody had reconciled the conflicts yet. So we chose to move on, for the moment, to actions.

The action choices were:

- Demolish facilities that are poorly located and/or in disrepair
- Take on tenants to share facilities with low occupancy and good conditions
- Sell or otherwise dispose of facilities that are underutilized and/or in disrepair

Following the Decision Requirements phase, we next tried to schedule a teleconference to identify intermediates and externals and to wire up some causal chains. Here we hit another brick wall: nobody wanted to do it!

Our internal champion explained that digging into the cause-and-effect mechanism would be too scary and complicated for this group—even though the decision customers agreed that if they took some of the listed actions, they would at least make progress on their desired outcomes. Now, most organizations don't mind seeing a few CDDs before building a simulation; indeed, they recognize the value of doing so to avoid rework. But sometimes you'll find that your customer needs you to do things differently, so you'll need to stay flexible and be willing to tailor the DI processes as needed. Here, we tailored the Decision Requirements phase: instead of requiring consensus on a diagram version of the CDD before moving on, we would "meet them where they're at" and animate the CDD using a low-fidelity interactive software model.

Was this a failure of DI? *Not even close.* Some people can look at the causal chains on a CDD and imagine the dynamic systems embodied within it. Others need to see cause and effect in action, in an interactive visualization.

Why Simulate Your CDD?

Recall that in Chapter 1 we identified two big problems that arise when people begin doing data-driven decision making. First: "How can decision makers identify the data they need to support their decisions?" Chapter 3 showed you how the Decision Modeling phase addresses this problem.

The second problem is: "How can the technological assets available to support a decision be used to show how a decision's outcomes depend on the decision maker's actions?" The solution is to use the decision model to simulate a large sample of lever choices and external assumptions and calculate the outcomes produced by each. This is the systematic method for transforming the technology represented by the annotated CDD into the form decision makers need: that is, a representation of how decision actions influence decision outcomes.

There are three main benefits to simulating a CDD:

- It drives a clearer and better-aligned *understanding* of the cause-and-effect structure of a complex decision—an insight that at best is otherwise achieved through the "invisible imagined" mental models of your staff, which is imperfect, impermanent, and not shared. Remember the early video games where you played with just words instead of interactive characters that moved? That's how many organizations are still making complex decisions today. A simulated CDD "brings the decision alive."

- You can see *what levers and externals really affect the outcomes*. So, if you want to improve your decision, you can use the simulation to learn what data, models, and human expertise really matter. This can save massively on costs, because many organizations spend a lot of time gathering, preparing, and governing their data.

- If something important is missing, or there is a serious *error* in the cause-and-effect pathway, you can see that more readily.

All three of these benefits emerged strongly when we presented our simulation for the facilities project previously described. Let's look closer at each one.

Better understanding of cause and effect

This group was strongly focused on data. Their decision assets included spreadsheets of old facilities maintenance budgets as well as projected budgets adjusted for inflation. They also had a newer ML model that mapped a building's characteristics to its likelihood in the past to be demolished. This ML model had been trained on characteristics of past and present buildings, plus data on which ones had been chosen for demolition.

We used this data and model to build a simple simulation with sliders that decision makers could move to choose levers. When they did, the bar charts moved up and down to show the changes in outcome values. We set up a teleconference and showed them the simulation—and the lightbulbs came on! In a nanosecond, the decision team went from "What is all this confusing spaghetti?" to "WOW!"

They were surprised, but we weren't: we've seen this reaction many times. That's what simulations are all about: *dynamic visualization of decision behavior*. You've heard that "A picture is worth a thousand words," right? Well, a dynamic interactive simulation of how actions lead to outcomes says what no words can convey.

Visualizing which levers and externals affect outcomes the most

As the managers eagerly tried different lever choices, they told us that the simulation taught them two things. First, they saw that demolishing buildings had only a tiny effect on the outcomes, so building a better ML model for analyzing demolitions wasn't going to be very useful. This is a great example of *outcome sensitivity*. If you can see that the outcomes aren't very sensitive to changes in a certain choice, you won't waste time improving the wrong data or building the wrong models based on that data.

This point is worth emphasizing: because many ML models are built without an understanding of the decision in which the model will be used, ML engineers don't know when to stop. They simply work to achieve the very highest accuracy possible. We've observed this suboptimal use of resources hundreds of times, and it can be very costly.

Identifying missing pieces of the puzzle—and accounting for them

The managers also noted that none of the lever settings got even close to achieving their budget objective (bringing total O&M spending within budget in three years).

Playing with the simulation activated the team, and they were willing to go back to brainstorming levers. One great suggestion emerged: "Replace HVAC, electrical, and plumbing systems that are obsolete, in poor condition, and/or expensive to operate." Later, when we moved back into analytic mode, we asked, "Who has the authority to replace obsolete systems?" It turned out that none of our customers did, but there was a department responsible for replacing obsolete systems that was not represented on the decision team. Due to project constraints, we couldn't include this missing team. But we could model system replacement as an external and add sliders to explore assumptions about it. Using an assumption slider in this way *is very effective* in dealing with uncertainty or missing information.

We took the project offline to do some analysis. Between the company's spreadsheets and some public domain data we dug up, we were able to make some rough calculations about how replacing obsolete systems would affect the outcomes: quite dramatically, as it turned out. We added a slider to show that effect and presented it at the next teleconference.

The levers the managers controlled had a modest impact on budget. Initially, they were spending six times the amount budgeted for facilities maintenance (which is why they had an ever-increasing maintenance backlog-cost problem). The levers they controlled could get them down to about four or five times the budgeted amount: better, but not great. But a change to an external—*someone else's lever*—moved them to just 1.5 times the budgeted amount. The lesson is that simulation and observed sensitivity can show you that your outcomes are controlled by an external more than anything else.

As we'll explain in more detail in "Silos, Whack-a-Mole, and the Measurement Effect" on page 195, when midlevel managers create CDDs, the outcomes they choose often reflect the KPIs for the managers in the room, with outcomes from other silos appearing as externals. We'll also look at how "zooming out" to consider how multiple departments interact can help you find the best solutions.

This is not the kind of realization you could arrive at by sifting through data for insights. Without a simulation that connects actions to outcomes, you can't know how best to use your technical resources (data gathering, preparation, and modeling) to guide decisions. That can leave you modeling the wrong things.

Deciding Whether to Automate Your Decision Simulation

The DI methodology does not require any simulation software at all. A CDD developed on a whiteboard, using PowerPoint, or with general-purpose online collaboration tools can align a team of decision makers around actions, outcomes, and causality. It can even help the team perform basic sensitivity analysis, using visual inspection to assess how much various inputs affect the outcomes of the decision. And sometimes you don't even need simulation—it's just simple calculations.

As the number and complexity of causal chains increases, though, it becomes more difficult for people to understand what's going on using just a static CDD. This is where simulation software becomes especially valuable: it lets you try different inputs, incorporate decision assets as software technology services, explore different scenarios, and see the results in an immersive visualization. And if you do choose to use software to help simulate your decision, the CDD you created gives you a great start.

There is no hard-and-fast rule that says you must create a software simulation if you have more than N boxes on your CDD,[2] or if your longest causal chain has more than M dependencies. Every decision is different. People and organizations have different needs and different capacities for dealing with complexity.

To help you decide when a software simulation will be most helpful, consider whether the following statements are true for your decision:

---

2 Since the remainder of this chapter focuses exclusively on automated simulation, we'll often say just *simulation* to mean "automated simulation," supported by a computer, in contrast to an imagined simulation you might do in your head.

- Even after you've cleaned up and reworked your CDD to aggregate where possible and reduce "spaghetti" dependency arrows, the decision customer (or team) feels overwhelmed by its complexity and finds it hard to understand.

- Your decision assets exist in software, as mathematical or ML models, and would be difficult to use without a simulation.

- There is a high cost to not meeting the objectives for the outcome, especially if it will be difficult to monitor the decision adequately without software support. (See Chapter 7 for more about the Decision Monitoring process.)

- Some people in the organization need to understand the cause-and-effect behavior involved in the decision quickly, without spending the time to understand the CDD in detail.

- You need decision optimization: an automated system that determines the best actions to take to achieve the best outcomes (as opposed to going the opposite way, as we previously described, visualizing how changes to actions and externals affect outcomes).

- You would like to use the CDD to give you a more structured and valuable mechanism to track KPIs after the decision is made (see Chapter 7).

If one or more of these factors are true for your decision, it might be a good candidate for a software simulation. See "Technology Options" on page 144 later in this chapter for more about the many possible ways to create your simulation using software.

To get you started thinking about how decision simulation software looks so that you can decide whether it's worth automating or not, take a look at this TEDx Talk by coauthor Pratt (*https://oreil.ly/y163M*), this C-SPAN TV show (*https://oreil.ly/9vx4p*), and this Live Decision Model Gallery (*https://oreil.ly/IFhty*). As you'll see, there is quite a diversity of ways to visualize action-to-outcome decisions. As more organizations build such visualizations, they're beginning to become a little more standardized, but we always expect a diversity of representations and designs to fit the needs of different audiences.

Showing your simulation to stakeholders can help them understand your rationale and can help you solicit input and feedback. For instance, Figure 5-2 shows screenshots from an immersive, gamelike simulation of Covid-19 particle infection patterns in a building. Our client used this simulation when explaining their decision to require masks, install new ventilation systems, and other choices designed to keep its event venue safe during Covid-19.

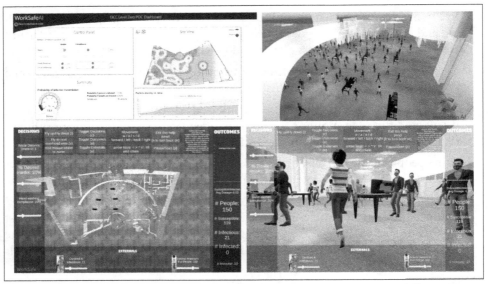

Figure 5-2. An immersive decision simulation. Source: Data Innovation AI (https:// oreil.ly/T13fX) (reproduced with permission).

By now you're probably wondering how to go about building this software system, or whether you can buy one or hire a consultant to build one. Our approach has been to work together with our team at Quantellia to custom-build a number of action-to-outcome DI software systems. This chapter collects some of the best practices we've learned along the way. We'll look at the formal process description for building a simulation software system next, then examine the steps in more detail.

Developing the Simulation Iteratively

When you begin building a decision simulation system, it can be tempting to build *too much*. Instead, the best practice is to use Agile methods (or similar) to work iteratively. Start small: try a low-fidelity simulation of key decision elements, using a limited number of causal chains and the simplest decision assets. Then you can improve the simulator and assets, one iteration at a time.

As you move from one iteration to another, you'll need to decide what parts of the model to include in the simulation. For the first iteration, human experts are often the only sources available; you might solicit their opinions through a poll or an anonymous technique like the Delphi method (*https://oreil.ly/Y8_sV*),[3] or by

---

3 The basic idea of the Delphi method is to collect opinions independently and anonymously. A leader or facilitator collates anonymous responses and summarizes them for the group. This can be followed, optionally, by additional rounds of independent and anonymous answers and summaries, building to consensus.

consulting secondary sources like scientific research papers. Another approach we've seen used increasingly is for a Large Language Model (LLM) like ChatGPT to give decision advice (see coauthor Pratt's "ChatGPT Does Decision Intelligence for Net Zero" (*https://oreil.ly/fK-QK*) for an example of how ChatGPT advises the net zero example described in this book).

For later iterations, you might improve your model in several ways: analyzing your simulation according to risk, provenance, and sensitivity as described in Chapter 6, conducting research to identify new decision assets (part of step 12 of Decision Design), and/or investigating new assets as you did in Process B2: Decision Asset Investigation.

Formal Process Description: Decision Simulation

Description

> Plan and build a software system to help the decision team understand the cause-and-effect behavioral dynamics of the CDD, determine how actions and externals lead to outcomes, and select the best action(s) to take.

Prerequisites

- A CDD, optionally annotated with decision assets (see Chapter 4).

- A rough sense of the desired fidelity of the first iteration of your system, plus the time and/or effort you'd like to expend. (For some decisions, you might decide that building decision software isn't justified and skip this process entirely.)

Responsible role

> Decision team leader, optionally working with a software project manager and/or a *DI engineer* (someone with expertise in building decision simulations and a number of technical skills, perhaps with a certification or a degree in DI)

Steps

1. Read through this process and tailor it, as appropriate, to your situation.

2. Examine the CDD and decide which causal chains, lever choices, and external assumptions you will model for this iteration.

3. Select the lever choices (or ranges of choices) you will simulate in this iteration. If you have several binary choices, you might use a shorter list at first; if you have ranges of data, you might restrict the range.

4. If any of your externals are uncertain, select for each one the assumption(s) you will simulate in this iteration.

5. Examine the CDD you are modeling and decide how you will represent choices and assumptions, show outcome values, and compute values for intermediates and outcomes. Note that your tailoring might omit certain element categories

(such as, for example, externals), because your decision makers might only want to see visualizations of some elements. Be sure to consider:

Levers
Decide how to represent each lever's choices: for example, using a slider or a set of radio buttons.

Externals
Examine the decision assets representing each external's value or assumptions and decide how to represent them visually for this iteration. This might be as simple as selecting a single value or as complex as adding controls to select among assumption models and to select ranges or values for each external.

Outcomes
Decide how to visually represent a value for each outcome. This may be a simple visualization, like a moving bar graph, or part of an immersive visualization that looks like a video game.

Objectives
Decide how you will visually indicate that the outcome has achieved its objective. This might mean a bar on the bar graph that changes color, something that lights up, or an animation (like showing plants growing) in an immersive visualization that looks like a video game.

Intermediates
Decide how you will calculate the value for each intermediate. Recall that each intermediate is the right-hand element of one or more dependencies (arrows). You'll compute its value using the values of the left-hand elements on these dependencies, the dependencies themselves, and any associated decision assets. If you have a dependency that isn't yet associated with an asset, you'll need to create one.

6. Select the technology you will use to build your simulation.

7. Plan and execute the development of your simulation software.

8. Run the decision simulation software—perhaps in collaboration with your decision customer. Try different configurations: for example, you could run the simulation in action-to-outcome mode, optimization mode, or both. You might decide to run many scenarios, changing the externals and/or actions to see what happens. You might run it using assumptions you consider likely, as well as moderately or extremely optimistic or pessimistic ones.

9. Publish an interactive decision simulation to stakeholders. This can help them understand your rationale and can help you solicit input and feedback. You may want to show them several scenarios, like best case, worst case, and expected case

or good case. You might also show the consequences from multiple sets of good or bad choices. You might also publish an LLM-powered tool like ChatGPT to support a dialogue between your users in which they can explore the decision model and its rationale.

10. Analyze the results you've produced using the decision simulation software to see what you can learn from them. Specifically:

    - Identify any outcomes that are especially sensitive to one or more decision elements or causal chains (you'll learn more about sensitivity analysis in Chapter 6).

    - Identify any changes that result in outcomes meeting, or getting close to meeting, their objectives.

    - Investigate feedback loops. Include identifying any positive (virtuous) or negative (vicious) cycles.

    - Identify any causal chains that meet a short-term goal but produce long-term unintended consequences.

    - Identify any causal chains that meet a long-term goal but produce a short-term negative effect.

11. Create a Decision Simulation Report. Document what scenarios you simulated, what assets you used, and any conclusions you draw. Include screenshots or scenario output as appropriate.

12. Decide whether to improve the simulation through another iteration. If you decide to do so, return to step 2. If not, move on to Process C2, Decision Assessment (which could suggest that additional decision simulation is warranted).

Deliverables
- Simulation software
- Recommendations for actions
- (Optional) A Simulation Report

Creating a Decision Simulation

This section provides additional guidance on how to design and run a decision simulation.

Simplifying the CDD

Decision simulation involves many judgment calls, especially as you decide which causal chains are the most important to start with. Sometimes the decision customer or an expert can help you narrow it down, or you might ask your team to vote.

Here's a handy tip: if your goal is to identify sensitivities, consider running your simulation using an intermediate as a proxy for an outcome. If you have a causal chain with several intermediates that lead to an outcome and no other dependencies are coming into that chain, you can save yourself a little simulation work. The first intermediate's sensitivity to a lever choice or external assumption will determine the entire chain's sensitivity.

Lever Choices

Your lever choices may be discrete choices, like "plant sweet potatoes" versus "plant peanuts." You might have a long list of discrete choices, but in early iterations of a simulation, it's best to simplify by limiting them to a binary or just a few. Lever choices can also be ranges, like "amount to spend on advertising."

Sometimes you can simplify a long list of discrete values by approximating it with a range. In the facilities management simulation earlier in this chapter, we could have provided a list of buildings that were candidates for sharing with tenants. Since that would have been an unwieldy list, we instead used a range representing the value (in millions of dollars) of the shareable buildings. The managers could use a slider to select the value to try in the simulation. This approximation simplified things enough to let us build a useful simulation quickly.

On the same project, we later had several options for refinement, such as looking at individual buildings or classifying them into shareability tiers using ML. Classifying lists of discrete values into tiers or other "bundles" can help keep them manageable.

While the values of levers are choices that you make, you might want to start by limiting levers to choices that have been made in the past, perhaps based on historical data. This can help you understand what choices may lead to undesirable or unintended consequences.

Externals and Assumptions

For each external, you may select the assumption model or value to use in a simulation or allow the people who use the simulation to choose different assumptions or assumption values each time they run the simulation. Allowing people to change an uncertain value and observe its impact is an important DI mechanism for handling uncertainty. For an initial simulation, it's a good idea to include only the most important externals.

In the facilities management simulation, for instance, we knew the values for several externals, including the age, maintenance backlog, and current state of repair of each building and its systems. (And, yes, initial conditions like these are externals, even if you could have changed them if you had acted differently last year.) We could set those values directly.

For other externals we had only what public information we could find, like the estimated costs of relocating an office or demolishing a building. In those cases, we provided sliders with broad ranges that the managers could set to values they thought applied best. Similar to using tiers with lever choices, this was a way to bundle related externals that would avoid complicating our computations or overwhelming the simulation users.

You may also need to compare competing models for how to make assumptions about an external. Our decision model for the Covid-19 particle spread example needed to incorporate Covid-19 safety plans. However, this was early in 2020, and no research had yet been completed on how the virus is transmitted—a factor that would, of course, be crucial in determining how to keep buildings safe for employees. To handle this uncertainty, we proposed a model that would allow users to select between three kinds of transmission risks to mitigate: surfaces, droplets, and aerosols.

Intermediates and Outcomes

You may choose to show some, all, or no intermediates in your simulation software user interface, depending on the needs of the decision makers. You could select the intermediates that are important to them, or those that are the best predictors of the outcomes. If your audience is easily overwhelmed, you might want to omit intermediates from your visualization, at least at first.

In the facilities simulation, we initially treated the maintenance backlog as an objective. Later, however, we realized it was actually an intermediate, because it was part of the computation for the objective "keep total O&M spending within budget." Although this client didn't want to see all the intermediates, we decided to include this one because it was a KPI connected to performance reviews for one of the managers on the team.

Sometimes you need to create a calculation function for a decision element. Start by looking at all the dependencies coming into it. Whether or not you show values of intermediates, you'll need to compute them, as well as the values of the outcomes. Sometimes one of your decision assets, such as a model or a function, will have all the elements on the left sides of those dependencies as its inputs and the element on the right side as its output.

Sometimes you don't have a detailed functional form for a dependency function; you just know that if the left side goes up, so does the right (or vice versa). You could code this with a simple straight line with a slope of 1 or −1, or just a graphic that demonstrates the direction of influence, as shown in Figure 5-3. A small refinement to this approach might be to provide a slider that lets the user change the slope of the line.

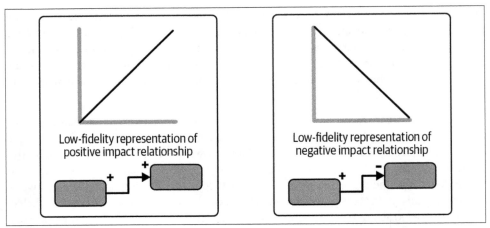

Figure 5-3. Low-fidelity ways to show how one decision element affects another.

In addition to computing the values of intermediates, you may want to include some comparison information. To see which choices and assumptions could lead to intended or unintended changes, try comparing historical datasets (and models based on them) with intermediate estimates from simulations. If your simulation could lead to values that have never appeared before, that might indicate that you should think again about that intermediate's functional form.

You might also need help from a human expert. In this case, it's best to let the expert provide information in a way that is comfortable to them.

Another way to test or validate a simulation is to set constraints on the value of an intermediate: for instance, "startup costs should be between $20,000 and $50,000 starting one month after the decision." If the intermediate breaks the constraint when you run the simulation, you might see unintended consequences.

Decision Simulation Fidelity

A simulation that doesn't *exactly* match how things work in reality can still be of great value. The reason is that you can still learn the basic dynamics of a system from such a simulation—like our building managers did when they gained insight about the minimal effect of demolishing old facilities.

This is worth repeating because it's not at all intuitive to data scientists, who have been trained to believe that "The decision is only as good as the data." In fact, even for low-quality data, the dynamics of many systems end up "washing out" the particular data values. System dynamics are, as a general rule, *more important!* This means that it's often possible to greatly improve your understanding of what's going on from a simulation, even if that simulation is based on imperfect—or even missing—data.

So what's good enough? There is no "bright line" between a low- and high-fidelity simulation, but in general a *low-fidelity* action-to-outcome simulation uses simple qualitative models. For instance, it might only show directionality between decision elements, as was shown in Figure 5-3 ("When X goes up, Y goes down"), or give you a "ballpark" estimate of the magnitude of dependency connections' sensitivity. You might only have rough concepts of your externals: "Our competitor's price is above $10, but we don't know exactly what it is."

One best practice when you build your first simulation is to simply guess at the functional forms of your dependencies. Even if you're completely wrong, showing a simulation to your users can still spark their intuition. Of course, you need to be careful to explain that the simulation is based on "fake" data and models (in software development parlance, you're "stubbing out" these models), but you'll be surprised at how valuable a discussion can arise from a low-fidelity simulation. In particular, it might drive discussion around the relative sensitivity of outcomes to different choices and assumptions, or suggest where a little more refinement would provide clear evidence of sensitivity.

When data and models are not available at all, a low-fidelity model is a valuable first simulation step for people who struggle to understand cause and effect on a CDD.

To improve the sophistication of your simulation and create a *high-fidelity* action-to-outcome simulation, you'll want to add more accurate models to the dependencies, more precise data to the externals, and probably also identify additional decision elements. Moving from a low- to a high-fidelity simulation is usually an iterative process, where each step informs the best refinement for the one that follows it.

Running the Simulation "Backward": Decision Models for Optimization

You can also run your action-to-outcome simulations "backward": ask the software team to build a system that uses your desired objectives to search for the best actions to achieve them. For this, the system can run in "batch" mode overnight, without any human intervention, to explore thousands of action combinations and find the best ones. In fields like operations research and AI, this task of searching for best actions is called *constraint-based optimization*. Applying best practices in optimization to CDDs is an active area of research and development today.

These simulations are designed to automate running many scenarios. They produce visualizations that display decision behavior patterns or let you identify optimal choices (see Figures 5-11 and 6-3). While they do not require "operational-quality" curated decision assets, they do require reasonably good assets, so you will often need to do several rounds of interactive simulation, asset assessment, and refinement before you move on to a fully automated simulation.

Automating a simulation does not remove *all* user interaction. Typically, simulations include control panels in which you can select scenarios to include and change your choices and assumptions. But once you click the Run button, the simulation calculates a group of scenarios and displays results.

Technology Options

If you do decide to automate your decision (for action-to-outcome experimentation and/or for optimization), you have a number of choices about what technology to use. Your software developers will have a lot to say about this, but here are a few choices to use as a starting point, listed in order of technical sophistication:

- Imagine the simulation in your head, without writing anything down. This is the baseline, so tell your software developers that their goal is that, by using a computer, you can do better than this.
- Run the simulation by hand, taking notes and using a calculator.
- Code the simulation in a desktop tool like Excel, using Microsoft Visual Basic or a similar programming language (this is appropriate if the calculation is not complex and there are no circular loops in the model).
- Write the simulation in a web language like JavaScript and run the simulation in a browser.
- Architect a software asset that separates the visualization from the simulation logic (this is justified when the simulation requires more compute power than is available within a browser).
- Build the simulation in a gaming environment like Unity or Unreal Engine.

By the time you read this, there may even be available dedicated low- or no-code action-to-outcome simulation environments available that could save you the work of coding these. (This is a big focus for the authors of this book; drop us a line!)

As you select your technological tool, consider what you're trying to accomplish with it. For example, you might ask:

- What kinds of decision assets do you need to include?
- Where will they come from?
- Are they qualitative or quantitative?
- How will you incorporate them into software?
- Do you plan to explore multiple simulation scenarios manually, or automate your optimization?

Figure 5-4 shows some of these possibilities.

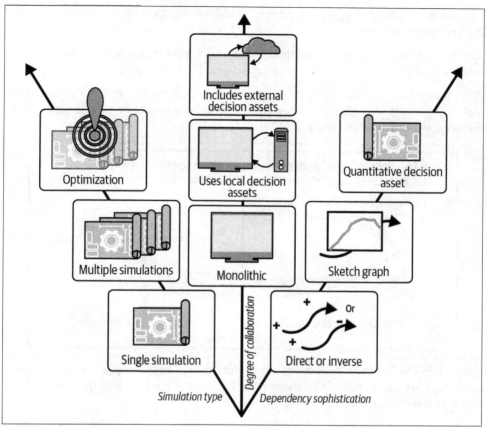

Figure 5-4. DI software tools, sorted by type and sophistication.

Simulation Report: Identifying Patterns and Feedback Loops

Simulations can teach you important things about the context of a decision, which helps you to think about it more clearly even before the computer makes a recommendation. After you begin running and iterating on your simulation, you'll look at the results and try to identify patterns, feedback loops, and anything else you notice that might have some predictive power.

Your Simulation Report (listed as a deliverable in the "Formal Process Description: Decision Simulation" on page 137) is a way to capture the key findings you gain from running your decision model. Its audience is your decision customer, who might choose to share it more broadly to justify a decision to stakeholders and/or decision implementers. The report might show the CDD and discuss how the simulation was created, who created it, how it was validated, the simulation results in summary (including especially anything surprising), and how the decision will be executed and tracked going forward.

This section shows some common patterns we've observed when running simulations, which you may choose to use as ingredients for your report.

First, a simulation helps you to investigate both long-term and short-term outcomes and objectives. Otherwise, you may miss long-term benefits or unintended consequences, as illustrated in Figure 5-5.

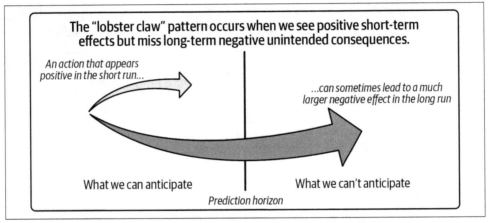

Figure 5-5. The "lobster claw" pattern illustrates the need to investigate both short-term and long-term cause-and-effect behavior. See L. Y. Pratt's book Link *(https://oreil.ly/kINon) for more details.*

Here are some additional patterns that you might want to look for:

Multiple actions changing the outcome
Sometimes you need to apply two actions at the same time to achieve an outcome, such as in this decision model (*https://oreil.ly/Mhdmn*), where an investment in both policing and legal system improvement were needed to change the level of conflict in a country.

Important versus less important actions or externals
You can observe through simulation which actions and/or externals have a bigger impact on the outcomes than others, as previously illustrated with the building decommissioning action (lever).

Sensitive versus less sensitive range of values
Sometimes there's a particular range of values to which the outcome is very sensitive. You might find, for example, that if your competitor's price is less than $4, then no matter whether it's $0.50 or $3.50, your outcome will be the same.

If the competitor's price is higher than $4, then whether it's $5 or $50 makes no difference to your success.

Butterfly effect

Sometimes a very small change to a lever or external can have a very big impact on outcomes. For instance, if you lower your price from $4 to $3.99 when your competitor is charging $4, then that could lead—through perhaps a feedback effect—to a very big improvement in your profits.

Short-circuit effect

Sometimes an external can act as an amplifier on a feedback loop, sometimes because there are dependencies that are not obvious. Suppose you make purchase decisions from different suppliers based on several factors, like cost, discounts, availability, and transportation costs. Your decision model would typically include feedback loops because of causal connections between suppliers, such as them all being affected by weather or a pandemic. Anand Thaker, an investor, entrepreneur, and go-to-market expert with deep experience in DI, writes:

> I've seen short-circuit effects when intermediates have an unintended impact on each other, usually causing a surge on the outcome. This is different from the butterfly effect, where the lever is the problem. A DI example I've repeatedly encountered deals with feedback loops on intermediaries occurring due to external factors. I've seen this happen in particular when restructuring or a renovating of system or organization. We solve this short-circuit effect by combining intermediates, or in extreme cases, we rebuild the CDD and use it to discover a new solution.

Feedback loop

Many CDDs include causal chains in the form of loops, as shown in Figure 5-6. There, the value of decision element A contributes to the values of B and C, and the value of C in turn contributes to A. It's important to identify any feedback loops in your CDD and investigate the behavior patterns that can arise from them.

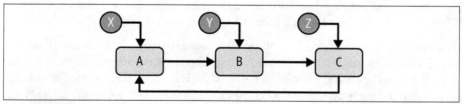

Figure 5-6. A simple feedback loop.

Feedback loops can have positive or negative effects. A feedback loop becomes positive, or a *virtuous circle,* if some change in A causes a desired change in B, which leads to C, which then causes further desired changes in A, resulting in continuous improvement. For instance, if you hike more, you build your muscles and stamina, which makes hiking easier, which makes you hike more. Or if Starbucks charges a bit more for coffee, then invests that in worker programs like 401(k)s and health-care plans, then that makes the workers happier, which leads to a more cheerful café environment, which means they can successfully charge even more for coffee, and so on.

Conversely, a feedback loop becomes a *vicious circle* if some change in A causes an undesirable change in B, which leads to C, which then causes further undesirable changes in A, resulting in continuous deterioration. For instance, if a student misses school for a while, they struggle with understanding the lesson when they return, which makes school harder, which discourages the student, which leads to them missing even more school. A corporate example: a bad brand reputation leads to fewer buyers, which leads to less money to improve the reputation, which leads to even few buyers, and so on.

Decision elements in a feedback loop may also have dependencies from decision elements outside the loop. These are illustrated as X, Y, and Z in Figure 5-6. These dependencies may act as *accelerators,* amplifying a virtuous or vicious cycle; as *dampers,* slowing down a cycle; or as *triggers* that tip the cycle from virtuous to vicious or vice versa. When feedback loops have dependencies on externals, the external is often a trigger—which means that changing the external (or the assumption about the external during simulation) can tip the cycle between virtuous and vicious. Such triggers pose a risk to the decision. You can mitigate that risk by decreasing the uncertainty around the external or by monitoring the external (as part of Decision Monitoring, described in Chapter 7). Similarly, the behavior of a feedback loop may depend on one or more lever choices.

The main point regarding feedback loops is not to forget them! Before CDDs were widely used, people would oversimplify complex situations, leading to unexpected results of actions. By modeling your feedback effects, you can gain a much better understanding of how to make great decisions.

The remainder of this chapter will present some use cases illustrating computerized decision simulation. First, we'll revisit the European government agency's model that helped it to weigh travel policies to help reduce its carbon emissions. For this agency, we created a simple actions-to-outcomes simulation. Then we'll take another look at our puzzle toy example, where the simulation focused on identifying patterns and gathering data on them. You'll then have an opportunity to try a simple simulation for yourself.

Net-Zero Emissions Use Case: Simulating the Decision Model

As you'll recall from earlier chapters, our European government agency client was seeking to reduce its carbon emissions to net zero in a few years, and asked us to model the impact of potential new travel policies on this decision. The organization asked us to "please keep it simple," so we started building our simulation visualization with just actions and outcomes (Figure 5-7). We included only a single lever, which let the decision makers choose different spending amounts (a range). As they adjusted the amount, our calculations changed the GHG emissions and relationship score outcomes. These calculations happened behind the scenes, hidden from users to avoid overwhelming them. The outcomes were visualized on a dial, and the objective included a simple yes-or-no "Objective met?" icon to indicate clearly whether the chosen amount satisfied the goal.

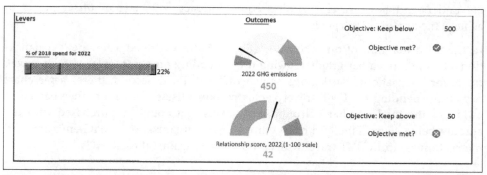

Figure 5-7. Net-zero emissions use case: our first and simplest iteration of the decision simulation.[4]

The second iteration of this simulation is shown in Figure 5-8. It still shows only levers and outcomes, but one of the outcomes has been made more specific based on the decision customer's feedback. It now includes a new lever: investment in carbon offsets, which allows organizations like this agency to reduce their net GHG emissions. Adding this lever required an external, too: the price of a carbon offset. The user can still move the levers back and forth and observe how they change the outcomes.

---

4 For print readers, the color versions of this figure and the following figures are available in the supplemental materials repository (*https://oreil.ly/DIH-supplemental*).

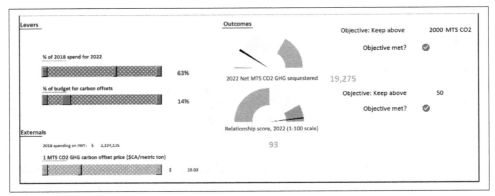

Figure 5-8. Second iteration of the net-zero emissions use case simulation.

Importantly, the simulation was much more effective than text in helping stakeholders understand how travel spending could interact with carbon offset prices to achieve the organization's goals.

In the third iteration of our simulator (Figure 5-9), we added a few new visualizations. First, there's a bar graph showing total spending on a particular type of travel: travel for international workshops, which we'll call IWT. Second, there's a pie chart depicting spending on IWT travel versus carbon offsets. Third, another bar chart estimates the total number of round-trip tickets that could be purchased with the amount being spent. Finally, a chart compares the organization's GHG emissions (in metric tonnes) from IWT travel with carbon offsets against those GHGs.

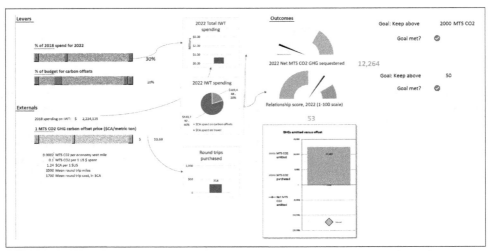

Figure 5-9. Third iteration of the net-zero emissions simulator user interface, showing some intermediates in more detail.

These visuals allowed the decision customers to observe some counterintuitive dynamics as they moved the levers and saw how those changes affected the outcomes and whether they met their objectives.

Note that these simulations serve a similar—yet enhanced—purpose to the business intelligence dashboards used by many businesses. They don't just show things that are being measured; by showing their relationship to actions and business outcomes, they bring what is otherwise a static dashboard "alive," allowing for root-cause analysis and decision simulation.

In our final simulation for this use case (Figure 5-10), we added visualizations of some intermediates that we had previously hidden. This iteration also breaks down the relationship benefits in-person travel can achieve. These simulations, along with the CDDs from Chapter 3, ended our DI work on the first phase of this agency's project.

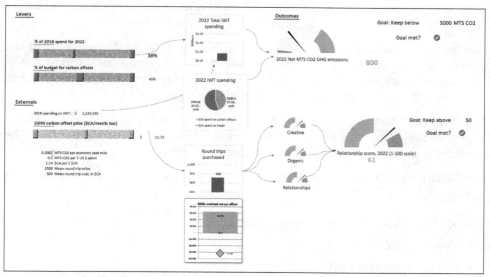

Figure 5-10. Final iteration of the simulation.

Visualizing Emergent Patterns in the Puzzle Toy Use Case Simulation

In Chapter 4, we showed you how to find the decision assets for the puzzle toy use case. You might want to review the CDD in Figure 4-10 and the dashboard in Figure 4-5.

At this point, you know that your revenue depends on how many units you sell. You have identified three key externals that affect revenue—market size, base demand versus price, and increase in demand versus marketing spend. Your analytics team has provided data assets that provide predictions and assumptions for these externals. Your costs depend on another external, manufacturing order size, and you also have an asset for that.

Now, that's helpful information—so why do you need to simulate anything? Your CDD identifies the missing information needed to make the decision. Why don't you just decide now?

The problem is that even though you have some very valuable information, nothing yet directly connects profit (the outcome you are trying to optimize) with the range of values you are considering for the three decision levers (sale price, manufacturing run size, and marketing spend). Nothing tells you, "If I take this course of action, what will the outcome be?" You *can't* determine the answer to this question based on these charts alone: it's just not obvious at all. Simulation can help.

You start to document your simulation in a *Simulation Report*. You decide that the purpose of your simulation is to find the combination of choices for the three action questions that will yield maximum profit. As you develop the simulation, you add to the report, shown in "Completed Simulation Report" on page 154.

For this simulation, instead of bar graphs or gauges, you decide to show various action choices (amounts of marketing spend) on an x-axis—combined with the resulting y-axis outcome result, profit (or loss, when the value is negative).

Specifically, each point on the x-axis represents a unique combination of the three levers:

- Marketing spend as a percentage of profit
- Unit retail sale price
- Size of production run

In Figure 5-11, these are indicated individually in the three sub-axes below the main x-axis. The profit corresponding to each combination of levers is shown as the oscillating line.

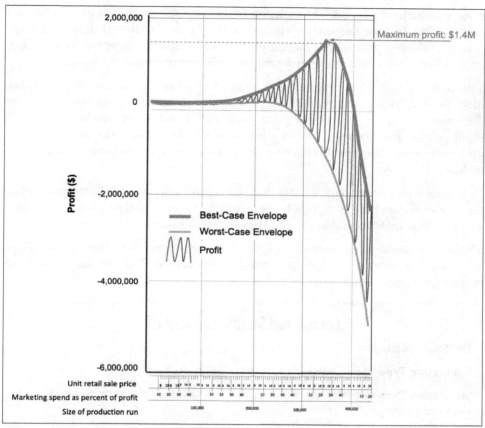

Figure 5-11. The result of a DI simulation for the product launch use case. Source: Quantellia (reproduced with permission).

The oscillating line is the profit—it computes as:

profit = price × units_sold − cost_of_units_manufactured

In addition, the best- and worst-case "envelope" curves in Figure 5-11 show the boundaries on profit and loss across the range of lever choices you may select. The heavy boundary at the top is called the *opportunity envelope* and the lower, lighter boundary is called the *cost envelope*. The highest peak of the profit curve corresponds to the decision that will yield the highest profit of $1.4 million, and the lowest point on the loss curve shows the maximum loss that may be incurred, around −$5 million.

You designed this simulation and graph to show you not only maximum profit and loss, but also to answer the question, "What levers or externals have the most impact on my profit?" The profit oscillates because demand rises and falls based on unit price and marketing spend. The variation in the outcome graph (but not the amount of oscillation, because the order of choices on the x-axis is arbitrary) shows that *profit is very sensitive to pricing*. The highest profits (the peak of the opportunity envelope) occur when you are selling the most units at the lowest manufacturing cost.

You incur losses for two reasons. First, sales drop off sharply when the price is too high. Second, you have a limited market, so as the market nears saturation, you sell fewer units regardless of the price. Note that if you target maximum profit, a small pricing error could result in a loss of about $1 million. However, there are opportunities for lower profits where a small pricing error would incur a small loss or no loss.

Designing a visualization on a CDD that shows sensitivity is a great research project for human factors people, especially those looking to leverage their data visualization expertise into studying and improving decision visualization.

This look at sensitivity is a sneak peek into Decision Assessment, the topic of Chapter 6. But first, here's the completed Simulation Report. You'll create one of your own in the final section of this chapter, "Try It Yourself."

Completed Simulation Report

Use Case: Puzzle toy

Simulation Type: Quantitative, leading to optimization

Simulation Purpose: Find the combination of choices for these three levers that will yield maximum profit:

- Sales price
- Production order size
- Marketing spend as a percent of profit

Simulation CDD: The entire CDD (as shown in Figure 4-10)

Simulation Scenarios:

Lever choices (note that the ranges match the ranges provided by the external assumptions used for this simulation):
- Sales price: $8 to $18
- Production order size: 100,000 to market size
- Marketing spend as a percent of profit: 0% to 50%

External assumptions:
- Unit cost versus number produced: data from analysts (typically you would reference an entry in your Decision Asset Register)

- Base demand versus price: ML model from analysts
- Market size: data from analysts
- Marketing-driven demand uplift: predictive function from analysts

Simulation Controls: None. This is not an interactive simulation (for now), just a report.

Simulation Visualizations: Graph showing maximum profit and maximum loss

Simulation Calculations:

profit = price × units_sold – cost_of_units_manufactured

Profit will be calculated using three loops: the innermost loop is sales price, the middle loop is marketing spend as a percentage of profit, and the outer loop is production order size. (This produces the oscillating graph in Figure 5-11.)

Simulation Code and Run Parameters Repository: MyCompany's GitHub contains all the code, input, and instructions to rerun the simulation.

Simulation Results: Maximum profit is about $1.4 million. Maximum loss is about $5 million. Because profit is highly sensitive to price, if you target maximum profit, a small pricing error could result in a loss of about $1 million. However, there are opportunities for lower profits where a small pricing error would incur a small loss or no loss. (Typically you would include some sample output, like the graph.)

Recommendations: Because profit is very sensitive to pricing, focus further work on pricing, such as vetting the base demand model or simulating with a different model. Add pricing experts to the team before the next iteration.

Try It Yourself: Decision Simulation for the Telecom Use Case

In Chapter 3, you worked through Phase B, Decision Modeling, including the Decision Design and Decision Asset Investigation processes for the telecom use case. In this section, you will complete Process C1, Decision Simulation, for the same use case.

Exercise

Before you continue reading, review the annotated CDD from Decision Asset Investigation for this use case (Figure 4-13) and the Decision Asset Register (Table 4-3). Recall that one of Dr. Smith's major concerns is that a competitor will launch an unlimited plan. You want to build a very simple qualitative simulation to explore that aspect of the decision. What parts of that CDD might you want to start with to simulate?

Deciding on a CDD to Simulate

You decide to start your simulation with a tiny subset of the CDD, shown in Figure 5-12. You have observed that your market is in a steady state. That is, recently, more marketing by you or your competitor does not motivate many customers to move between companies. You believe that introducing the new unlimited plan and advertising it will convince customers to move to your company. So in this CDD, "Marketing/Advertising" represents the *additional* amount of marketing and advertising spend for an unlimited plan, so if your competitor does not launch an unlimited plan, their "[additional unlimited plan] Marketing/Advertising" will be zero.

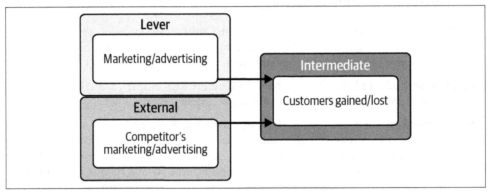

Figure 5-12. A very simple CDD for initial simulation.

Exercise

Did you make a very simple CDD like this one? Of course, there are many possible solutions.

Before you continue reading, please imagine that it's your job to create your simulation. You will need to use simple controls (like a slider or toggle button) to select lever choices and to provide a visualization for the intermediates.

Draw a picture of your visualization. You might want to include images of typical computer interface elements, like bars in a bar chart or sliders.

Designing CDD Visual Elements

You decide to visualize your intermediate using a bar graph. The center line will represent your current number of customers; the bar will go above the line for customers gained and below it for customers lost (Figure 5-13).

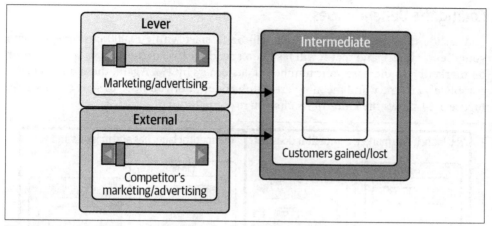

Figure 5-13. Selecting visual elements for the simulation.

You choose sliders for the lever choices. You need some numbers and calculations to make the simulation work interactively, so you give the sliders a range from 0 to 100. But your range of values stays behind the scenes: users won't see any numbers on the sliders or the bar, to keep things simple: this is a *qualitative* simulation, not a quantitative one.

In fact, numbers can confuse matters. If you show the arbitrary numbers you've chosen, people will assign meaning to them. They'll read it as something like "the competitor is spending $100" or "we gained 100 customers." That would be incorrect and entirely beside the point. The point isn't specific numbers—*the point is to know whether a certain lever choice will result in gaining or losing customers* and to gain intuition about the decision model's behavior from this low-fidelity relationship.

Exercise

Check your controls. Did you use some similar controls? Make sure you did not include numbers, because this is a *qualitative* simulation and the numbers would be meaningless.

Before you continue reading, write some code, pseudocode, Excel formulas, or even just equations that use the values of the lever choice controls to calculate the value of your outcome(s).

Coding the Dependencies

You decide that your simple formula will be to start with 100,000 customers (that's your "center line"), and that it will take you spending 10% more than your competitor on marketing to increase your number of customers by 1%. Again, these numbers are completely arbitrary and meaningless ("stub code"), but you need to start somewhere. Figure 5-14 shows the kinds of results you're going for here.

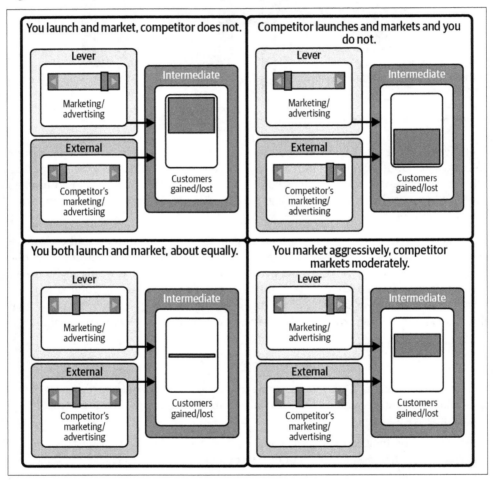

Figure 5-14. Simulation screenshots.

You decide to code your dependencies in JavaScript and run the simulation in your browser. You set your "constants" like this:

```
initialNumberOfCustomer = 100000;
percentDifferenceToDriveAOnePercentGainOrLoss = 10;
```

You decide to call the number from your slider *ourMarketingSpend* and the number from the competitor slider *competitorMarketingSpend*. You have a function that can display a number as a bar:

```
spendDifference = ourMarketingSpend - competitorMarketingSpend;
customersPercentChange = spendDifference /
    percentDifferenceToDriveAOnePercentGainOrLoss;
customersGainedLost = .01 * customersPercentChange * initialNumberOfCustomer;
displayOnBar(customersBar, customersGainedLost);
```

You could also do the simulation using Excel formulas:

1. Name a column *initialNumberOfCustomer* and set it to 100000.

2. Name a column *percentDifferenceToDriveAOnePercentGainOrLoss* and set it to 10.

3. Name a column *ourMarketingSpend*. Create a bar graph that displays the number in this column. You will change the number in this column instead of using a slider. (Note that in developer mode in Excel you can create ActiveX slider controls, but teaching you about them is beyond the scope of this book.)

4. Name a column *isCompetitorMarketingSpend*. Create a bar graph that displays the number in this column. You will change the number in this column instead of using a slider.

5. Name a column *spendDifference* and set its formula to = *ourMarketingSpend – competitorMarketingSpend*.

6. Name a column *customersPercentChange* and set its formula to = *spendDifference / percentDifferenceToDriveAOnePercentGainOrLoss*.

7. Name a column *customersGainedLost* and set its formula to = $.01 \times$ *customersPercentChange* $\times$ *initialNumberOfCustomer*.

8. Create a bar graph to display the number in this column. Style the bar graph in Excel to look like the bar graph in Figure 5-14.

Time to take your simulation for a test run!

Exercise

Before you continue reading, run your simulation (either through manual calculations or you could implement it in some software system) to be sure that:

- You gain customers if you launch and market and your competitor does not.

- You lose customers if your competitor launches and markets and you do not.

- There is little change if you and your competitor both launch and market about equally.
- You gain a little if you both launch and you market a lot more than your competitor.

Your results might be similar to those in Figure 5-14.

Testing Your Simulation

The very simple simulation in Figure 5-14 suggests something useful: that, regardless of whether your competitor launches an unlimited plan, your company will never be worse off if *you* launch one. Of course, this insight depends on your fake numbers and formulas, but if you move the levers and watch the outcome bars, you'll observe that you gain some intuition you don't get from just the numbers.[5] There is something counterintuitive going on here that bears repeating: even with "stub" code, you've creating a connection between math and a visualization of that math in a way that is very intuitive and natural for people. You're asking them to think in terms of an action they take (the lever) in some context (the external) and its result. This is like throwing a ball and catching it (*https://oreil.ly/NFhsC*)—something that is a lot easier on human brains than reading math and trying to translate it into something understandable.

A side note: externals, actions, and outcomes are largely similar to the "antecedent/behavior/consequence" identified in psychology as *operant conditioning*, a widely accepted model for how people naturally think. We've observed over the years that this model form is uniquely helpful in driving intuition and understanding, *even when the model fidelity is extremely low*, as it is here. Of course, given that the model has low fidelity, it can also be misleading, so you'll need to be careful in this regard.

Exercise

Create your Simulation Report before you read ahead. Phase C, Worksheet 1: Decision Simulation Report, available in the supplemental materials repository (*https://oreil.ly/DIH-supplemental*), provides a template. Then check to see if yours is similar to the one in the next section.

You create a brief Simulation Report with this conclusion from your simulation and some screenshots like those in Figure 5-14.

---

5 To explore this concept further, see this presentation of a qualitative model for a carbon tax, by coauthor Pratt (*https://oreil.ly/C8gLi*) (starting around 12:13).

Writing a Simulation Report

Use Case: Unlimited Usage Plan

Simulation Type: Qualitative

Simulation Purpose: Understand how a competitor launching a similar plan will affect your profit. Since customers gained or lost directly affects profit, to make the simulation simpler, I used customers gained or lost as a proxy outcome.

Simulation CDD: A subset of the CDD. (Typically you would include Figure 5-12 here.)

Simulation Scenarios:

Lever choices

> Our marketing/advertising spend on an unlimited plan. Zero spend means we do not launch a plan.

External assumptions

> Competitor's marketing/advertising spend on an unlimited plan. Zero spend means they do not launch a plan.

Simulation Controls: Sliders: one for us, one for the competitor

Simulation Visualizations: Bar graph showing our gain or loss of customers

Simulation Calculations:

Coded in JavaScript:

```
var initialNumberOfCustomer = 100000;
var percentDifferenceToDriveAOnePercentGainOrLoss = 10;
```

The number from your slider is ourMarketingSpend and the number from the competitor slider is competitorMarketingSpend. Using a function that can display a number as a bar:

```
var spendDifference = ourMarketingSpend - competitorMarketingSpend;
var customersPercentChange = spendDifference /
    percentDifferenceToDriveAOnePercentGainOrLoss;
var customersGainedLost = .01 * customersPercentChange *
    initialNumberOfCustomer;
var displayOnBar(customersBar, customersGainedLost);
```

Simulation Results: Launching a correctly priced plan never hurts us. If our competitors do not launch a plan and we do, we gain customers. If our competitors launch a plan and we don't, we lose customers. If we both launch a plan, our gain or loss of customers depends on our marketing spend.

Recommendations: While this simulation suggests that launching the plan is a good competitive strategy, we might improve it by making it quantitative, adding our current number of customers, an estimate of our competitor's number of customers, and using the human knowledge from Decision Asset Investigation that "it is 'common knowledge' that a targeted advertising campaign will convince about 2% of potential customers to move to the company running the campaign." We also might do further simulation to investigate what lever choices lead to the best profit.

Conclusion

How much effort should you invest in Decision Simulation? It's a judgment call. There is a risk to "overthinking"—spending a long time building the model when a lower-fidelity one would have value. There's also risk in "underthinking"—building a model so simple that it is misleading. It's not as straightforward as "simple simulations for low-stakes decisions and sophisticated simulations for high-stakes decisions."

A simple simulation might tell you that the outcomes of a high-stakes decision depend almost entirely on one causal chain. This makes it easy to bound your simulation work. Or, if a high-stakes decision is easy to modify, you might decide to invest your time in better Decision Monitoring (see Chapter 7) instead of more simulation. Conversely, an apparently low-stakes decision might be an operational decision you make dozens or thousands of times every day. Many small differences can add up to big effects on outcomes in aggregate, so such a decision might be worth investing more simulation time.

There's a lot you can do to make a model better over time: investigating feedback loops, looking for unintended consequences, performing sensitivity analysis, adding refinements, optimizing, and so forth. How deep you decide to dig into any of these will depend on the resources allocated to this decision; the uncertainty, risk, and potential costs and benefits of the decision, your time frame, and many other factors.

In the next chapter, we'll explore Process C2, Decision Assessment, in which your decision team and decision customer evaluate the work you've done so far to assess the risk and upside potential from your decision model. You'll learn how to judge whether a decision is based on good data (*provenance*) and what parts of the decision model are the most important to get right (*sensitivity*), and at the end of the chapter, you'll reach a decision.

CHAPTER 6

Decision Reasoning: The Decision Assessment Process

Congratulations: you're a good way through the DI processes. You've modeled your decision and you've run it through, from actions to outcomes. You might have even run it backward, to see if a computer simulation can help you find the best actions. You have a recommended action in mind. Are you done? Or is it time to go around the loop again, maybe building a better model, to gather more data, interview more experts, dig up more research? Or have you learned what you can from the decision model?

Welcome to Process C2, Decision Assessment. This second process in Phase C, Decision Reasoning, is where you make the most important concerns, risks, sensitivities, and uncertainties of your decision explicit. These may stem from single elements of the decision (like an external element on the CDD that represents the weather) or larger subcomponents (like a financial modeling part of a CDD). Either way, in this process, you'll record them so that you can assess and manage the risks and opportunities that arise from how you built your decision model. Much like Process C1, Decision Simulation, this process can involve both human and computer techniques.

Figure 6-1 shows the Decision Reasoning phase in the context of the other process phases.

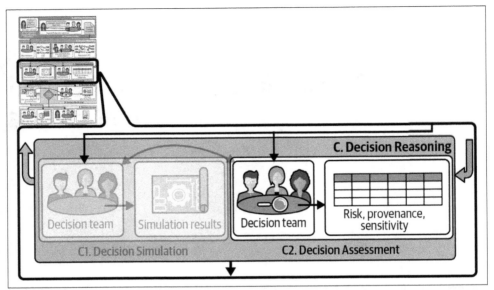

Figure 6-1. The Decision Reasoning phase includes Process C2, Decision Assessment (this chapter), and Process C1, Decision Simulation (Chapter 5). Typically, you'll iterate between these two processes several times until you are ready to take action in the real world (Chapter 7).

In some sense, every model is wrong. In other words, it's not an exact match to reality, because that's the nature of models. Remember the George Box quote from earlier in this book: "All models are wrong, but some are useful." By definition, there will be some *risk* in going with any model's recommendations. Process C2 will help you to assess this risk, as well as assessing the *upside opportunity* of going with your model's recommendation (that is, the opposite of risk: the good things that could happen if you're lucky).

Your model is a human artifact representing your decision. It's your map of the decision territory. You've chosen your model's level of detail. In consultation with your team, you also chose which CDD elements—levers, intermediates, externals, dependencies, and outcomes—to include, whether and how much simulation to employ, and what data and knowledge to use in your simulations. What you have discovered, and added, while completing processes A2 through C1 means that you probably have more than just a higher-fidelity version of the invisible model in your head when you first wrote down the Decision Objective Statement.

Maybe seeing the model on paper or in a simulation has helped you to understand a complex decision, and you have little doubt in the value of documenting it. On the other hand, maybe the model is telling you to do something that conflicts with past decisions, your "gut" intuition, or the recommendations of a trusted advisor. You can't assess your decision model's risk and upside opportunity in a vacuum: whatever your model tells you, you'll always compare it with the other ways you might make the decision. So this chapter will also help you to make these kinds of comparisons.

We've observed two categories of approaches that our clients like to take at this stage: observation and automated assessment.

In *assessment by observation*, humans examine the model, reaching conclusions like:[1]

- "Hey, let's include another outcome!"
- "I think we could do a better job with this dependency link."
- "This model is great. I've learned a lot. Time to take action."

In *automated assessment*, in contrast, you use computer software—including simulation—to help to assess the model. The computer might provide conclusions like:

- "No matter how you move this lever, it won't have much of an impact on the outcome." In the facilities management example in Chapter 5, for example, simulation showed that demolishing buildings had little effect on deferred maintenance.
- "This dependency model matters a lot—it's important that you get it right." In the puzzle toy example in Chapter 5, simulation showed that the dependency of profit on pricing is very important.

In this chapter, we explain how to go about the assessment that leads to these kinds of results, and how to record them on the *Decision Assessment Register*. We'll finish with an opportunity for you to try it yourself.

Research Opportunities in DI

More than any other DI process, Decision Assessment could benefit from new methods and is particularly ripe for academic research initiatives. If you're looking for a PhD topic in an area like cognitive science, behavioral economics, computer science (including ML), statistics, or human factors, look no further than this chapter. Each topic receives here only the lightest touch, but we envision a future DI body of research and active investigation that will span the 21st century, building on existing work in such diverse fields as cybernetics, Bayesian reasoning, journalism, complex systems analysis, decision analysis, and causal reasoning in AI. We've labeled the areas we particularly think are ripe for research—because they're needed and also because they build on preexisting work—with the words *research opportunity*.

---

1 Specifying how do to this in a systematic way is a research opportunity for human factors researchers and cognitive scientists.

Introduction to Process C2, Decision Assessment

As it turns out, DI gives us two "magic" powers. In particular, you can make great decisions from imperfect models, and you can make great decisions based on imperfect data. "The decision is only as good as the data" is a highly misleading statement. The truth is that the decision is only as good as the data to which the decision is sensitive.[2] *Sensitive* in this context means "having a significant effect on outcomes." Let us explain.

The *accuracy* (closeness to the true value) and *precision* (reproducibility) of the elements (like data or an ML model) that make up your decision model are important, of course. But you only need to be accurate and precise about parts of the model—CDD elements and data—to which the outcomes and objectives are *sensitive*. Certain factors matter less than others. By way of an extreme example: you don't need to know the phase of the moon to decide whether to go to the grocery store or not. More generally, you don't need to collect, prepare, or model from data that is irrelevant to the decision. The sticky part is that in most situations, the relevance of any given data asset is less obvious than in this example.

To drill into this, you only need accuracy and precision when they lead to a change in the recommended outcome. To the degree to which a decision element (like an external, lever, or dependency model) has the power to change a "yes" to a "no," it needs to be more accurate and precise than others. For instance, I don't need to know the exact outdoor temperature to decide whether to take my dog for a walk; I only need to know if it's over 20 degrees Fahrenheit or not (any colder than that and the ground will hurt his paws). So it's not only certain factors that matter or don't; it's also that only some *values* of those factors make a difference.

In addition, if a decision contains complex system dynamics driven by feedback loops and effects,[3] these dynamics often swamp any other component of the decision. If a factor determines whether you are in a particular dynamic, such as a virtuous or vicious cycle, precision and correctness are important. A more accurate motto than "The decision is only as good as the data" might be "The data only needs to be fine-grained and accurate enough in areas to which the decision is sensitive to tell you whether you've met your objective or not."

---

2   The term *sensitivity* in this process means "the degree to which the factor affects the model's outcomes." It is not the same sensitivity as reflected in receiver operator characteristics (ROC) curves, commonly used to evaluate ML models.

3   We don't cover system dynamics much in this book, but a good reference as to how this applies to DI is L. Pratt and Mark Zangari's paper "The System Dynamics of Aid" (*https://oreil.ly/fIBHC*), which describes how decisions regarding policing and rule of law converted a "vicious circle" of violence into a "virtuous one" in sub-Saharan Africa. You can also watch a video showing this model on YouTube (*https://oreil.ly/mzFoQ*).

Another way to think about this "magic" of decision modeling is that, by connecting actions to outcomes, we gain a data management focus we might not otherwise have. In contrast, when data scientists have to collect, prepare, and manage datasets without knowing how they'll be used in a decision, they often wind up wasting enormous amounts of time and effort. If they don't know which datasets are crucial versus which are tangential and don't require a high degree of quality, then they have no choice but to collect, prepare, and manage all fields of all datasets equally. That's a lot of work, much of which typically isn't needed or used for decision making. So DI allows decision makers to give their data teams the information they need to prioritize their work appropriately, focusing their efforts and resources on the places where it matters most. Understanding this is an incredibly powerful way to reduce technology costs—that's more than magic, it's money in your pocket.

Again, you don't get this value unless you connect data and models to outcomes, because the only way to assess sensitivity and objective-crossing is relative to some outcome and some objective. That's part of why the early DI phases place such emphasis on crisply articulating outcomes and objectives: they are critical for effective and efficient data and model governance.

It's worth taking a moment to contrast this approach to data governance with what needs to be done when your data represents transactional information, like bank accounts or purchase transactions. Of course, those need to be as perfect as possible. The same is not true of data to support decisions.

Formal Process Description: Process C2, Decision Assessment

How you go about Decision Assessment will depend on your situation and the decision you're making. Thus, this process—more than the others you've seen so far—is less prescriptive. You'll be doing a lot of thinking about how to tailor it to your particular situation.

The list in the following process contains a set of what we call "lenses" through which you can assess your decision. The list is very exhaustive—just considering one or two may be enough.

Keep in mind throughout that all you're trying to do is improve on how the decision is being made today, for which very few of these considerations were made. Focus on incremental and iterative improvement. We've seen organizations fall into a quagmire of "analysis paralysis" considering too many of these factors before moving forward with a decision because these elements can be reasonably expensive to assess. None of these lenses are—strictly speaking—required to make a good decision.

Description

Assess a decision diagram and/or simulation to decide what to do next. Is it time to implement the recommended actions, or do we need to do more decision modeling?

Prerequisites

- A CDD.

- Decision assets (captured in the Decision Asset Register).

- Simulation observations and results. If you built decision software, these may be in the form of screenshots and/or a report that was generated by your simulation. If you just used a diagram, then this might be the results of your inspection of the decision model.

Responsible role

Decision team leader

Steps

1. Revisit the Decision Objective Statement. Plan the rest of this process by selecting from the decision lenses in the following list and assessing your CDD and/or software, along with the amount of benefit the organization will realize (or risk it will avoid) from a good decision. Keep in mind that many of the analysis lenses that follow are costly to perform, and that this cost may outweigh their benefit.

2. Assess the *baseline* against which you are assessing your model, which is how this kind of decision was made before the organization began using DI. If your baseline is a sophisticated optimization model built by 10 PhDs over several years, then it will be harder to exceed than if the decision has never been formally modeled.

3. Related to the previous step, consider the *cost of doing nothing*: not making any new decision and not taking any new action. This may or may not be the same as your baseline.

4. Assess your decision model's *accuracy*.[4] You can measure accuracy if you have some data source that tells you the "right answer," against which you can evaluate your model.

   If you don't have any data that lets you assess overall model accuracy, then for model accuracy, you might substitute the accuracy of individual decision elements, especially those for which there is high decision sensitivity. All other things being equal, a decision model made of higher-accuracy elements will be more accurate than one made of lower-accuracy elements.

---

4 The term *accuracy* in this process means "closeness to the true value or to the demonstrable correct decision."

5. Assess your decision model's *bias*, meaning that the model is accurate and/or high-fidelity for some situations but not others. For example, a medical model built and tested only on white male patients, which does not include patients of other ethnicities or genders, would be biased.

6. Assess your decision model's *sensitivity* to each of its components.[5] For example, your model might make the same decision about a product feature regardless of whether you are selling to teenagers or young adults. In this case, we say that it's *insensitive* to the age of the customer. Another example: it might be OK to have a low-accuracy weather predictor in an external, if the weather has little impact on your decision.

7. Assess your decision model's *fidelity*. This is the degree to which the decision model matches reality. Note that you can have a low-fidelity model that produces high accuracy. For example, a decision model could predict that all humans are less than 10 feet tall using the rule: "If this human has fewer than eight eyes, they will be less than 10 feet tall." It would always be right, but it wouldn't exactly match how the world works!

8. Assess the *uncertainty* in the elements that make up your decision. Are you highly confident, for instance, that your competitor's price is between $2 and $20, but less confident that it's exactly $5? Based on historical data, maybe you can calculate that, on 80% of days, you'll sell between 80 and 100 units of your product, on 10% you'll sell less than 80, and on 10% you'll sell more than 100? If you have this kind of statistical information throughout your model, then you might tap the mathematicians in your organization to use a method like Bayesian inference (*https://oreil.ly/00L1r*) or some of the techniques from Six Sigma (*https://oreil.ly/7klcQ*), as appropriate, to calculate how actions lead to outcomes.

   - For many decisions, though, these kinds of statistics are not available. In this case, you might ask a less precise question: "What do I think is my *overall uncertainty* in this model as a whole?" You might say, "Well, this model pretty well captures how my best decision makers say they make choices, and they're pretty accurate a lot of the time, so let's say that this model uncertainty is pretty good, maybe plus or minus 5%." Although this kind of informality may make your mathematicians uncomfortable, it is nonetheless all that is available for many decisions made by organizations.

   - Part of your uncertainty consideration might include the *provenance* of the decision assets on which your model is based. Is a given set of data from a trustworthy source internal to your organization? An external source, like a

---

5 The term *sensitivity* in this process means "degree to which it affects the model's outcomes." It is not the same sensitivity as reflected in ROC curves, commonly used to evaluate ML models.

refereed journal or an expert with known credentials? Or did someone just make a guess? If you have several models or datasets or expert opinions, are they from equally reliable sources?

9. Assess the level of *consensus* around the model. To what degree is there agreement to the model structure?

10. Assess the level and nature of *noise* in your decision model's source data. Was it, for instance, measured using a "What do you think of our product" questionnaire that the same person might answer differently at different times, even if their opinion hasn't changed? Note that noise and uncertainty aren't the same: noise is one source of uncertainty, but so are other things, like bias.[6]

11. Assess your decision model's *timing*. Do some levers have time constraints attached to them? Is there a cost to delaying the decisions for too long? How else does time affect the decision?

12. Assess your decision model's *approach*: how different aspects of decision reasoning will guide not just how this decision is made, but also how you'll use decision assets and decision elements and how the organization will manage risk.

13. Assess your decision model's *risk*. The greater the uncertainty, the greater the chance of unexpected bad things to happen (risk).

14. Assess your decision model's *upside*. The greater the uncertainty, the greater the chance of unexpected good things to happen, too.

15. Use your assessments from the previous steps to decide between three options for next steps: improve the model, accept it and move on to action, or discard the model.

16. Record your assessment in a Decision Assessment Register.

Deliverables
- Decision Assessment Register
- A recommendation for next steps

Decision Assessment Lenses

The formal process description introduced you to the set of "lenses" through which you might want to view your decision model (or some of its components) during the Decision Assessment process. In this section, we'll dive deeper into several of them.

---

6 A great place to learn more about noise is Daniel Kahneman, Olivier Sibony, and Cass R. Sunstein, *Noise: A Flaw in Human Judgment* (New York: Little, Brown, 2022). Designing new methods for how to handle noise in CDDs is another *research opportunity*.

These lenses are meant to be used one at a time and applied iteratively; there's no way you can hold them all in your head and apply them all at once. Read through them and decide on one that looks like it will provide valuable insights. Apply it and document your findings in your Assessment Register. Then consider what to do next. The results of your assessment might suggest that you need more simulation, that you need to further refine your CDD or find a better data source before you do more assessment, or even that your next task is to assess your model through another lens. Every situation is different.

Baseline

It's common for data scientists on decision modeling teams to focus on the formal methods they know: reinforcement learning, ML, Bayesian optimization, Monte Carlo analysis, and so on. When you start from "applying methods to data," however, you can end up doing the project "upside down." You might gather data and use it for, say, a supervised learning project. Then, only once that is complete does anyone think to ask, "What decisions will this model be involved in making? What are their outcomes and actions?"

Why does this happen? Because academic data science programs are method-driven: they provide students with a toolkit of approaches, but they don't necessarily teach them how to select the right tool for the job based on the requirements of that job. In addition, people often implement software systems with the primary purpose of offloading work tasks by automating them. When you're supporting decision makers, you are doing something different: you're helping people to *think* better (*https://oreil.ly/S-qQL*). Which means you need to start with their thinking, not with your tools.

To start understanding how people think, the first three questions you should ask are:

- How are decisions like this one already being made? (In other words, how was the organization making decisions before it began using DI?)
- How can we measure the quality of today's decision?
- How will we know if the new decision is better?

Most of the time, we get answers like this:

How are decisions like this one already being made?
"We talk about it, and often whoever tells the best story prevails."

How can we measure the quality of today's decision?
"We can't, really, but we're pretty confident that if we improve our decision processes by using data and including a diverse set of experts, it can't be any worse."

How will we know if the new decision is better?

> "Well, we used data and more experts and we drew a CDD, so it seems pretty obvious that the decision is going to be better."

If you're a data scientist, these answers are going to be very unsatisfying. But you need to acknowledge that this very low baseline is widespread. Take the time to do proper decision design, investigate your decision assets, and justify your plan, and *then* you can use those great methods you learned in grad school. You can't skip those steps. In the meantime, be assured that simply being a bit more disciplined and formal—as you're learning in this book—will take you a long way.

Accuracy of the Model, and of Its Parts

How can you know that your decision model will help you to make the right choice? Is it possible to measure that?

There is a wide literature for assessing and reporting on model *accuracy* if:

- Your decision is one that's been made many times before (for example, the insurance underwriting decisions described in *Noise: A Flaw in Human Judgment*).
- You have some data that tells you what the "right" decision is (also known as the *ground truth*).
- You know that data from the past is relevant to the future.

If your possible decision outcomes are "yes" and "no" ("Should we do X?"), you can measure the decision against a reference dataset of known values. You can count up the number of true positives, true negatives, false positives, and false negatives, then divide the total number of true values by the total number of false values.

If, instead of a yes or no, your decision produces a number ("How much should we spend on X?"), you can calculate the average difference between the model and the truth based on your ground truth.

We won't get into any more detail here about accuracy measurement, because any statistical or ML text will tell you how to do it. Chances are, though, that if you're using DI, you don't have a repeated decision with ground truth that is relevant to the future. Maybe you're making a one-time decision, like whether to acquire a particular company. Maybe you're making the same decision but in a changing situation, like choosing what crops to plant in the face of a changing climate.

For cases that aren't clear-cut, you have four basic methods to choose from:

Human inspection

Ask some smart people to evaluate your decision model—either the CDD in a diagram or a simulation. Does it match their understanding of how things work in this domain? This approach is common in assessing decisions that have never been formally designed before.

Gauging the accuracy of parts

Even if you don't have repeated data for the decision as a whole, you might for parts of the decision. Say you're running a model meant to help you to decide when to reopen your building after a pandemic lockdown. You might never have run anything like it before, but it might include a dependency calculation to gauge something for which you *do* have data: how effective "Wear your mask" signs are in getting people to actually wear masks.

Leveraging general-purpose models

Even if you don't have a model that addresses something as specific as number of "Wear your mask" signs to mask-wearing rates, you might have some research that relates signage to behavior change in general. If so, consider adapting it to your situation.

Using good processes

Standards organizations, like ISO (*https://oreil.ly/NVGLq*) and CMM/CMMI (*https://oreil.ly/u5piC*), help manufacturers ensure a high level of quality. These methods don't assess the built artifacts themselves, but whether the builder has adhered to a particular set of best practices or processes. As DI matures, we expect standards organizations to assess the decision-making maturity of organizations, using processes like those in this book, completely aside from any assessment of the decisions themselves.

Bias

Bias is a tremendously important and substantial topic, and it is largely out of scope for this book. Due to their inspectable and transparent natures, DI models are inherently less subject to bias than models that hide their mechanisms. But their components—such as ML models—remain "black boxes" in many regards.

Generally speaking, to assess bias, you identify certain sets of situations in which the model has low accuracy compared with others. For instance, our model for sweet potato growing may be biased toward farms in the United States. It might not be as accurate for a farm in the Sudan. Similarly, a decision model built to help a Fortune 500 company retain high-value customers might be less accurate for a startup company.

There is also a growing interest in understanding how bias disadvantages historically underrepresented groups, such as people of color and disabled people, as well as how those groups intersect.

As with accuracy, you can assess bias for the model as a whole or for individual model elements, such as an ML model used in a dependency calculation. An example might be a model that predicts adherence to a medical screening test, which might be biased against certain populations due to cultural norms against them.

There is so far little research about how methods for identifying and removing bias in statistical and ML models can transfer to decision models—that's another great *research opportunity*.

Sensitivity

Imagine I'm trying to decide how to get across town. My outcomes are:

- How much time it takes to travel
- How much it costs
- How safe the trip is

My objectives are:

- Get there in as little time as possible
- Minimize cost
- Stay safe

My levers are the kinds of transportation I can use (car, helicopter, or walking) and the speed at which I'll travel. My externals are the amount of traffic and the weather.

If I choose to use a helicopter, then my "how fast" outcome will not be sensitive to traffic (an external). If, instead, I decide to drive, then my safety outcome is highly sensitive to my speed (a lever).

No matter what I decide to do, none of my outcomes are highly sensitive to my gender (an external) or to whether I feed my dog before I leave (a lever).

As you can see, my choices and the external circumstances change what parts of the model need to be accurate to achieve a good outcome. That's the essence of model *sensitivity*.[7] You've learned throughout this book that you can assess sensitivity in a

---

7 Formal methods for sensitivity assessment in decision modeling are fantastic *research opportunities* for computer scientists and mathematicians. They can draw from statistical methods for variable importance analysis (like the widely used Gedeon method (*https://oreil.ly/EsQC6*)), but they need to be able to handle the heterogenous nature of CDDs, which can include many different kinds of submodels.

computerized model by moving levers and externals and observing if they make a big difference to the intermediates and ultimately the outcomes. If all you have is a CDD, you can use it as a guide to discussing sensitivity.

Here's another example. To keep things simple, let's assume that there's never much traffic in my town. But there are two exits near each other, one that leads to a 50-mile-long road, and the other that leads to a 1-mile shortcut. Clearly, my choice of which exit to take affects my travel time: you could say that this outcome is highly sensitive to this choice. If we change the objective to a yes-or-no: "get there in half an hour," there's still a lot of sensitivity to this choice: I'm not going to make this goal if I take the wrong turn. But let's imagine a different yes-or-no: "get there in 10 hours." Assuming my town is only 30 miles wide, and, as mentioned, there's never much traffic, then now it doesn't matter too much which exit I take; I'll still reach my goal. Now, because the goal has changed, the sensitivity to my choice of exit ramp is much lower. So my model doesn't even need to include those two exit ramps; indeed, I could probably wander through town without any map and meet my goal if I just kept pointing toward the setting sun. My model can do just as well with much less fidelity. Voilà, that's another example of DI magic!

In the facilities management example at the start of Chapter 5, you saw another example of where even a low-fidelity simulation can provide sensitivity information. We were surprised to learn during that project that the outcomes had almost no sensitivity to demolitions. This meant that a better demolition ML model or more targeted information on demolition costs wouldn't affect the outcomes of the simulation. Demolitions were not a useful lever. On the other hand, the outcome of keeping the project within budget was highly sensitive to one external: replacing building systems like HVAC. We thus refined the simulation to include assessing and improving our model's assumptions about systems replacement. This bears repeating: a super-low-fidelity simulation produced very valuable insights. Given how many decisions are made "between the ears," without any visual decision model at all, it's actually no surprise how often this happens.

For another example, look back at our puzzle toy example in Chapter 4. The profit outcome oscillated in response to different levers, because demand rises and falls based on unit price and marketing spend. The variation in the outcome graph shows that *profit is very sensitive to pricing*. The highest profits (the peak of the opportunity envelope) occurs when you are selling the most puzzle toys at the highest price point and the lowest manufacturing cost. You incur losses if the price is too high, which causes sales to drop off sharply, or when you have a saturated market, which means you sell fewer units regardless of the price.

Designing visualizations to show sensitivity on CDDs is a great *research project* for human factors people, especially those looking to leverage their data visualization expertise into studying and improving decision visualization.

Uncertainty and Risk

One more time for the people in the back: there are no perfect data sources, datasets, models, or human expert judgments. Every CDD includes elements of concern and implicit or explicit uncertainty. This process makes the most important concerns and uncertainties explicit and records them so that you can assess and manage the risks they impose on your decision. Determining what is "most important" is a judgment call.

Donald Rumsfeld, a former US secretary of defense, once wrote of military strategy (*https://oreil.ly/Lsoww*) that "there are known knowns; there are things we know we know. We also know there are known unknowns ... things we do not know. But there are also unknown unknowns—the ones we don't know we don't know," as illustrated in Figure 6-2.

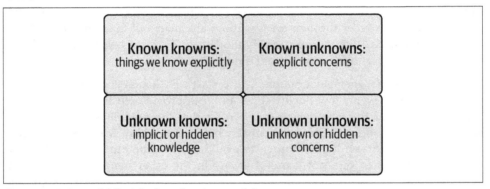

Figure 6-2. Rumsfeld's risk classification model.

Let's look at how DI addresses these four quadrants:

Known knowns
> During Decision Framing and Design, we surface knowledge from as broad a group of people as possible and integrate it into a single picture of the decision, which is the CDD, which shows all the elements that are known by the people who contributed to it. These elements are the *known knowns*.

Known unknowns
> An external whose value you don't know is the most representative *known unknown*. You've identified that a value is needed, but you have some or complete uncertainty as to its value.

Unknown knowns

Part of the art of elicitation is surfacing the *unknown knowns*: decision elements that are not top of mind for people but that can be elicited with enough brainstorming. Another kind of unknown known is an element that is unknown to one group of people but known by the larger group of people who contribute to the decision model. For example, when we worked with sweet potato growers, our plant pathology expert didn't just walk to a whiteboard and write down the missing functions for the CDD in Figure 4-4. We elicited it one piece at a time, thinking about ranges and narrowing them down, to document as many decision elements as possible, thereby reducing the number of unknown knowns.

Unknown unknowns

Unknown unknowns are elements in the world that affect your decision outcomes, but which you don't know. They are the essence of the difference between your model and reality: the more unknown unknowns, the lower the fidelity of your model to the real world. We gave an example of unknown unknowns in Chapter 4, where we discussed the toilet paper industry basing its annual predictions on data before the Covid-19 pandemic: the idea of a pandemic as an important external was not on anyone's mind, but it had a big impact on consumers' panic buying of toilet paper.

Decision Assessment focuses on the known unknowns, like risk, and also helps us to assess the model through a series of decision lenses that help us to convert unknowns into knowns.

To understand the relationship between sensitivity and risk, please take a look again at Figure 5-11, which showed a big oscillation in the profit outcome based on particular choices made about its sales price, marketing spend, and the size of the production run. Let's assume that, as previously described, we don't know any specific statistics representing uncertainty in the various model elements, but we do have reason to believe that the model has some uncertainty and lack of fidelity here and there.

Figure 6-3 shows an analysis of some specific numbers associated with that graph. Here, the big swings in profit representing sensitivity translate into risk: if we make a choice in the region labeled "Risk interval around maximum profit" and we're even a little bit wrong, we could go from a big upside of $1.4 million to a big loss. We can steer clear of this risk by making a choice with a lower downside, but it also has a lower upside (one of the choice combinations in the region labeled "Risk interval around second-highest profit"). Although a complete discussion of mathematical approaches to modeling risks and upsides in complex decisions is outside the scope of this book, you can see that these kinds of visual models do help to communicate the pros and cons of making high-stakes decisions.

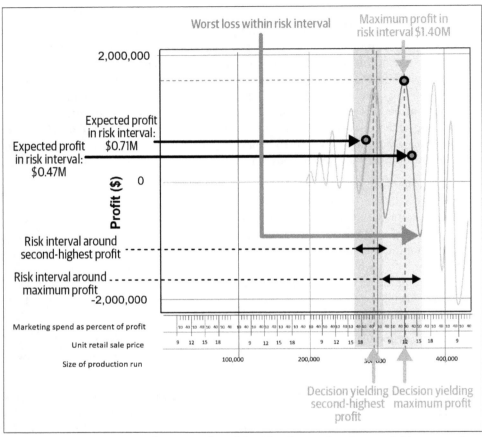

Figure 6-3. Sensitivity translates to risk and upside when a decision model is uncertain.

Provenance

Provenance is the degree to which you trust an asset or DI model because you trust its parts, or the people or methods that created it. Provenance applies to decision models as a whole, and to dependency calculations, submodels, and externals. In general, better provenance translates into decreased uncertainty, as we describe next.

Material from refereed journals has strong provenance. A weather report from the National Weather Service has a stronger provenance than the data from your 14-year-old niece's rooftop weather station. If you read a claim on Twitter that an uprising has just begun in Iran, its provenance is weaker than if you hear the same claim from the US State Department. Or is it? Maybe you disagree with this third statement. When we lack ways to verify what we are told, what constitutes better or worse provenance is often a matter of opinion.

You don't need to do provenance assessment if you have an objective way of assessing accuracy. If you can see a funnel cloud, you don't need a tornado warning from the National Weather Service to know that you should take cover. Maybe your cousin in Iran is calling you from the street to tell you what's going on! Historically, assessing the veracity of sources—and hence the provenance of claims about the world—is the domain of journalists and intelligence professionals.

As you assess each source's provenance, we recommend being transparent and flexible. A good decision modeler is clear about their degree of trust—or lack thereof—in the decision model and its parts, especially those to which the outcome or objective is sensitive.

You might find that some of your information conflicts. If you have information such as dependency models, externals, or submodels from multiple credible sources, what should you do if those sources differ? Be flexible: give your decision customer a chance to select which sources the model uses. (You can see this done in coauthor Pratt's *Book TV* appearance on C-SPAN (*https://oreil.ly/4KHWF*), around minute 19:20).

Investigating methods for assessing, displaying, and using provenance in decision models is a great *research opportunity* for journalists, intelligence professionals, and data scientists.

Fidelity

Fidelity means the degree to which your model and reality match. A model that perfectly matches reality will—by definition—produce good decisions. But the opposite isn't true: as we noted earlier in this chapter, a decision model can have low fidelity and still reliably lead to accurate decisions.

Like all of the assessment methods described here, you can assess fidelity—at least in part—through inspection. Does the simulation change the way that you think reality operates?

If all you have is a CDD, you can use it to guide a conversation about fidelity, to keep everyone on the same page. This is especially helpful if your model has too many elements for everyone to reliably track.

Part of this will involve assessing the *graph topology*—this is what's connected to what in your CDD (see Process B1, Decision Design, in Chapter 3). This will include debugging problems with correlation versus causation.

Consensus

Don't overlook simple consensus as an important source of information for assessing your model. If you present your CDD to the board of directors and everyone says,

"Nope, that's not correct at all," that's a consensus that the model is a failure, even without specific statements about provenance, accuracy, or fidelity. Conversely, even if you haven't looked through any of the other assessment lenses yet, if lots of human beings say it's a great model, that's evidence that it might be.

That being said, consensus is imperfect: there is such a thing as groupthink. There is collective bias, especially confirmation bias. The board of directors could be in denial about a problem, or the right conclusion could be totally counterintuitive! For this reason, we recommend that consensus should not be your only lens. Also, consensus among diverse groups who have not previously communicated much has more value than consensus among homogenous groups.

As with the other assessment lenses, consensus can apply to the model as a whole or to parts of it, and can be based on a CDD or a simulation. This is an important *research opportunity* for those in the social sciences who are interested in DI.

Timing

Sometimes there is a risk to not making a decision at the right time. If you want to be the first to market with a new product, you can't wait too long or someone will beat you to market.

Likewise, some lever choices require action in a specific time frame: a sweet potato grower must spray for nematodes after the soil thaws and before planting. Other lever choices have greater value within a particular time frame, like releasing a new toy in time for Christmas. Delaying some decision choices can have a cost: if a building manager waits another year to replace an obsolete plumbing system, another year's worth of high maintenance and repair costs will accrue.

Some lever choices are "one-time" choices that you can't modify after you take action: once you start to scramble an egg, you can't start over and cook it sunny-side up. Others can be partially modified over time: you can add a little salt to the egg as you cook it, then add more at the table if that wasn't enough.

Many decisions include both one-time and modifiable lever choices. You can manage the timing risk of these decisions by letting the one-time choices drive when you take action—so you can take action in the optimal time frame—and monitoring the decision (see Chapter 7) over time and adjusting the modifiable choices as needed. It's better to have a lever that you can reverse if things start to go awry during execution.

Try It Yourself: Decision Assessment for the Telecom Use Case

In Chapter 5, you built a small qualitative simulation for the telecom use case. In this section, you will complete a brief decision assessment for that use case.

After running your simulation several times, you review the results with your team. Three things are very clear:

- If your competitor launches a plan before you do, you will lose customers.
- If you launch a plan before your competitor, you will gain customers.
- If you both launch at about the same time, you will be in a marketing competition with your competitor—and you can win.

The team concludes that timing and urgency pose considerable risk to your decision.

Do you agree that there is an urgency risk?

Next, you look at your levers to see which choices are modifiable:

Choose unlimited plan
    A one-time choice.

Marketing/advertising
    Modifiable many times as the decision rolls out.

Pricing
    Modifiable, but there will be a cost if you don't have the right pricing at launch.

Invest in call center training
    Partially modifiable. You can't "untrain" workers, but you can train them incrementally.

Invest in more call center personnel
    Partially modifiable. If you hire too many people, layoffs are costly, but you can hire incrementally.

Did you correctly identify the modifiable lever choices?

Exercise

Before you continue reading, open Phase C, Worksheet 2: Decision Assessment Register, available in the supplemental materials repository (*https://oreil.ly/DIH-supplemental*). Identify one or two elements (including dependency calculations) that you think are going to cause the greatest problems with model fidelity. Also identify one or two elements that you think volume and/or profit are most sensitive to. Generally, the combination of lack of fidelity or uncertainty with sensitivity to the things you have uncertainty about indicates a place to look for risk or upside opportunities. What are the possible upside opportunities? If you have identified risks, how will you manage them?

Looking at the CDD with "fresh eyes," you realize that volume depends on competitor behavior (things like competitor pricing and marketing) and on the wider economy (things like inflation and unemployment), as well as on pricing and marketing. (This is normal. When you take another look at a CDD, you will often see ways to improve it.) You also realize that both competitor behavior and macroeconomics are hard to model at high fidelity. How pricing, marketing, the economy, and competitors' behavior all affect volume is a web of complicated relationships. Your decision is urgent because your competitor might be making launch plans. How much modeling is enough?

To answer that question, your team examines the model with an eye toward sensitivity. You look at historical information for all your products about sales volume versus pricing, competitor pricing, and marketing. You find that in the short term marketing attracts customers, but over the long term, lower prices and especially lower prices than your competitor help you both attract and retain customers. Given this information, you decide that volume is especially sensitive to your choice of pricing. This choice is modifiable, but it would be costly to fix it after the launch.

You decide to brainstorm about how to improve the parts of your model that depend on pricing. Several ideas emerge:

- Use a pricing dataset from another product—one that your team believes is similar to this one—in the simulation.

- Suggest that Dr. Smith make an intuitive choice on pricing and use that choice in the simulation.

- Find out whether (and how soon) your competitor plans to launch a competing product and at what price. Use competitor pricing information to help you determine your pricing.

- Build an ML model for pricing.
- Do additional simulations to see how sensitive sales volume is to pricing.
- Use the Delphi method to discuss pricing with some internal experts.

Your team now analyzes the brainstorming results. You agree that an evidence-based approach would be optimal. You could estimate a price-to-sales-volume function from the dataset. You could even build an ML model and use it to test how sensitive sales volume would be to price versus to marketing/advertising spend and the externals.

When you ask your company's competitive-research expert if she has information available about the competitor's plans, she tells you no: they're being very tight-lipped at the moment. That worries you: maybe they're planning a launch, too! This increases your sense of urgency.

You now have two risks/upsides:

- You have a lot of uncertainty about whether your competitor will launch an unlimited plan and, if so, what their pricing will be. There is a risk that they will launch before you and an upside if you launch before they do or launch if they don't.
- Your sales volume is sensitive to price. There is an upside if you hit the right price—and a risk of lower volume if you don't.

Your team decides that the upside of launching quickly is more important than the risk of launching at the wrong price. You decide this is not the right time to build a higher-fidelity pricing model. Instead, you identify three internal people with pricing experience. You realize that using the Delphi method with them would be much faster than running additional simulations and could provide some risk mitigation as well. Your team decides to recommend a collaborative, intuitive approach, using the Delphi method with Dr. Smith and several pricing experts to develop a pricing candidate and assess its risk.

As you assess, you also identify ways to manage any risks you identify. Some of these recommendations concern things you can manage before you make the decision; others you'll need to monitor after you make the decision. You record them all, along with the other information you have discovered during Decision Assessment, on the Decision Assessment Register, as shown in "Sample Decision Assessment Register for Unlimited Usage Plan."

Sample Decision Assessment Register for Unlimited Usage Plan

Decision Assessment Register for CDD: Unlimited Usage Plan
Decision urgency/timing risk: High
• If competitor launches a plan before we do, we will lose customers. • If we launch a plan before they do, we gain customers. • If we both launch at about the same time, we will be in a marketing competition that we can win.
Lever choice modifiability and approach:
• *Choose unlimited plan:* This is a one-time choice. Although we could test it on a sample of customers or in one region, that would take time, and our timing risk is high. • *Marketing/advertising:* Modifiable many times as the decision rolls out. • *Pricing:* Modifiable, but there will be a cost if we don't have the right pricing at launch. An evidence-based approach would be optimal but may take too long. Recommend a collaborative, intuitive approach, such as using the Delphi method with Dr. Smith and several pricing experts to set a price. • *Invest in call center training:* Partially modifiable. We can't "untrain" people, but we can train them incrementally. • *Invest in more call center personnel:* Partially modifiable. If we overhire, layoffs are costly, but we can hire incrementally.
Sensitivity:
• Volume (customers gained/lost) is sensitive to whether our competitor launches a plan before us and how aggressively they market it. • Volume is also sensitive to pricing.

Elements Assessed and Recommendations		
Decision element	**Assessment**	**Recommendations**
Lever: Choose unlimited plan	Volume is sensitive to the timing of the choice. If we launch a plan after the competition launches one, we will lose customers.	• Consider the time value of the decision in assessing other elements. • Once we decide to launch, we need to continue to watch our competitor and react if they also launch.
Causal chains that start with price	There is considerable uncertainty in the pricing model. However, there is a time cost to creating a better model. Incurring this time delay could put us behind our competitor in launching the plan.	• Use the Delphi method to evaluate the price with our experts. • If our competitor launches a plan, monitor their prices closely and adjust ours.

Exercise

Did you identify pricing as one of the biggest risks? How did you recommend managing it?

After a brief Delphi method session (see Chapter 5) to find a pricing choice, your decision maker, Dr. Smith, will be ready to take action. Then your team will be ready to start Phase D: Decision Action.

Conclusion

Before you began the Decision Assessment process, you built a CDD and added to its value by identifying data and knowledge assets to show how the actions and externals lead to outcomes. You used those assets to add further value by simulating the CDD—possibly only in your head—with a qualitative simulation like the telecom use case example, a low-fidelity quantitative simulation like the facilities management example, or a high-fidelity quantitative simulation like the puzzle toy use case. Then you stepped back to do a Decision Assessment. You looked at your decision model through one or more lenses to determine its attributes like sensitivity, accuracy, and risk. Based on your assessment, you may decide you need to return to a prior chapter to do more modeling, find better data, models, or knowledge, or perform further simulations. Or you may be ready to take action. If so, then we'll see you in Chapter 7.

Decision Action

Digital transformation has modernized how data is employed, as witnessed by the increase of intelligent tools designed to assist us in processing and harnessing the power of data. Yet this technology remains in the hands of a few. We won't see the full democratization of the power of data until decision intelligence (DI) is readily available. DI will help decision makers to transform their data so that they can consume it effectively, both to help them make decisions in the first place and then to help to monitor those decisions as they play out in reality, to ensure that predicted decision outcomes materialize as desired.

—Teasha Cable, CEO and cofounder, CModel

So far, you've framed your decision, assembled experts to help you to model it, and created a CDD. You might also have built some software to simulate the CDD, using some preexisting data, knowledge, models, or other assets. These *decision artifacts* have been used in *Decision Reasoning*, and you've decided what action(s) to take. Now it's time to take action. Welcome to the *Decision Action* phase.

Now, how you go about taking action is outside the scope of this book. So the sole process here in Decision Action is about how you will use the assets created earlier to monitor the decision as it plays out. In particular, your decision model isn't just for making a decision. It provides a more sophisticated framework that builds on KPIs to track how the action corresponding to your decision plays out over time. This way, you can use data to *monitor* the decisions that you make—and if you receive evidence of a discrepancy between what's happening now and your original decision, then the decision model gives you two things: (1) a mechanism to go upstream from a KPI that's "off the rails" to determine what action you took led to it—this is root-cause analysis (*https://oreil.ly/irOaJ*) using a decision model—and (2) a system that helps you choose the best corrective action (using your decision model to reconsider your choice given what you've learned). This is, in a sense, a "perfect marriage" of data science (which includes collecting, preparing, and modeling data) and DI, which helps you to prioritize data monitoring and understand the implications of the data you gather.

In this chapter, we'll examine Phase D, Decision Action, and its single process, Decision Monitoring. After going over some basics, we'll present the formal process description, walk you through some of its finer points, and then look at a few case studies, including one that allows you to try it yourself. If you need a refresher on levers, outcomes, objectives, externals, and the other decision elements, we suggest you look back at Chapter 3 before reading on.

Decision Action Phase Overview

Phase D, Decision Action, starts when you select one or more lever choices from your CDD and take action corresponding to it. This phase has just one process: Process D1, Decision Monitoring. Decision Monitoring covers making sure your decision is on track, making adjustments as needed, and knowing when the decision has become obsolete. During Process D1, Decision Monitoring, you track the results of your decision to see how your predictions play out. This includes monitoring not just outcomes but also intermediates, which sometimes act as leading indicators that can provide early warning of an impending disaster. Figure 7-1 shows the Decision Action phase in the context of the other process phases.

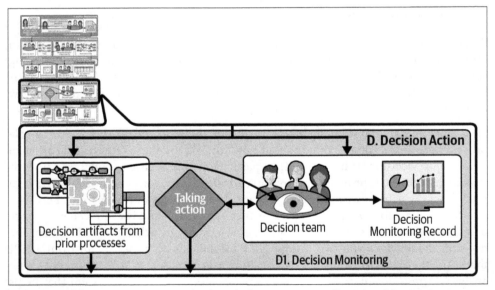

Figure 7-1. The Decision Action phase includes one process: Decision Monitoring.

Decision Monitoring continues until either the decision is complete or you find a problem. You can consider the decision to be complete at the end of the time frame for your decision objectives. If you find a problem with the decision, you'll loop back to revisit it.

Decision Monitoring is one of several DI phases where you can find and debug decision problems. Process B1, Decision Design, was your first chance to improve your decision. You then did some more debugging in Process C1, Decision Simulation. Decision Action is a single-process phase that gives you yet a third chance to head off disasters (and maximize benefits).

Process D1: Decision Monitoring

During Process C1, Decision Simulation, you made certain assumptions and/or predictions about intermediates and externals, like how they would behave and what ranges you could expect for certain numerical values. Your assumptions and predictions will almost certainly be wrong a lot of the time. But how wrong is wrong enough that you need to reconsider your decision? In this process, you'll track intermediates and externals to detect if they are drifting so far from their expected values that you need to reconsider your decision. You'll record your findings in a Decision Monitoring Record to help you spot patterns over time.

According to the Gartner Group (*https://oreil.ly/21c-A*), "Leading indicators are a defined set of metrics that are predictive of financial or other desired outcomes." In a decision model, a leading indicator can be an intermediate or an external, because they are causally upstream of—and therefore happen before—outcomes. One of the great benefits of a decision model is that it helps you to think in a structured way about these leading indicators so that you can detect problems long before changes to outcomes become visible: they can warn if the decision is going off track.

Examples of leading indicators that are externals are customer behavior, competitor behavior, the macro economy, and climate. These externals can change over time in ways that violate your assumptions and predictions. And these unexpected values for externals can put your outcomes at risk.

This process shows how to *decide what to monitor*, and what kinds of corrective actions you can take to head off impending problems, like updating the decision model or investigating new scenarios using the values you're observing in the real world. It also covers monitoring and updating repeated decisions to reflect current realities and identify obsolete decisions.

While monitoring key organizational data provides situational awareness, monitoring through a causal lens provides more. Annotating CDDs with data/models/knowledge sources and causal links ties data to the business dependencies that drive outcomes. Monitoring a decision element not only gives you information about that element, it also lets you see how changes to that element affect outcomes (through downstream causal chains) and can support root-cause analysis (through upstream ones). If you have a simulation of the path from the element to an outcome, you can use the CDD to assess how changes to that element will affect your outcome.

Note that this process is not about *how* to monitor. Every organization has its own processes and instrumentation for monitoring information of interest, especially dashboard tools like PowerBI, Tableau, Pyramid, and Qlik. There are so many great methods and approaches for this kind of monitoring that covering them is beyond the scope of this book. Indeed, the actual monitoring work will often be done by a resource outside the decision team like operations or IT. Instead, this chapter focuses on two things: first, using your CDD, simulation results, and assessments to decide *what* to monitor; and second, how to use that monitoring data.

Unlike many other DI processes, Decision Monitoring may occur over a substantial time period: the life of the decision until you either complete or modify the decision action. For decisions where results of an action play out over a long time period, you will monitor leading indicators and externals until you can measure the final outcomes. During the monitoring period, you may need to revisit the decision and revise your actions based on your monitoring.

Many decisions—especially operational decisions like pricing and marketing spend—occur repeatedly. For such decisions, Decision Monitoring is part of a decision maintenance cycle that begins when you complete your first CDD and act based on your initial assumptions. Then you monitor the values of intermediates and externals and adjust your actions and the CDD as needed. CDDs for repeated decisions are long-term organizational assets.

So, when do you decide what to monitor, and when do you start monitoring? In many organizations, a monitoring system is already in place, in the form of a BI dashboard. Process C2, Decision Assessment, lets you bring a deeper analysis to such a monitoring program (or to a new decision whose values you haven't monitored before on a dashboard), by identifying the intermediates and externals to which the outcome(s) are most sensitive. As part of that process, you may have noted some of these as monitoring candidates. If not, you should identify what to monitor before or immediately after you act so that you can begin monitoring right away.

Formal Process Description: Process D1, Decision Monitoring

Description

Monitor and modify the decision as it plays out over time. The amount of time depends on how long it takes to complete the decision action(s) and measure the outcome(s). This can be anywhere from a few days to a few years.

Prerequisites
- You (or the decision maker) have decided what actions to take. You may be ready to act or you may have already taken action.
- You have determined the appropriate scope and amount of time and/or effort to dedicate to this process.
- You have agreed that this decision is worth monitoring.

Responsible role
Decision team leader

Steps
1. Read through this process and tailor it, as appropriate, to your situation.
2. Before or immediately after taking decision action, determine which decision elements you will monitor or measure, and at what time intervals. These include actions, intermediates, externals, and outcomes (for repeated decisions).
3. Use the sensitivity analysis methods described in previous chapters to determine, as you see fit, the values of externals and/or intermediates that are far enough away from your assumptions that they should trigger a reexamination of your decision (the "safe" versus "not safe" boundary).
4. As the decision plays out over time:
   - Monitor decision elements as determined in step 2.
   - If the measurements produce values outside of the acceptable range, determine the root cause(s).
   - Take corrective action as needed: this could include revisiting any of the prior process steps. (See the section "When Do You Need to Revisit Your Decision?" on page 194.)
   - Recommend process improvements as needed.
   - Update decision documents and decision assets as needed.
5. Record your Decision Monitoring work on Phase D, Worksheet 1, Decision Monitoring Record.

Deliverables
- Corrective actions, if needed
- Process-improvement recommendations, if needed
- Updates to decision documents and decision assets, if needed
- Entries in the Decision Monitoring Record

When Is a Monitored Value Wrong Enough to Matter?

We promise: your intermediates and externals will rarely exactly match what you thought they were going to be when you built your model. But the failure to match exactly won't always be enough to merit reconsidering your decision. So "how wrong is wrong enough" to reconsider?

As you assessed sensitivity and uncertainty during Decision Assessment in Chapter 6, we described how you might identify "safe values" for externals and intermediates: that is, the values that you believe will lead to the outcomes you predicted from your chosen actions. For instance, during Decision Design, you might have assumed that your customers' price was between $4 and $6. If you learn that actual price is outside this range, that merits revisiting the decision.

The "safe values" are also important information to monitor. You might build a dashboard that uses a gauge to monitor a specific external, with green, amber, and red zones to indicate if the external's value is drifting away from your safe area. Connect it to a real-time data source, and you have a mechanism for tracking your decision execution that is well grounded in the best understanding that you and your team have of the situation.

For instance, in the decision about travel policies for net-zero GHG emissions, you might want to set "safe zones" on intermediates you will monitor, such as the average number of conferences each employee attends, their ratio of economy to business-class flights, and dollars the organization spends on carbon sequestration. You might calculate the values of those intermediates that lead to outcomes that cross a line from what you consider a "good" to a "bad" outcome. If intermediate values go outside of these "safe zone" ranges, it's time to revisit the decision. A more sophisticated treatment of "safe zone" calculations for intermediates/externals as "leading indicators" of good/bad outcomes is a terrific *research topic*.

More generally, you'll be monitoring intermediates and externals. Their "safe zone" calculation determines what values of that element are OK and what values are cause for concern.

You can determine the "safe zone" by human judgment or by the previously mentioned kind of calculation. If you don't have enough precision in your CDD, you might need to use your judgment. If so, here are some factors you might consider in determining the "safe zone":

- Is this a one-time or repeated value outside of the zone?
- Over time, are the values trending toward the edge of the safe zone? Can you predict in advance that you will cross into it?

- Has the behavior of the element changed over time? For example, were the values earlier clustering around a "good" value and now they are all over the place or clustering around a different value?
- Are the values of downstream elements (those closer to the outcomes) also in the warning-flag range?

What to Monitor

To decide what to monitor, you'll need to consider sensitivity and uncertainty.

During Phase C, Decision Reasoning (Chapters 5 and 6), you experimented with lever choices, externals, intermediates, and dependency calculations and discovered that your outcomes are more sensitive to some changes than to others. You also assessed which elements had the greatest combination of sensitivity and uncertainty.

For example, in the puzzle toy example, we found that the product launch model is very sensitive to pricing (a lever choice), and that unit price drives sales volume. All other things being equal, your best candidates for leading indicators are intermediates that depend on the most sensitive lever choices and externals, and intermediates on the most sensitive causal chains. In the puzzle toy example, volume would be a good candidate for monitoring because it lies along the most sensitive causal chain.

Based on these considerations, you'll probably want to select a subset of your CDD to monitor: perhaps one or two externals and one intermediate. Here are four ways you can use data to enhance Decision Monitoring:

Measure an external.
As you begin implementing the action, you might choose to set up a mechanism to measure a specific external. You might track, for instance, a competitor's price through an API or a typical customer's perceived value for your product through market research. Or if you're looking for a new job in a certain position, you might track average salaries for that job position.

But just monitoring an external requires that human eyes know what to check for to know that it needs attention. For this reason, you'll probably want to take the next step:

Add a test onto the external to detect when it's outside the "safe zone."
This is especially helpful if there are too many externals to monitor with human eyeballs, if you think the external is changeable or uncertain, if the "safe" versus "not safe" range has complex dependencies on other externals, and/or if the decision outcome is highly sensitive to this external.

In our job hunting example, you might set the "safe" versus "not safe" threshold at 10% higher than your current salary. As long as the job pays at least 10% more, you won't change your strategy to find a new job with that title. But if the salaries change such that you won't make more than 10% more in the new position, then you want to be alerted so you can reconsider your decision to try to change jobs.

Track an external that makes a prediction.

Time-based weather prediction is a good example of an external that makes a prediction. You might want to keep updating the forecast for the next two weeks as time moves forward. For example, in the sweet potato model we described in Chapter 4, soil temperature is a key factor that changes the efficacy of fumigant nematicides: if it gets too hot, your fumigant evaporates before it can control the pests. (That, in turn, decreases the quality of the sweet potatoes and thus their selling price.) So you might choose to monitor predictions of soil temperature closely during the fumigant activity period so that, if the predicted soil temperature goes out of the "safe" bounds, you can reconsider your decision.

Monitor intermediates for changes that could be leading indicators of a problem.

Measuring an intermediate as your actions play out can provide an early warning that a decision's implementation is drifting away from its intended outcome(s). The sweet potato CDD includes, for example, an intermediate representing nematode level in the soil after the crop is harvested in the fall of the first year. You can compare this level to what was expected when you made your year-1 nematode treatment. If it's too far from what was expected, then you probably want to reconsider your decision about what to do about the nematodes in year 2.

When Do You Need to Revisit Your Decision?

If your intermediates or externals leave their "safe" ranges, then it's time to revisit the "decide" phase of the OODA loop (introduced in Chapter 3).

Update your CDD with any new understanding of the situation that you've gained from monitoring, and return to your team. After quickly revisiting your framing materials to ensure that you're still on the same page, you'll probably want to return to Phase B, Decision Modeling.

As you revisit the decision after a reset, you might correct external values (such as the price in the previous example) and add any missing external elements to your CDD (such as a pandemic that decreases interest in your product). Some of your levers may no longer be levers; because their action has already occurred, they will now be externals. You might also realize that a feedback loop is leading to an emergent behavior you hadn't expected, or decide that one of your link computations could have higher fidelity. In response, you might change a lever setting, remove a lever, or add a new lever. If needed, you could simulate your decision again with the new settings, then move on, taking action again with a new time frame.

Decision Monitoring Records

This section focuses on what to record during Decision Monitoring and how to use that recorded information. We do not discuss how to set up data monitoring systems, which is outside the scope of this book. Many organizations already have monitoring tools and processes. If your organization has not yet started to track data using computer tools, then companies like Astral Insights (*https://oreil.ly/lwYs6*) and Pyramid Analytics (*https://oreil.ly/wvxkL*) can help you get started organizing your data so that it will support your DI work. If you're working mostly with pencil and paper or with spreadsheets, then you can find a blank version of Phase D, Worksheet 1, Decision Monitoring Record, in the supplemental materials repository (*https://oreil.ly/DIH-supplemental*) to get you started with recording your Decision Monitoring results (see "Phase D, Worksheet 1: Decision Monitoring Record for the Unlimited Usage Plan" for an example).

You need three types of information about each decision element you're monitoring:

"Safe" range
> First, you need the element's "safe" range: the range of values for this element that you need to achieve your outcomes. You discovered or estimated these values during Decision Simulation in Chapter 5. If you did a simple simulation by hand, these are the values you used or assumed. If you automated your simulation, then you will have a lot more information. In addition to a "safe" range, you might also create a "warning" range to indicate values you should start tracking more frequently. In the job search example, for instance, your "warning" threshold may be when the salary for the job you're seeking drops below 15% higher than your current salary. You might not want to take action right away when that value is between 15% and 10% higher, but it's a good idea to pay closer attention.

Current value
> Second, you need the decision element's current value so you can determine if it is within your "safe" or "warning" ranges.

History
> Third, if you keep a history of the element's values over time, you can mine it for patterns in the future. This important decision asset can improve your simulations for future decisions by creating better predictions, dependencies, and other model elements.

Silos, Whack-a-Mole, and the Measurement Effect

Let's face it, adding measurements and data isn't always a good thing. How would you feel if your job performance rating incorporated 10 new measurements every month? But wait, it gets worse: what if the only way you could achieve your numbers was if someone in another department could *not* achieve theirs? As you might imagine, this zero-sum game wouldn't be a great recipe for success. Yet, as more organizations use data to guide their management, it's a risk.

This problem isn't limited to corporate settings. In his groundbreaking book *Team of Teams,* General Stanley McChrystal, who led US forces in the 2003 invasion of Iraq, explains that, to succeed in a unique battlefield situation, he had to turn old habits inside out.[1] Military teams had maximized their *within-team* performance—their ability to work together—but had ignored *between-team* interfaces, the ways different teams connect (or fail to connect). Outside of the military, similarly, there are often *silos*—groups, teams, or departments with their own data, processes, organizational culture, KPIs, and incentives. McChrystal observed, in particular, that whatever efficiencies are gained within silos are outweighed by the consequences of interface failures, or those times when teams fail to connect and align their objectives.

When midlevel managers create CDDs, the outcomes they choose often reflect the KPIs for the managers in the room, with outcomes from other silos appearing as externals. The facilities management example from Chapter 5 is a great example of this. If multiple departments work as one to maintain CDDs, they are more likely to align their objectives and incentives.

While many organizations believe that their KPIs and related incentives are causally linked to organizational outcomes like profit, few have actually drawn the causal chains to assess these connections. Without doing that, it's easy to establish KPIs that have unintended consequences, or whose objectives conflict with each other or with organizational objectives. Remember, these KPIs drive bonuses, raises, and promotions. Some sort of analysis method is essential to fix these problems within the complexity of modern organizations. DI provides a solution.

As you assess and simulate interacting CDDs from multiple departments, you might find that there is no possible situation in which every manager can achieve their objectives. This creates a conflict between them. Running the simulation sometimes helps generate ideas for resolving that conflict. Aligning everyone's goals and making success possible for everyone increases the likelihood that everyone will work together and that, as the decision plays out over time, if measurements on dependencies indicate a problem, that the team will problem-solve to achieve a common set of objectives.

If you don't fix conflicts like this, in contrast, people will compete to make sure they are the ones who meet their objectives and collect their incentives. That's how the very act of measurement can spark unintended consequences and undesirable behaviors.

---

1 Stanley McChrystal, Tantum Collins, David Silverman, and Chris Fussell, *Team of Teams: New Rules of Engagement for a Complex World* (New York: Penguin, 2015).

Case Study: Network Upgrade: When the Decision Is Already Off the Rails

Here's an example of an early, very complex DI project that generated big cost savings for one of the largest companies in the world.

A European company decided to upgrade its telephone systems. These systems connected more than 10,000 distinct business locations in over 50 countries, from simple offices to large office towers and call centers. The company had grown organically as well as through mergers and acquisitions, so the existing network was a patchwork of systems. Some were aging, others were up-to-date. The company's supply chains had become overly complex, and it maintained more than three hundred different service agreements with vendors. There was considerable duplication, with multiple contracts from multiple suppliers, local and global, providing the same services to the same locations. These inefficiencies were expensive, and new telephone technology would be much cheaper, so it was easy to justify the cost of upgrading this mess.

The company assembled some of its best staff and equipped them with best-in-class project management and business process tools. Their remit was to plan and run a successful program to upgrade each of the ten thousand business locations to the new technology and renegotiate service contracts along the way.

One year later, the program was on the rocks. Fewer than half of the attempted site upgrades had succeeded, because resources were not available at the needed times.

The company decided to try a DI approach. Upon creating a CDD, the DI team learned about several important things affecting the program:

Finite resources

> The team's decisions about timing and resourcing for each site-transformation project were changing resource availability and contracting, creating externals that could affect every other site.

Legacy infrastructure

> Several complex externals were driven by the preexisting network infrastructure. Sites' equipment and contracts overlapped in every possible way. For example, the contracts were written such that if one site wanted to decommission an expensive shared asset, there would be no cost savings until *all* sites using that same asset were converted. If they failed to decommission even one last tiny site that was using such a shared asset, they effectively postponed substantial cost savings.

Interacting rules and constraints

> Using shared equipment and contracts imposed rules and constraints on how the upgrade could take place at each site—anywhere from a dozen or so rules for a small site to hundreds for a complex site. For example, sites needed to

be upgraded before any outstanding contracts expired. And if a site provided network capacity to a downstream site, it had to be upgraded before the sites that depended on it. All these rules and constraints interacted to form causal chains so complex that not even the best managers could hold it all in their heads. It surfaced that almost all the early failures had occurred because a rule or constraint had not been satisfied in time. Therefore, much of our work was aimed at monitoring the decision elements that were constrained and using "safe zones" to detect risks. See Figure 7-2.

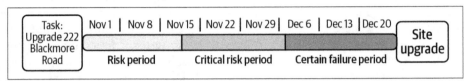

Figure 7-2. Monitoring display showing "over the horizon" risks for telephone infra-structure upgrades.

Faulty assumptions about ROI

The top-level decision also had a problem. The decision had a measurable outcome with the following objective: the network's return on investment (ROI) at the end of the project should exceed the previous year's ROI by a specified amount. However, there were no causal chains with intermediates to connect the "initiate project" lever to the outcome. The project team had made an untested assumption that ROI would steadily improve as sites were upgraded. It did not, for two reasons.

First, the complex interactions previously described meant that the project wouldn't realize its financial benefit until late in the timeline, after lots of money was spent on upgrades. Second, the project team had created an incentive system that favored upgrading the easiest sites first—but this strategy produced the least benefit to ROI.

The DI team created a CDD to capture this complexity and to help team members from diverse departments gain a shared understanding of what was going on. They tracked intermediates from the CDD as leading indicators, then used them to build a simulation for decision making. Every few days, they input new data from all of the sites, which changed all the externals. Then they used the resulting simulation findings as they planned the next set of transformations.

The CDD showed a high sensitivity to sites being transformed on time successfully, so the team focused on that. The simulator also tracked all causal chains representing upstream requirements that had to be satisfied before the upgrade. It combined this information with human expertise to calculate an "over the horizon" risk for each site: if the prerequisites were not completed by a certain date, the site risked being delayed, up to a threshold date where, if a given prerequisite was not done, then the upgrade would definitely be late (Figure 7-2). Typically, once DI has identified the elements to be monitored, there are systems in place to do the monitoring and reporting. However, in this case the DI team was asked to help with monitoring as well.

The CDD analysis further indicated that the following externals were critical in determining whether a particular site would be upgraded on time, and therefore whether ROI would be realized effectively:

- Sites that (a) were "upstream" (scheduled to be upgraded before the target site), (b) were running late, and (c) shared resources with the target site

- Contracts that were due to expire before the target site's upgrade date, and that would be expensive to extend

- Upstream sites that would have to be upgraded before the target site because of a dependency, such as a connecting trunk cable

Identifying and acting on these issues helped get the project on track.

A software tool was essential for this project because it was just too big for unassisted humans: the dependency network was too complex, the data volume was too great, and the decision time frames were too short. The humans still ultimately made the decisions, but the tool helped them understand the implications of their decisions by propagating information between site-upgrade decisions and testing choices against rules and constraints. It would have been very difficult for them to navigate this complex web of contracts, resources, technology connections, and financials without a DI approach.

As this example illustrates, even when Decision Modeling is brought in partway through a project, it can align a team around the causal chains to which the outcome is most sensitive. It can identify which intermediates are the critical leading indicators and support the measurements and monitoring needed to execute the decision effectively. In this case, the DI project was so effective that the company estimated its cost savings at several tens of millions of euros.

This example is not as unusual as it appears. In many organizations, especially those with mature data-driven processes and technology, Decision Monitoring is the entry point for DI. These organizations have a robust infrastructure for recording, monitoring, displaying, and analyzing data. But without DI, that data is not connected to organizational outcomes. When a monitored value like "number of sites successfully upgraded" is out of its "safe" zone, there is nothing to connect that value to either outcomes and objectives like "X% better ROI than the prior year" or actions like "convert site A before site B." It is at times like this that a CDD is not only helpful, but essential for success. The company in this example valued the CDD alone at over six million euros because it showed chains between corporate silos that affected its ability to complete the project. DI software provided additional value because it pinpointed the risks to intermediates and outcomes like "this upgrade will definitely be late" and suggested optimal actions like "this site can be converted because all its constraints are satisfied."

Try It Yourself: Decision Monitoring for the Unlimited Usage Plan Use Case

In Chapters 5 and 6, you built a small qualitative simulation for this use case and performed a Decision Assessment; now it's time to decide how you'll monitor that decision.

Exercise

Before you continue reading, review the Decision Assessment Register you created at the end of Chapter 6. Choose one or two elements you would want to measure or observe as the decision plays out over time. What values would you consider "safe" for those elements? What values would give you cause for concern?

Dr. Smith, your CEO, makes the final decision: the company will launch an unlimited usage plan. At the next executive meeting, he tells the other executives to commit people and resources to launching the plan. Teams begin preparing marketing and advertising campaigns and start getting ready to hire and train call center employees. He appoints a project manager to work with the executive team to produce Gantt charts, schedules, and project reports.

Your decision team meets to discuss whether decision monitoring is warranted for this decision. Because your model predicts that demand will be sensitive to price, you agree to monitor sales volume every month. You also decide to monitor your competitors' behavior weekly, since you'll lose your advantage if a competitor launches an unlimited plan at the same time as you, or be at a competitive disadvantage if a competitor launches an unlimited plan before you do.

Exercise

What elements did you decide to monitor? Did you focus on the elements that the outcomes are most sensitive to? What did you decide were their "safe" ranges?

Assume that sales are below your estimates. What might you do? Would this change if your competitor launched an unlimited plan?

In month four, the company begins actually selling the new unlimited plan. Sales volume is lower than expected: it consistently averages about 2% below the lowest value your demand model predicted.

Initially, the CEO wants to watch volume without adjusting prices. After a year of sales at this reduced volume, though, he decides he wants to revisit the decision model. He's thinking it's time to raise the price to make up for the reduced volume.

As your decision team reconvenes around your CDD simulation, a member from the competitive tracking team reports that a competitor will be launching its own unlimited plan shortly. You rerun the CDD simulation and it shows that, with your competitor in the mix, a price increase would be a terrible idea. Instead, you recommend increasing the company's investment in marketing. You also resolve to watch the competitor's behavior carefully, since you assess it will have a big impact on your success.

Exercise

What did you decide to do if your sales volume was low? Did you decide to resimulate when the competitor launched their own plan?

Assuming the information from the prior section, fill out Phase D, Worksheet 1: Decision Monitoring Record, available in the supplemental materials repository (*https://oreil.ly/DIH-supplemental*).

You capture this monitoring plan in Phase D, Worksheet 1: Decision Monitoring Record. Note that in most data-driven organizations the actual values from monitoring would be recorded in organizational databases; you would use a form like this to record your evaluation, action(s), process improvements, and artifact updates.

Phase D, Worksheet 1: Decision Monitoring Record for the Unlimited Usage Plan

Decision Monitoring Record for CDD: Unlimited Usage Plan		
List of Decision Elements to Monitor		
Decision element	**Monitoring interval**	**Reason**
Volume (intermediate)	Monthly	In Decision Assessment, we identified a lot of uncertainty in our model that predicts the demand based on the price. Lower volume than expected indicates issues with that model, and we may need to adjust pricing.
Competitor behavior (external)	Weekly	If we detect a competitor's intent to launch an unlimited plan, we may need to accelerate our launch schedule.

Unexpected Measurement Results					
Date	**Volume**	**Evaluation**	**Action**	**Recommended process improvements**	**Decision artifacts and assets updated**
Month 4 (sales begin)	2%	Below expected lowest value	Does not warrant revisiting the decision yet. Continue to monitor.	None	None
Month 5	1%	Below expected lowest value	Does not warrant revisiting the decision yet. Continue to monitor.	None	None
Month 6	3%	Below expected lowest value	Does not warrant revisiting the decision yet. CEO floats the idea of a price increase in month 15.	None	None
Month 12, week 3	N/A (because the issue here is not sales volume but the fact that your competitor is launching)	Your competitive information team discovers that a competitor is planning to launch an unlimited plan in month 15.	Revisit the decision simulation.	None	None
Month 17	2%	Below expected lowest value	Does not warrant revisiting the decision yet. Continue to monitor.	None	None
Month 18	1%	Below expected lowest value	Does not warrant revisiting the decision yet. Continue to monitor.	None	Dataset for demand model

Exercise

Did you record information similar to that in Phase D, Worksheet 1? Specifically, what did you write about evaluation and action? Do you have organizational processes and technology for capturing the data produced by Decision Monitoring?

Do you have an appropriate repository for keeping the evaluation and action information? If not, how would you integrate this activity with your current decision and knowledge management processes?

Conclusion

Decision Monitoring lets you keep your decisions on track to produce the outcomes you need. It takes your BI or other monitoring practice to "the next level." Understanding the causal connections between your KPIs mean you can:

- Reduce your monitoring to the elements that matter most to decision making
- Do root-cause analysis when something goes off track
- Have a principled way to calculate "safe" and "unsafe" ranges of data elements
- "Look around corners" into the future to explore the impact of today's decisions on tomorrow's outcomes, given the data you've gathered so far

In sum, DI monitoring is the "next generation" of existing BI monitoring systems. By pairing it with Decision Review, the topic of Chapter 8, you can enable your organization to continuously improve its decision making.

Decision Review

One of the great benefits of DI is that documenting decisions lets you reuse them and improve them over time. This increases efficiency so much and allows for such continuous improvement that *this benefit alone* justifies the effort of bringing DI into your organization—especially if you'll be making a decision (or similar ones) repeatedly.

Understanding how your experts make decisions is one of the most critical forms of organizational knowledge, so it's a little shocking how rarely organizations document decisions in ways that allow for reuse. A senior Pentagon official in charge of conducting a comprehensive review process every four years once told us, "We throw everything out and start again every time." Another US federal employee told us that their organization doesn't always capture decisions, but if they do, it's in PDF documents, which are very hard to reuse. Imagine if every time Pratt & Whitney built a rocket engine, it threw away its design and relied on engineers' memories to build the next one!

This chapter presents the final DI phase: Phase E, Decision Review. This phase comes after you've taken action based on the decision. Its purpose is to ensure that you learn from the decision-making experience and capture any artifacts you could reuse for later decisions.

You learned in Phase C2, Decision Assessment (Chapter 6), how to assess your decision before taking action, such as applying sensitivity and provenance analysis to the decision artifacts. There you asked, "Do I trust this decision model enough to follow its recommendation, and to move forward into action?" Then, in Chapter 7, you learned how to assess the decision as it plays out in reality: between the action and the outcome. Like these processes, Decision Review also involves assessing the decision, but from a perspective that takes future decisions into account as well.

Unlike the previous processes, you'll be doing elements of this process at the same time as other processes, as we'll describe in more detail.

Coming into this process, you should have a well-documented, well-structured decision with a clear frame, design, and CDD, as well as (potentially) a Decision Monitoring Record documenting data and analytics gathered during Decision Monitoring.

The Decision Review Phase: Overview

This phase includes two processes: Process E1, Decision Artifacts Retention, and Process E2, Decision Retrospective.

In Process E1, Decision Artifacts Retention, you'll curate your decision artifacts, your CDD, and all other documents and decision assets and place them in appropriate repositories for study and reuse.

In Process E2, Decision Retrospective, you'll reflect on and learn from the decision. You'll examine your decision artifacts and ask whether your decision process was sound. Regardless of whether the decision action achieved the outcomes you wanted, you'll determine possible improvements to your process, information, knowledge, and/or model.

In some situations, there is a *ground truth*: that is, eventually you learn what the right decision was (and thus whether or not you made the right choice). Even when there is no ground truth, however, you can still measure the quality of a decision. You can measure decision quality even when there's lots of noise to cut through. You can document experiences when good decisions lead to bad outcomes, and vice versa. We'll discuss how to do all of these measurements. We'll particularly emphasize repeated decisions and the improvement opportunities they present. We'll finish the chapter—and the book—with some reflections on what a mature DI culture looks like, and how to assess your organization's DI adoption and maturity.

Figure 8-1 shows the Decision Review phase in the context of the other process phases.

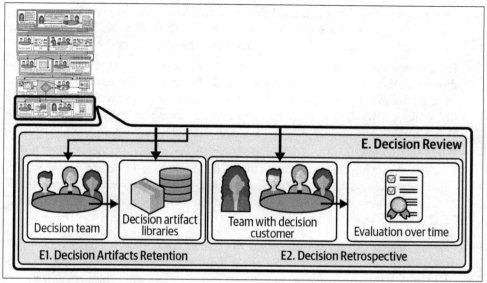

Figure 8-1. The Decision Review phase includes two processes: Decision Artifacts Retention and Decision Retrospective.

Process E1: Decision Artifacts Retention

The primary goal of Decision Artifacts Retention is to create a repository of the connections between organizational data and the business dependencies—the cause-and-effect chains—that drive outcomes. This repository makes it easier for you to model, simulate, optimize, and monitor new one-off decisions, and it drives continuous improvement of repeated decisions. New one-off decisions can often reuse causal chains or parts of causal chains from earlier CDDs. Each additional DI process you complete on a CDD and its causal chains adds reuse value. For example:

- A published CDD (from Process B1, Decision Design) contains causal chains, some of which may be reused for future decisions. The Decision Framing Document (Phase A, Worksheet 2) from Process A2, Decision Framing, also provides context.

- The annotated CDD and Decision Asset Register (Phase B, Worksheet 2) from Process B2, Decision Asset Investigation, shows how data, knowledge, and models inform the business dependencies captured in the causal chains. If you have a data governance lexicon and data dictionary, this process connects your causal chains to them.

- You can reuse simulation code from Phase C, Decision Reasoning, to access data, models, and knowledge, and to calculate each element in a causal chain from prior elements. A Decision Simulation Report (Phase C, Worksheet 1) provides documentation on how you used that code and what you learned from using it. This will help you estimate the code maturity if you want to reuse it and remind you about things like emergent properties that the simulation showed you.

- The Decision Assessment Register (Phase C, Worksheet 2) provides information about a CDD's important properties, causal chains, and elements. These include lever modifiability, outcome sensitivity to certain elements, uncertainty, volatility, and data, knowledge, and model provenance. These help you ascertain each CDD's quality and decide whether parts of one CDD are appropriate for use in another.

- The Decision Monitoring Record (Phase D, Worksheet 1) documents the leading indicators you identified and any unexpected observed values for them. Observed values can suggest useful simulation scenarios when you reuse the CDD (or parts of it).

Like one-off decisions, repeated decisions may incorporate reusable parts from other decisions as well as providing reusable parts. However, certain repeated decisions are especially important: the decisions embedded in your most important organizational business processes. A single decision can be embedded in more than one business process, like a pricing decision model that is helpful for more than one product.

How you build your data artifacts repository depends on how your organization captures data and knowledge. It might already have a document management system or a knowledge management (KM) system you can use (although most KM systems today don't have a structured way of capturing action-to-outcome decision logic). If you're just starting with DI, you might store your decision artifacts—the CDDs you have built and the forms you have filled out as you completed each DI process—on paper or virtual paper, or use spreadsheets to keep track of the artifacts for each decision. You might use views in a relational database or multiple tabs in a spreadsheet to enable you to find artifacts in different ways, like showing all the artifacts for one decision, all the CDDs that show total sales as an outcome, or all the CDDs that use a specific competitor pricing model.

If your organization has or is developing a data governance architecture and a data lexicon, you can integrate your Decision Artifacts Retention with your data governance. At the most mature end of the spectrum, you could create an automated library of CDDs, stored as executable software models, that connect to data assets via your data governance lexicon and data dictionary. Your automated library will work with your data governance system, letting you quickly answer these questions:

- What actions and data drive this outcome (for any outcome in any CDD or business process)?

- What business outcomes depend on this business element?

You might even search your library of assets and decisions using an LLM like ChatGPT that's been fine-tuned for your private data, or with a new generation of semantic search methods.

This is the hallmark of a decision-driven organization: at your greatest decision maturity, you can find the right knowledge and data to inform your decisions and to thereby maximize the likelihood of achieving your desired outcomes.

Legal, Regulatory, and Policy Issues

How and whether some decision artifacts are stored may depend on legal or regulatory requirements or on organizational data retention policies. This is especially true of any artifact that includes financial information, proprietary information, intellectual property (IP), or personally identifiable information (PII). Your business must retain certain tax information for a specific time period. Contracts you sign limit how you can use and disclose a third party's proprietary information or IP, and many governments limit how PII can be used and stored. Regulations and policies may require very secure storage of a decision for a long time, while an anonymized version must be retained for study or reuse.

A number of years ago, one of the authors of this book worked on a decision-improvement project for a national health-care system. The system was concerned about making decisions around sepsis (*https://oreil.ly/Dou_K*), a potentially lethal condition common in hospitalized patients that is much less lethal if caught and treated early.

In this project, the artifacts around each hospital sepsis decision were retained in two sets of repositories in very different ways. First, the decision for a particular patient became part of their medical record, which was stored in a secure national patient-medical-records database, accessible by any doctor treating the patient at any hospital in the country at any time in the future. Second, every sepsis decision also had to be stored in a national decision-improvement database. The records in that database could not contain any PII, but they had to include all the data used to make the decision—including days of recordings from electronic medical monitoring systems. They also included the "ground truth" (whether the patient developed sepsis), nature and timing of treatments, and patient outcome. The purpose of the second repository was to find patterns, develop better sepsis models, and find ways to optimize sepsis decisions nationwide. Separating decision artifacts into two kinds of repositories—one centered around a specific decision, the other for reuse and decision improvement—is common whenever decisions include "sensitive" data, knowledge, or models.

The USDA sweet potato project we mentioned in Chapter 4 has an interesting regulatory twist. Because it is a research project, we learned that asking the growers to use DI tools and provide feedback would be considered "experimentation with human subjects." If we were doing the same thing at a trade show or in a focus group, we would call it "market research." There are few regulations on market research, but because of past abuses (*https://oreil.ly/Lgiap*), there are many regulations on human subjects experimentation. This is another reason to carefully segregate reusable artifacts from this project from those that might contain PII. Your ability to share artifacts with other researchers is limited by the level of informed consent given by the human subjects.

When Should Decision Artifacts Retention Begin and End?

Artifacts retention should begin *immediately* after you make the decision. This ensures that you'll gather up and protect your artifacts before you stop thinking about them. If the decision takes a while to roll out and you haven't begun this process, you may lose track of valuable artifacts while you wait to see your final outcome(s).

It's even better to make artifact retention an ongoing process for the life of the decision. It can start as soon as you create your first artifacts. As soon as you complete the Decision Objective Statement and the Decision Framing Document, store them in the appropriate folders or repositories. Then you'll know where to find them whenever you need them, and you won't need a separate place to keep them while you're completing the other processes.

You can't complete artifact retention until you have completed your Decision Retrospective and Decision Quality Report. This means that, although this process appears later in the book than Process D1, Decision Monitoring (Chapter 7), it will in many cases happen simultaneously. We cover artifact retention at this point in the methodology primarily for pedagogical reasons: there's a natural workflow from the Decision Objective Statement through Decision Monitoring, where each process adds value to your decision making. Discussing artifact retention earlier would disrupt that flow and burden you with one more thing to think about. Therefore, we placed the process here, at its latest reasonable starting point. By now you should understand most of the decision artifacts, so it makes sense to discuss their reuse value and how they fit together. You'll meet a few more artifacts in the next section, Process E2, Decision Retrospective, but for retention purposes you won't handle them much differently than any other documents.

Formal Process Description: Process E1, Decision Artifacts Retention

Description
    Store each decision artifact in the appropriate repository.

Prerequisites
- A Decision Objective Statement

- One or more decision artifacts from previous phases: Decision Objective Statement, Decision Framing Document or worksheet, published CDD, annotated CDD and Decision Asset Register, simulation code and Simulation Report, Decision Element Assessment Register, Decision Monitoring Record, or any other artifacts associated with the decision

 As discussed in the previous section, you do not need to complete all the prior processes and have their artifacts at hand to begin Decision Artifacts Retention. You may want to place artifacts into repositories as you create them. In the case of decisions whose actions take a significant amount of time, you may not want to wait for Decision Monitoring to complete before safeguarding your other artifacts.

Responsible role
Decision team leader

Steps
1. Read through this process and tailor it, as appropriate, to your team.
2. Determine the appropriate repository for each decision artifact. Consider any applicable legal, regulatory, or policy requirements that may affect your choice of repositories or require you to separate reusable artifacts from those that require specific kinds of storage and handling.

   If your organization has a knowledge manager, someone in charge of data governance, or people with similar responsibilities, consult with them to decide where each type of decision artifact should reside. Registers, reports, and other documents may go into document repositories, simulation code may belong in code repositories, and you may need references to your data lexicon and data dictionary. Since you want both reusability and access to individual decisions, you may want to set up several ways of locating each decision artifact (such as by decision, by associated organizational process, by the data/knowledge/models they use, or simply through keyword search).

   If you don't have formal "librarians" of this type, then you can start by keeping it simple. For example, you could set up a shared folder and subfolders in Google Docs, SharePoint, or Dropbox, or a page on an intranet, and use a spreadsheet to track which artifacts go with which decisions. Different tabs on a spreadsheet (or views in a relational database) might show different ways of locating artifacts.
3. Submit the decision artifacts to the appropriate repositories or place them in the appropriate folders.

Deliverables
Entries in the appropriate repositories

Try It Yourself: Decision Artifacts Retention for the Telecom Use Case

---

Exercise

Before you continue reading, list some of the decision artifacts from the prior Try It Yourself exercises. What artifacts do you have? Do any of them contain sensitive information that might require special handling? How might you set up a simple repository for them? What are the different access paths you want to use?

At the start of Chapter 7, the decision you made turned into an action, and you monitored the decision action for several months. You have the following decision artifacts: Decision Objective Statement, Decision Framing Worksheet, published CDD, annotated CDD and Decision Asset Register, simulation code and the Simulation Report, Decision Element Assessment Register, and Decision Monitoring Record. You assemble your team to consider how to retain these artifacts.

First, you all agree that none of your artifacts contains information whose storage is constrained by legal, regulatory, or organizational policy considerations. You also agree that your artifacts' sensitivity is such that storage in a third-party cloud environment is an appropriate choice.

Everything is in Google Docs except the simulation code, which is in GitHub. Everyone agrees that you will keep the artifacts in folders in your Google Workspace and include in one of the folders a shortcut to the code on GitHub.

Next, you consider how future users will access the artifacts. You decide that other teams typically won't want to look at the entire body of documentation for one decision—instead, they'll want to see examples of each artifact type as they encounter it in the DI methodology. They'll use existing artifacts as starting points and might partially reuse them. They may also want to reuse causal chains that end with a specific outcome, start with a specific action, include a specific external, or use a specific decision asset, like data or knowledge or a model.

This leads to you to create your primary folder as follows:

- One folder for each type of decision element (action, outcome, dependency link, causal chain, and so forth)

- A naming convention that makes it easy to find all the artifacts for a specific decision. Naming conventions are a simple, low-tech way to keep things organized. You decide on *<decision name>_<artifact type abbreviation>_<date>*, so your Decision Framing Worksheet might be named *TelecomUnlimitedPlan_FramingWksht_20230623.docx*. Every document for this decision will be named

TelecomUnlimitedPlan_xxx_xxx, and every Decision Framing Worksheet will be named *xxx_FramingWksht_xxx*.

You also decide to create a spreadsheet with several tabs to let you find artifacts in other ways:

Decisions

One row for each decision with a column for the decision name, along with a column for each artifact type with the name of the artifact.

Outcomes

One row for each outcome/decision pair; one column for the outcome and one for the decision name. Sorting this tab by outcomes lets you find all decisions that use a specific outcome.

Actions

One row for each action/decision pair; one column for the action and one for the decision name. Sorting this tab by actions lets you find all decisions that use a specific action.

Externals

One row for each external/decision pair; one column for the external and one for the decision name. Sorting this tab by externals lets you find all decisions that use a specific external.

Assets

One row for each asset/decision pair; one column for the asset and one for the decision name. Sorting this tab by assets lets you find all decisions that use a specific asset.

You create the folders and the spreadsheets, change the artifact names to match the naming convention, and fill out the spreadsheets.

Exercise

Did you identify some of these decision artifacts? Did you find sensitive information? What kind of repository did you specify—a simple set of folders in Google Workspace, SharePoint, or a cloud repository like Dropbox? Or did you decide on some more sophisticated repository? How did you decide the information in the artifacts would be accessed? Did you store them by decision, artifact type, or some other way? How else did you decide they need to be accessible? Did you use a spreadsheet to enable alternate access, a database, a wiki, or something else?

Process E2: Decision Retrospective

The goal of Process E2, Decision Retrospective, is continuous improvement. It aims to ensure that all of your DI work and artifacts realize their full value by contributing to the quality of future decisions and—ultimately—the success of your organization as a whole.

As we explore the Decision Retrospective process, it's important to keep in mind that a good decision can produce a bad outcome. Many people believe the opposite: that if you get a bad outcome, it's because you made a bad decision. Psychologists call this incorrect belief *outcome bias* (*https://oreil.ly/Ibrab*). This error can be costly, because it can lead people to reject decision *processes* even when the outcome error arose from imperfect or incomplete information or predictors, and not the processes themselves. Recall our discussion of "unknown unknowns," too—externals aren't always predictable. A "black swan" event like the Covid-19 pandemic can torpedo even the best decisions.[1]

Whether you're happy with the decision outcomes or not, it's important to isolate what worked and what didn't. And, if the decision outcomes weren't what you hoped for, was there something you could have done to improve the decision?

This section begins with a brief discussion of what it means to measure the quality of a decision. We'll then present the formal process description and review several related concepts to help you understand how to measure decision quality and use the Decision Retrospective process effectively.

One-Time Versus Repeated Decisions

Some decisions are made just once, like the decision in our case study about pricing a new product. Other decisions may repeat many times, such as promotion and hiring decisions in a large company. Of course, in repeated decisions, every instance is still different—but with enough repetitions, you'll begin to detect patterns. For instance, the hiring team might discover that employees with project management certifications are more effective at certain tasks than those who hold master's degrees.

When you use a decision model to support repeated decisions, you'll assess its overall quality differently than you would for a one-off decision. A repeated decision may result in continuous retrospectives and improvements, whereas a retrospective exercise for a one-off decision may only produce reusable assets for other, very different decisions. For instance, let's say our one-off pricing decision model has a subcomponent: a model that compares price sensitivity among consumers in Canada

---

1 Nassim Nicholas Taleb, *The Black Swan: The Impact of the Highly Improbable* (New York: Random House, 2007).

and in the United States. The organization could reuse that subcomponent model in decisions about completely different products (like home security systems) that will be sold in the same markets.

Measuring Decision Quality

How right was your decision? And how do you assess that? We called this *decision quality*, and the Decision Retrospective process is all about how to measure decision quality. The first step is determining whether or not ground truth is available for your decision.

Measuring against ground truth

In some situations, you eventually find out what the *right* decision was—and, thus, whether your choice was objectively the right one or not. The idea of *ground truth* captures this concept. Near-future predictions have ground truth: if you predict that a stock price will go up or down by a certain date, you'll eventually see it play out and know whether you were right or not. If the weather forecast predicts a sunny Saturday, but Saturday brings six inches of snow, the forecast was wrong. That's a ground truth. These are ground truths for predictions, but ground truth also helps us to measure the performance of an action-to-outcome decision-making process.

In the net-zero GHG use case we've followed throughout the book, it is conceivable that the organization could measure the actual GHGs sequestered or emitted as a result of its policy decision. It could also conduct a survey to measure the reputational impact of employees traveling to meet in person versus attending virtually. That team could then compare the model's predicted outcomes in these categories with the actual outcomes measured. How close those values are will tell us a lot about the decision's quality.

One-off and repeated decisions can both have ground truth. If your decision repeats, you have an opportunity to measure the quality of your decision repeatedly, too. This can give you an increasingly robust understanding of your model's reliability in different circumstances.

You can measure the ground truth of the entire decision by comparing the predicted outcomes to the actual outcome. You can also measure the ground truth of intermediates. And when part of the decision involves a prediction—such as an external weather prediction—you can also compare that prediction to the ground truth.

Sometimes, with repeated decisions, external reality diverges from the reality reflected in the decision model. You can detect this as an increasing discrepancy between the decision model's predicted elements and their ground truth: it means that the decision's fidelity is decreasing over time. This is called *decision quality drift*. If such a drift becomes evident, it's a good idea to treat this as a trigger to revisit Process B1, Decision Design.

When there is no ground truth for decision outcomes

Not every action-to-outcome decision has ground truth for all outcomes available in the complex environments for which we use DI. Decisions occur in a rich context that includes known and unknown values of externals, and particular external contexts seldom repeat exactly. The context can also change while you are implementing the decision or soon thereafter.

You might wonder how, given that you had measurable outcomes and well-defined objectives, you could have a decision with no ground truth. Either you met your objectives or you didn't, right? Not exactly. The concept of ground truth assumes a consistent context over the lifetime of the decision. Unknown unknowns like the 2020 toilet paper crisis mentioned in Chapter 4 or $9.6 billion (*https://oreil.ly/LE-bW*) of lost trade due to a ship stuck in the Suez Canal in 2021 are one cause of inconsistent contexts. Exactly how much the context needs to shift to make ground truth irrelevant is yet another DI judgment call. If, for example, a key resource was on one of the 369 ships blocked in the Suez for six days, then a production manager might reasonably argue that their decision context had changed significantly.

Table 8-1 shows ways to measure decision quality based on whether the decision is one-off or repeated, and whether ground truth for the decision outcome(s) is available or not. We'll discuss this table more next.

Table 8-1. Approaches to decision quality depending on the type of decision

	One-off	Repeated
Known outcome ground truth(s)	Assess decision quality by evaluating the decision processes and the difference between the predicted outcomes and known outcomes.	Assess decision quality using measurement techniques from machine learning and/or statistical models to compare the decision's outcome prediction with the ground truth.[a]
Unknown outcome ground truth(s)	Assess decision quality by assessing the quality of the decision *processes* and by assessing the quality of the individual components of the decision (its submodels and elements).	Same as for one-off decisions, but you can use your assessment to improve this same decision over time.
[a] For example: a confusion matrix, the residual sum of squared differences between truth and prediction, R^2, a *t*-test, or the percentage of time that the outcome was right (for yes/no outcomes).		

As shown in the lower-left box of this table (one-offs with unknown ground truth), when ground truth is not available, you can use process quality as a proxy. This is a widespread approach, used by quality systems like IEEE 730-2014 (*https://oreil.ly/kvLqE*) and CMMI (*https://oreil.ly/6bvlW*). The idea is that, if you can't measure the correctness of the decision itself, you can at least assess whether you followed a set of decision-making processes that are widely considered to be effective. You can also examine those processes to see how well they helped your decision team identify the critical decision elements, assets, uncertainties, and scenarios.

We'll have more to say about decision-process improvement later on in this chapter, under "Continuous Decision-Process Improvement" on page 220.

Another approach for the lower-left box of the table is to measure the quality of the individual elements that make up the decision model. All other things being equal, a decision model that consists of high-quality components will have higher quality than one that does not.

Sometimes you have ground truth for one of the decision model's dependencies or external predictors. For example, a decision model might include a dependency between time spent on a marketing awareness campaign (in hours per week) and the resulting awareness (measured through survey results). If you gather those two numbers every week, you can compare that ground truth to the model used in the original dependency and assess the accuracy of just that component.

Formal Process Description: Process E2, Decision Retrospective

Description

> After a decision has been made and its outcomes have played out, assess the decision processes and artifacts and improve them for future use. Capture your findings in a Decision Quality Report.

Prerequisites

- A completed decision and its outcomes
- All decision artifacts (from Process E1)
- Documentation of all tailoring to the DI processes
- A determination of appropriate scope, time, and/or effort for this process

Responsible role

> Decision team leader

Steps

1. Read through this process and tailor it, as appropriate, to your team.
2. Discuss whether you are assessing a one-time decision or one that will be repeated.
3. Is there ground truth available for the outcomes or any other elements? If so, you'll measure decision quality as the difference between the ground truth and

the decision's predictions using one of the methods described in Table 8-1. Are there datasets to update with this new ground truth? If so, update them.

4. If you are assessing a *one-time decision*, how close are the outcome values to the objectives? Capture this as one component of decision quality.

If you are assessing a *repeated decision*, assess this instance of the decision in the context of all the other times this decision has been made. Then look at other instances of this decision and assess:

- How close are the outcome values to the objectives this time? Capture this as one component of decision quality.

- Look at other repeats of this decision and assess whether decision drift is happening for outcomes and elements for which you have ground truth. If so, and the drift is happening quickly enough that you predict quality problems in the future, consider returning to Phase B, Decision Modeling. Work through all processes as appropriate to update the CDD and assets for the next iteration of this decision.

5. Assess decision processes:

- If you significantly tailored one or more processes for this decision, make sure that the tailored processes are captured as decision artifacts.

- Examine the processes you followed and capture any suggested improvements—including tailoring—for the next time you use those processes.

- If this is a repeated decision, assess whether to incorporate any decision-specific process improvements or tailoring next time. If so, follow your organizational procedures for tailoring decision-specific processes.

- Do you need to make improvements to the *template processes*, the processes that you have tailored to your organization that each decision team now tailors for an individual decision? If so, follow your organizational procedures for tailoring template processes. (See "Template processes and organizational culture" on page 220.)

6. If you trigger your periodic process reviews from this process, is it time to ask about or initiate such a review? If not, is it time to find the right people to help with this review and begin discussions? Note that decision team members or perhaps an organizational-level process team may be responsible here.

7. Is there a process in place to periodically assess the organization's DI maturity? If so, is it time to ask about or initiate an assessment? If not, is it time to find the right people to help with this assessment and begin discussions?

8. Record your retrospective results in Phase E, Worksheet 1, Decision Quality Report, and place it in the proper repository.

Deliverables

Phase E, Worksheet 1, Decision Quality Report, with the following information:

- Changes to datasets and models that capture decision results, such as a training set that contains new ground truth rows
- Results of drift analysis and any resulting updates
- Decision-specific process-improvement recommendations
- Organization-wide process-improvement recommendations
- Recommendations, discussions, and discussion notes regarding periodic DI process reviews and/or maturity assessment
- Overall assessment of decision quality, on a scale from 1 to 10

Phase E, Worksheet 1: Decision Quality Report

Decision Quality Report		
Is this a *one-off* decision or a *repeated* decision? For a one-off decision, if there is ground truth for the outcomes or other elements, fill out this table. For a repeated decision, if there is ground truth, fill out the table for *this instance* of the decision.		
Element	**Value from objectives**	**Actual "ground truth" value**
If it is a repeated decision, evaluate this instance in the context of all other instances:		
Estimate decision drift		
Are ground truth values trending away from objectives? Are they likely to fail to meet the objectives soon enough that it's time to update the CDD?		
Plot or sketch graphs of differences between predictions and outcomes or other values for which you have ground truth over time.		
Assess the decision process		
If you significantly tailored any processes, list them. (You'll need to capture them on your Decision Artifacts Register as well.)		
If this is a repeated decision, list any decision-specific process improvements or tailoring for next time. Follow your organizational procedures for tailoring decision-specific processes.		

If you identified any changes needed to template processes, list them here. Follow your organizational procedures for updating template processes.
Did this retrospective trigger a periodic review of all decision processes?
Did this retrospective trigger a periodic review of DI maturity?
What is your overall assessment of the quality of this decision, on a scale from 1 (worst) to 5 (best)?
Write a short paragraph explaining your quality number.
Comments:

Continuous Decision-Process Improvement

In addition to assessing a particular decision's quality, it is also often valuable to assess the decision processes you used to make the decision, to identify any process improvements to implement in the decision itself, if it is a repeated decision, or in the *template processes*, the processes you start with for new decisions, which decision team leaders can tailor.

Template processes and organizational culture

The phases and processes in this book are starting points. They show you the key steps of DI. But they cannot be *your* business processes if everyone thinks of them as "that new thing stuck on top of what we already do." To use DI effectively, you need to embed it into your organization. You need to use the DI processes, understand how they work, and then change and rewrite them so that they work within your particular circumstances. Your existing business processes might absorb parts of the DI processes, or vice versa. Along the way, you might decide to create a new set of *template processes*. Put them somewhere for easy access, probably stored either with your other organizational template processes or with your decision artifacts.

You'll be adapting your decision processes at two levels:

- Recommended tailoring changes for your organizational template processes
- Tailoring for a specific decision

As you use your organizational template processes, you will find that some of them need revision to be more effective. How you revise template processes is also a matter of organizational culture. In some organizations, any change will need approval from a change control board; in others, anyone who finds a problem with a process template simply revises it as needed.

If you tailor a process significantly for a decision, the new process is a decision artifact for that decision and should be retained with the other decision artifacts. What "significantly" means is a judgment call, depending on your organizational culture. If your organization follows processes "to the letter," any change might be significant. If your organization treats processes as suggestions, then most changes won't be significant. For a repeated decision, a decision-specific template may need to be further tailored over time. How this will happen depends on how your organization approaches process management.

In addition, we suggest you create a periodic process to review all DI processes in the context of your organization's other processes. If you have an organizational process-review process (yes, this is a bit redundant, but it's common in mature organizations), it can ensure that this review occurs. Otherwise, the Decision Retrospective process can trigger it.

Every time you do a DI process retrospective, you will typically ask, "What do I need to fix or improve?" It's also worth asking, "How do I make this process more usable and create less work for my colleagues?" Over time, the template processes that you start with for new decisions will not be the ones in this book, they will be the ones you have tailored for your organization.

Overcoming organizational resistance to DI process adoption

Usually when we ask a group of DI practitioners to articulate the greatest challenge of introducing DI into an organization, the first thing we hear is "overcoming organizational resistance to change." While that's undoubtedly true, addressing it is beyond the scope of this book: change management is a separate discipline with its own commercial (*https://oreil.ly/F0msL*) and academic certification programs (*https://oreil.ly/XDiw3*).

Beyond change management in general, there are also DI-specific challenges that often create organizational resistance. Let's look at three of the biggest:

Some organizations value "decision obscurity."
> Sometimes decision makers perceive transparent decision processes as a threat to their power or control. Alireza Farahany describes "decision makers' (especially C-levels') unwillingness to make clear decisions" as a "challenging barrier." Indicating that cultural context can be a factor, Farahany notes that "the bigger a

decision or a decision maker gets, the more unclear and obscure the decision becomes."

Some leaders can't see past the data to find the decisions.

Ever since big data became a buzzword, organizations have been striving to become more "data-driven." But, as we noted in Chapter 1, many decision makers take this too literally, focusing on the data *itself* rather than on how best to interpret, analyze, and use that data. Efrain Rodriguez writes of this mindset that "data is all it is": even when leaders should be focusing "more on decisions or expected outcomes, they only ask for data."

Once DI tells you what data you need, how do you navigate the data maze?

Even as business systems generate more data than ever before, it can be challenging to navigate a patchwork of platforms and silos to access it. DI helps you understand what data you need to support a decision, but you still have to get to it. Mehdi Vahabisani calls this "information systems integration" and notes that DI platforms, "being heavily data-dependent, need to be integrated with all of the organization's Transaction Processing Systems (TPS) databases, as well as analytical servers, to perform their expected routine tasks.

In addition to these challenges, many practitioners have identified the lack of a tool that helps them through the DI processes as a need. There is an active market of software vendors—including the authors of this book!—working to help to bring such a tool to market.

DI maturity

Even more broadly, you may wish to assess the overall value of your DI initiative to your organization. See "The DI Maturity Model" on page 20. As you perform Decision Retrospectives, ask, "What value did DI bring to this decision?" and "How is DI improving our organization as a whole?" You will probably want to document your conclusions and communicate them to the rest of the organization. You may decide to do this with the help of HR, change management, or organizational development experts, either within your company or as hired consultants.

Conclusion

If you've read through this whole book, congratulations! You're well on your way to improving your organization's decisions. What's more, you're now part of what we see as one of the most important initiatives of the 21st century—and not just for business, but for governments and civil society as well.

Importantly, this is the first book on DI processes, and the first edition of this book. As time moves on, you should expect to see an explosion of new materials on DI, addressing such topics as uncertainty propagation, repeated decisions, integrating DI with planning, integration with decision analysis and complex system analysis, and—probably of most interest to you—new technologies and platforms that will help you to do DI. You might even write some of these yourself as you pioneer DI in your own setting. We hope that you find—as we have—that being around at the beginning of a field that is not just new but is also widely enough recognized that its growth is inevitable, is pretty exciting. DI's potential to help solve some of humanity's hardest problems makes it a particularly fulfilling discipline to join.

In closing, as you know, the world has seen an explosion of diverse technology and data, developed over hundreds of years. Yet, so far, very little of that technology has been used to solve the next class of problems we face: complex organizational management in the face of "wicked problems" like climate change, inequality, poverty, and the new challenges and opportunities associated with generative AI.

These problems require a collaboration between people and technology: in particular, we can't solve them without the far-reaching eyes of data and the clarity that AI brings to deriving insights from it. We see DI as a way to crystallize diverse technological assets into a renaissance of solutions, with action-to-outcome decisions as a unifying principle, to solve some of the hardest and most important problems of our age.

This is our journey, and now it is yours, too. Welcome.

N. E. Malcolm, Sparks, Nevada, USA
L. Y. Pratt, Lakewood, Colorado, USA
April 2023

Framework for How Data Informs Decisions

Data can inform decision making in many different ways, which are diagrammed in Figure A-1. This diagram shows nine places where data informs a CDD during simulation, labeled *T(i)* through *T(ix)*. There are also seven places where the CDD acts as a framework for a data-tracking mechanism after the action is taken in reality, labeled *R(i)* through *R(vii)*.

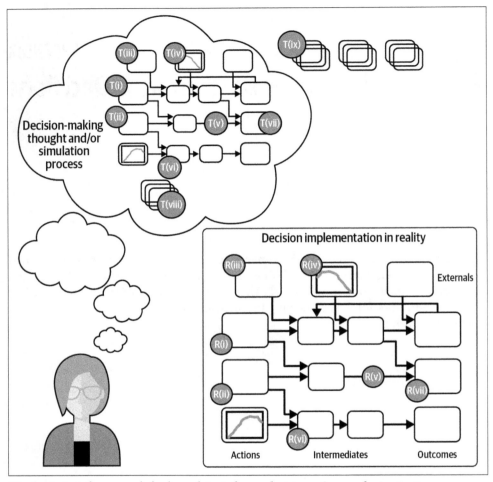

Figure A-1. A framework for how data informs decisions. Source: lorienpratt.com (reproduced with permission).

The data integration points circled in Figure A-1 are:

- *T(i)*: A simple lever, which in reality (*R*) will be an action, and which can be represented by data. For instance, the number of minutes you choose to spend reading this chapter can be represented by a number.

- *T(ii)*: A more complex lever, perhaps representing a plan. For instance, you might plan to spend 10 minutes studying DI today, 20 tomorrow, and a half hour on Wednesday.

- *T(iii)*: A scalar external: something you can't control, but whose value influences how actions lead to outcomes. For instance, the price of a competitor's product.

- *T(iv)*: A more complex external. For example, this might be a prediction of market salaries for your job position over the next three years.

- *T(v)*: A dependency link that represents how one factor influences another, and whose form may be a model informed by data.

- *T(vi)*: An intermediate, which can have a data value that's calculated from its upstream elements.

- *T(vii)*: An outcome: something that can be measured at the end of the dependency chain.

- *T(viii)*: When a decision model is computerized, the computer can experiment with many different sets of choices to determine which one, in simulation, leads to the best outcomes. This generates "data from the future," which you can analyze just as current BI and other data systems analyze data from the past and present.

- *T(ix)*: A computerized decision model creates a platform that allows for multiple vectors of environment (aka context, external) variables to be considered.

"*R*" items represent how a decision impacts a chain of events in reality, after its associated action is taken, as opposed to during simulation or ideation. The role of data shifts a bit here, as follows:

- *R(i)*: Corresponding to each *T(i)* lever is an *R(i)* action. For example, you are reading this chapter right now; that behavior is different than the idea of that action when you were considering doing so. An action, as it plays out in time, can be measured and captured as data.

- *R(ii)*: As with *T(ii)*, you might make a choice to take a series of actions, which in reality can take place over a period of time. That plan can be represented as data as well.

- *R(iii)*: Represents an external measurement that the decision maker may or may not choose to measure once the action is playing out through time.

- *R(iv)*: Represents a more complex external, such as a time-based prediction of the weather.

- *R(v)*: Represents a cause-and-effect dependency influence as it plays out in reality. Usually these are monitored through measuring their impacts, as in *R(vi)*, which we cover next.

- *R(vi)*: Represents an intermediate. Intermediates are sometimes understood as KPIs or leading indicators. In contrast to *T(vi)*, here we're not planning to measure KPIs but are actually measuring them as our actions play out. This can provide an early warning that a decision is going adrift from its intended outcome(s).

- *R(vii)*: Measuring outcomes of actions taken is a good complement to measuring leading indicators. To the extent that a decision is repeated, these outcomes can form training data for ML models.

You can read more about this data/CDD integration framework in the article "A Framework for How Data Informs Decisions" (*https://oreil.ly/JgoMN*) by coauthor Pratt.

Index

About the Authors

L. Y. Pratt, PhD, Chief Scientist at Quantellia, has been delivering artificial intelligence and machine learning solutions for her clients for over 30 years. These include the Human Genome Project, the Colorado Bureau of Investigation, the US Department of Energy, SAP, and the Administrative Office of the US Courts. She is a machine learning pioneer, having led the teams that invented inductive transfer and decision intelligence (DI). Pratt received the CAREER award from the National Science Foundation, an innovation award from Microsoft, and the Exemplary Research Award from the Colorado Advanced Software Institute (CASI). Formerly a computer science professor at the Colorado School of Mines, Pratt has appeared multiple times on national television and NPR, has given two TEDx talks, and is a respected AI and DI speaker worldwide.

Recognized by the Women Innovators and Inventors Project, Pratt continues to push the boundaries of technology as one of the creators and evangelists for decision intelligence, which is the next phase of artificial intelligence, and which will define how AI is used in the 21st century.

N. E. Malcolm, COO at Quantellia, has over 25 years of experience managing and delivering enterprise software, data science, machine learning, and decision intelligence projects. Malcolm has spent five years on the Quantellia executive team with Dr. Pratt, continuously improving and developing best practices for both decision intelligence and Agile AI methodologies and delivering AI and DI projects including:

- Data science and data management on several large enterprise projects to improve decision making in the telecommunications industry
- Machine learning to develop a digital twin of retiring key employees for a small financial company
- Machine learning to better understand medical device failures
- Machine learning for computer security for a medium-sized computer security company
- Machine learning for customer retention for a community bank
- Establishment of a decision intelligence center of excellence for a G7 national bank
- A NASA decision intelligence STTR

Malcolm holds a BS in mathematics from MIT and an MS in computer science from USC.

Colophon

The animal on the cover of *The Decision Intelligence Handbook* is an oriental scops owl (*Otus sunia*).

Oriental scops owls are native to eastern and southern Asia (there have also been a handful of sightings in the Aleutian islands of Alaska). They are a migratory species (although those who live in warmer climates do not migrate), and they tend to frequent forests. Their preferred nesting location is a hole in a tree or a nesting box, and females typically lay between three and six eggs at a time. Oriental scops owls are nocturnal (like most owls) and primarily hunt insects and spiders, with occasional forays into small vertebrates.

They are small in size and have ear tufts, referred to as such because of the tufts' location and general similarity in appearance to mammalian ears—not because of any role in hearing. When disturbed, these owls will freeze in place with their eyes half-closed.

The current conservation status (IUCN) of the oriental scops owl is "Least Concern." Many of the animals on O'Reilly covers are endangered; all of them are important to the world.

The cover illustration is by Karen Montgomery, based on an antique line engraving from *Meyers Kleines Lexicon*. The cover fonts are Gilroy Semibold and Guardian Sans. The text font is Adobe Minion Pro; the heading font is Adobe Myriad Condensed; and the code font is Dalton Maag's Ubuntu Mono.

O'REILLY®

Learn from experts.
Become one yourself.

Books | Live online courses
Instant answers | Virtual events
Videos | Interactive learning

Get started at oreilly.com.

Printed in the USA
CPSIA information can be obtained
at www.ICGtesting.com
JSHW051738210823
46934JS00006B/83